SKIPPER'S HANDBOOK

ROBERT GROSSMAN

Editor: Ellen & Steven Harden

Bristol Fashion Publications, Inc.
Harrisburg, Pennsylvania

Skipper's Handbook – Robert Grossman

Published by Bristol Fashion Publication, Inc.

Copyright © 2000 by Robert Grossman. All rights reserved.

No part of this book may be reproduced or used in any form or by any means-graphic, electronic, mechanical, including photocopying, recording, taping or information storage and retrieval systems-without written permission of the publisher.

BRISTOL FASHION PUBLICATIONS AND THE AUTHOR HAVE MADE EVERY EFFORT TO INSURE THE ACCURACY OF THE INFORMATION PROVIDED IN THIS BOOK BUT ASSUMES NO LIABILITY WHATSOEVER FOR SAID INFORMATION OR THE CONSEQUENCES OF USING THE INFORMATION PROVIDED IN THIS BOOK.

ISBN: 1-892216-24-6
LCCN: 00-133156

Contribution acknowledgments

Inside Graphics: By the author.
Cover Design: By the author.

Skipper's Handbook – Robert Grossman

Skipper's Handbook – Robert Grossman

ACKNOWLEDGMENTS

I wish to express my thanks and gratitude to several outstanding individuals. Their expertise and breadth of knowledge contributed significantly to this work.

Phil Arms, Ph.D. is a professor at the California Maritime Academy in Vallejo, California. Dr. Arms is retired from the US Navy. Dr. Arms lives in Vallejo, California.

Captain Robert Hannah, also of the California Maritime Academy, assisted Dr. Arms with the review of the text.

Dr. Brereton Strafford, MD is an orthopedic surgeon in Bellevue, Washington, specializing in sports medicine. Dr. Strafford is an avid boater and water skier.

Skipper's Handbook – Robert Grossman

Table of Contents

SECTION 1   Page 13
First Aid
- CPR
- First Aid

SECTION 2   Page 55
Rules of the Road
- Rights of Way
- Buoys
- Navigation Lights
- Dayshapes
- Sound signals
- Distress Signals

SECTION 3   Page 115
Navigation
- Conversion of Compass Points and Degrees
- Compass Variation and Deviation
- Compass Conversion Diagrams
- Dead Reckoning; Your Position
- Dead Reckoning; Distance, Speed, and Time
- Dead Reckoning; Set and Drift
- Dead Reckoning; Course to Steer
- Using Bearings

SECTION 4
Boat Handling
    Emergencies
    Propellers
    Cavitation and Ventilation
    Trim
    Turning and Steering
    Dock Lines
    Single-Screw Handling
    Twin-Screw Handling
    Rough Seas
    Special Situations
    Water Skiing
    Anchoring
    Launching and Trailering

Page 153

SECTION 5
Seamanship
    Fire Fighting
    Marine Radio Use
    Weather
    Knots
    Useful Formulas
    Personal Flotation Devices
    Boating Equipment
    Code Flags

Page 207

APPENDIX 1
State Boating Information

Page 259

APPENDIX 2
Glossary of Boating Terms

Page 263

APPENDIX 3
Index

Page 271

Skipper's Handbook – Robert Grossman

Skipper's Handbook – Robert Grossman

Skipper's Handbook – Robert Grossman

SECTION 1
FIRST AID

CPR / FIRST AID

RESCUE BREATHING - Person not breathing:

1. Check if conscious: "Are you OK?"
2. Check if person is breathing: look, listen, and feel. If not, **have someone call 911 or hail the Coast Guard on a marine radio, channel 16.**
3. Tilt back head, lift chin, pinch nose shut.
4. Give 2 slow breaths. Watch for chest to rise.
5. Check pulse for at least 10 seconds. If pulse present, but still not breathing, continue as follows:
6. Give 1 slow breath every 5 seconds. Do this for 1 minute.
7. Recheck pulse and breathing.
8. Continue cycle of breathing and checking pulse, for as long as possible or until help arrives.

If air does not go in (you do not see chest rise and fall) as you give breaths:
1. Retilt head back and try again. If this does not work:
2. Give up to 5 abdominal thrusts, then sweep mouth with finger.
3. Repeat rescue breathing from beginning.

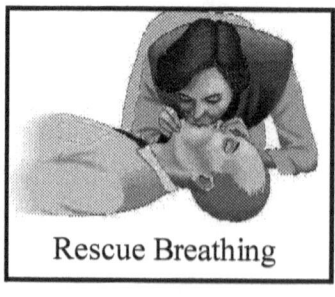
Rescue Breathing

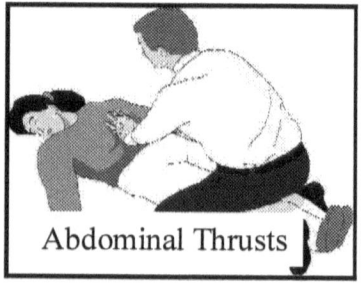
Abdominal Thrusts

CPR - Person not breathing, no pulse:

1. Check if conscious: "Are you OK?"
2. Check if person is breathing: look, listen, and feel. If not, **have someone call 911 or hail the Coast Guard on a marine radio, channel 16.**
3. Tilt back head, lift chin, pinch nose shut.
4. Give 2 slow breaths. Watch for chest to rise.
5. Check pulse for at least 10 seconds. If no pulse and not breathing, continue as follows:
6. Position yourself over chest area. Find notch where ribs meet breastbone. Put heel of hand just above notch. Put other hand on top of first hand, interlace fingers, and lift fingers up off of chest.
7. With elbows straight, and weight over hands, push down on chest 1½ to 2 inches deep. Give 15 compressions this way (at 80-100 compressions per minute).
8. Reposition head and give 2 slow breaths.
9. Do 3 more sets of 15 compressions and 2 breaths.
10. Recheck pulse and breathing.
11. Continue sets of compressions, breaths, and re-checking for as long as possible or until help arrives.

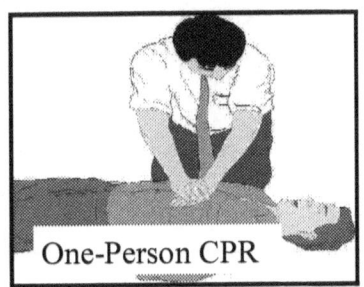
One-Person CPR

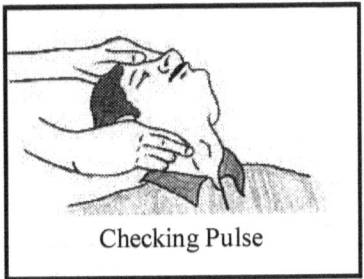
Checking Pulse

CPR CHARTS

	ADULT 8 years and older

1-Person CPR	Compression depth = 1½-2 in.
	Compress with 2 hands
	Compression rate = 80-100
	    (compressions per minute)
	Do cycles of 15 compressions +
	    2 breaths
	Recheck pulse every 4 cycles

2-Person CPR	Compression depth = 1½-2 in.
	Compress with 2 hands
	Compression rate = 80-100
	    (compressions per minute)
	Do cycles of 5 compressions +
	    1 breath
	Recheck pulse every 4 cycles

CPR CHARTS

	CHILD 1 to 8 years

1-Person CPR	Compression depth = 1-1½ in.
	Compress with 1 hand
	Compression rate = 80-100
	    (compressions per minute)
	Do cycles of 5 compressions +
	    1 breath
	Recheck pulse every 10 cycles

2-Person CPR	Compression depth = 1-1½ in.
	Compress with 1 hand
	Compression rate = 80-100
	    (compressions per minute)
	Do cycles of 5 compressions +
	    1 breath
	Recheck pulse every 10 cycles

CPR CHARTS

	INFANT under 1 year

1-Person CPR	® Compression depth = ½-1 in.
	 ® Compress with 2 fingers
	 ® Compression rate = 100-120
	  (compressions per minute)
	 ® Do cycles of 5 compressions +
	  1 breath
	 ® Recheck pulse every 10 cycles

2-Person CPR	® 2-person CPR is not used for infants

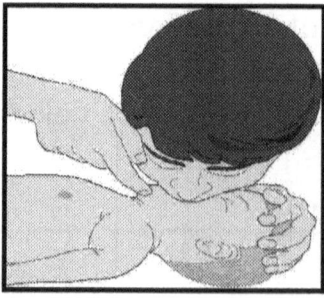

Cover infant's nose and mouth. Puff lightly into lungs. Do compressions with two fingers.

SHOCK

SYMPTOMS
Restlessness, anxiety.
Shallow, rapid, or gasping breathing.
Nausea, extreme thirst.
Cold, clammy, moist skin.
Trembling in arms and legs.
Drop in blood pressure.
Weak, rapid pulse.
Disorientation, fainting.

EMERGENCY ACTION
1. Check ABC's (Airway, Breathing, and Circulation).
2. Rescue breathing if necessary.
3. Stop any bleeding with direct pressure.
4. Elevate legs and keep head low (except when injuries prevent this).
5. Immobilize fractures.
6. Keep victim warm or cool as needed.
7. Monitor ABC's and vital signs every 5 minutes until help arrives.
8. DO NOT give victim anything to eat or drink.
9. **GET IMMEDIATE MEDICAL AID.**

TECHNIQUES

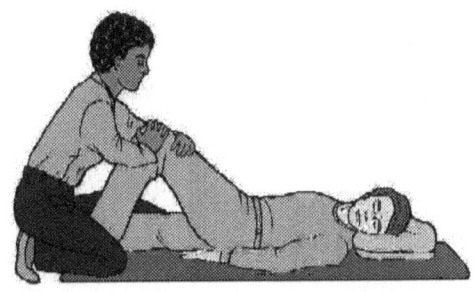

NEAR DROWNING, SUFFOCATION

SYMPTOMS
Unconscious.
Not breathing.
No pulse, or rapid, weak pulse.
Vomiting, gagging.
Bluish skin color.

EMERGENCY ACTION
1. Check ABC's.
2. Start Rescue Breathing or CPR.
3. Use abdominal thrusts if necessary on near-drowning victims.
4. If vomiting, turn victim on side for drainage.
5. **GET IMMEDIATE MEDICAL AID.**

TECHNIQUES

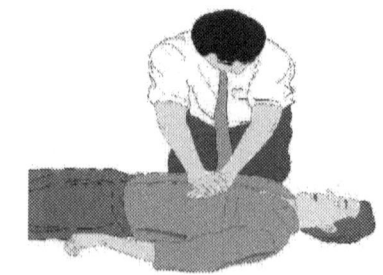

HEART ATTACK

SYMPTOMS
Sudden onset of weakness.
Nausea.
Pain across chest, radiating to neck, jaw, and left arm or both arms.
Erratic heartbeat or no heartbeat.
Sweating for no apparent cause.

EMERGENCY ACTION
1. Check ABC's.
2. Start Rescue Breathing or CPR if necessary.
3. Have victim sit or recline, or place in a position that promotes easiest breathing.
4. Assist victim in taking prescribed heart medication.
5. Administer oxygen if available.
6. Loosen constricting clothing.
7. Keep victim warm or cool as needed.
8. **GET IMMEDIATE MEDICAL AID.**

TECHNIQUES

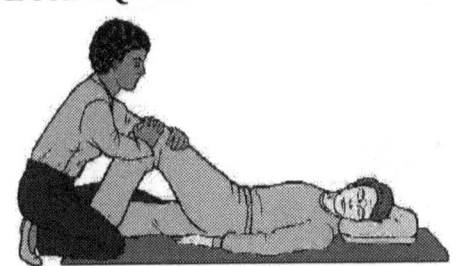

BURNS

SYMPTOMS
1st Degree: Redness, discoloration, mild swelling, pain.
2nd Degree: Red or mottled skin, blisters, moderate swelling, wet-skin surface, very painful.
3rd Degree: Charred skin, fat and/or muscle. Loss of skin. No pain except for surrounding areas.

EMERGENCY ACTION
1. Remove victim from fire, wash away chemicals, or disconnect live electrical wires.
2. **Check ABC's.**
3. Remove clothing and jewelry from burned area, but do not pull off any item that sticks to the skin.
4. Immerse burned area in cool water up to 30 minutes.
5. Cover 1st and 2nd degree burns with clean cloth. Keep it loose.
6. For inhalation of heat, smoke, or carbon monoxide, administer oxygen, if available.
7. Treat for shock, if necessary.
8. **GET IMMEDIATE MEDICAL AID.**

TECHNIQUES

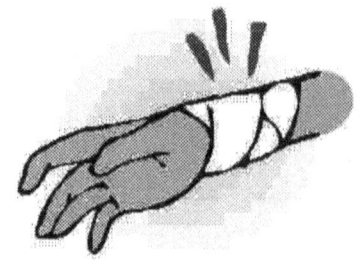

BROKEN BONES

SYMPTOMS
Deformity of limb or body area.
Pain, tenderness.
Loss of function of limb.
Swelling and bruising of area.
Bone ends exposed outside skin.

EMERGENCY ACTION
1. **Check ABC's.**
2. Control any bleeding.
3. Cover any open wound, exposed bone.
4. Splint and immobilize the fracture and the joints above and below the fracture. Use any materials you may have on hand: oars, life vest, dock lines, etc.
5. Treat for shock, if necessary.
6. **TRANSPORT TO MEDICAL FACILITY OR GET IMMEDIATE MEDICAL AID.**

TECHNIQUES

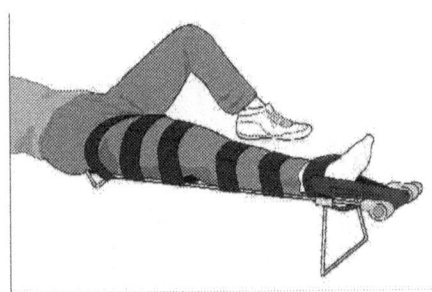

Apply splint. Immobilize injury area using any materials at hand.

DISLOCATIONS

SYMPTOMS Deformity of limb or joint area. Pain, tenderness. Loss of movement. Swelling.
EMERGENCY ACTION 1. Do not try to straighten the dislocation. 2. Splint and immobilize above and below the dislocated joint. Use any materials you may at hand: oars, life vests, dock lines, etc. 3. Place a cold-pack on the dislocation. 4. **TRANSPORT TO A MEDICAL FACILITY, OR GET MEDICAL AID.**
TECHNIQUES 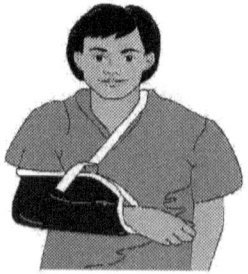Splint and immobilize. Wrap with cold pack.

SPRAINS

SYMPTOMS
Burning pain in the muscle.
Tenderness at area of sprain.
Swelling, redness, bruising of the area.
May not be able to move or put weight on the joint.

EMERGENCY ACTION
1. Wrap joint with a towel, snugly.
2. Apply cold-pack to affected area for up to thirty minutes at a time.
3. Elevate the joint area.
4. Rest the joint area.

TECHNIQUES

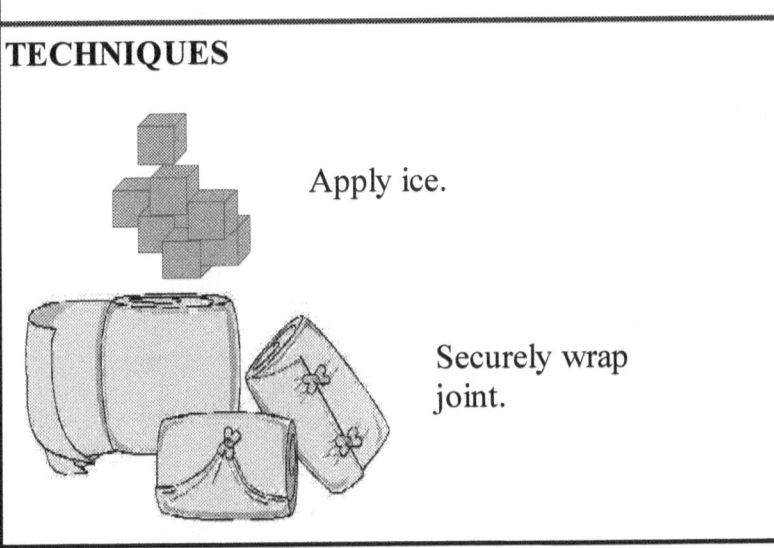

Apply ice.

Securely wrap joint.

OPEN WOUNDS: CUTS AND PUNCTURES

SYMPTOMS
Bleeding.
Ripped, torn, or cut skin.
Puncture holes.
Objects piercing and protruding from the body.
Skin scrapes.

EMERGENCY ACTION
1. **CHECK ABC's.** (Airway, Breathing, and Circulation).
2. Control any bleeding. Use direct pressure and elevation for severe bleeding. DO NOT USE A TOURNIQUET UNLESS A LAST RESORT.
3. Cut away clothing to expose the injury.
4. Clean dirt from around the wound. Do not remove imbedded objects, touch wound or pour water on wound.
5. Immobilize the injured part.
6. Wrap the wound with clean compress, dressing or bandage. Apply firmly.
7. Treat for shock, if necessary.
8. Preserve torn-off skin or body parts.
9. Get medical aid or transport to medical facility, if necessary.

TECHNIQUES

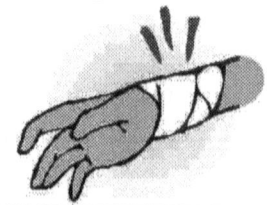

Control bleeding.
Wrap wound.

IMPALED OBJECTS

SYMPTOMS
Any foreign object that deeply penetrates and protrudes from the body.

EMERGENCY ACTION
1. **CHECK ABC's.**
2. Do not remove object. Cut away clothing to expose impaled object.
3. Control any bleeding.
4. Bandage wound and object in place. Use bulky dressings to immobilize object.
5. Treat for shock, if necessary.
6. **GET IMMEDIATE MEDICAL AID.**

TECHNIQUES

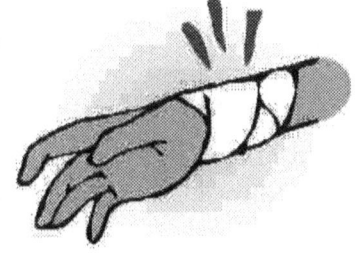

Control bleeding. Bandage object in place.

Skipper's Handbook – Robert Grossman

AMPUTATIONS: SEVERED BODY PARTS

SYMPTOMS
Any portion of the body that is separated from the rest of the body.

EMERGENCY ACTION
1. **CHECK ABC's.**
2. Control bleeding using direct pressure on artery. Use a tourniquet only if absolutely necessary.
3. Wrap the injured area or stump with clean dressings. Use elastic band or dock line to replace hand pressure for bleeding.
4. Treat for shock.
5. Wrap severed part in clean, damp towel, place in a sealed plastic bag, and store on ice. Transport with victim.
6. **GET IMMEDIATE MEDICAL AID.**

TECHNIQUES

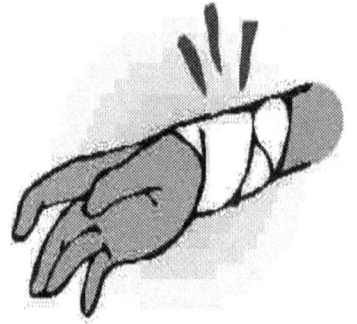

Control bleeding.
Use a tourniquet only as last resort.

GUNSHOT AND STAB WOUNDS

SYMPTOMS
Deep slashes or lacerations to body.
Deep punctures.
Entrance/exit wounds.
Major tissue injuries.

EMERGENCY ACTION
1. **CHECK ABC's.**
2. Stabilize and leave impaled knife in place.
3. Control any bleeding. Do not use tourniquet.
4. Cover all open wounds with dressings.
5. Immobilize area of the body that is injured.
6. Administer oxygen, if available.
7. Treat for shock.
6. **GET IMMEDIATE MEDICAL AID.**

TECHNIQUES

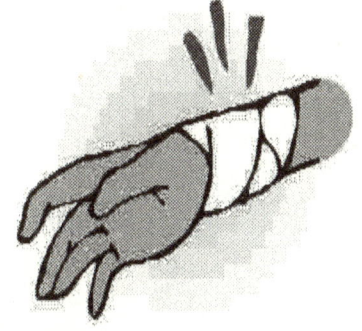

Control bleeding.
Immobilize injured area.

EVISCERATION: EXPOSURE OF INTERNAL ORGANS

SYMPTOMS
Internal organs, or any portion of an internal organ, that is exposed outside the body.

EMERGENCY ACTION
1. **CHECK ABC's.**
2. Control any bleeding.
3. Cover exposed organs with clean, wet cloth. Do not try to replace organs into the body.
4. Have victim recline and remain still.
5. Treat for shock.
6. **GET IMMEDIATE MEDICAL AID.**

TECHNIQUES

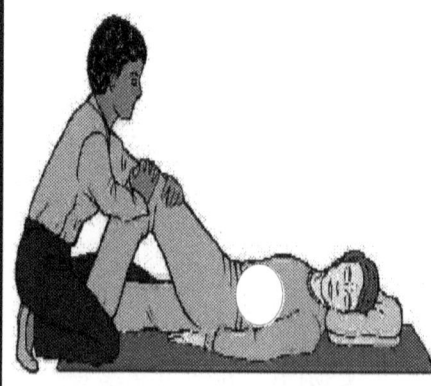

Control bleeding. Cover area with clean, wet cloth.

EYE INJURIES

SYMPTOMS
Object impaled or imbedded in eye.
Eye knocked out of socket.
Dirt or foreign object in eye.
Chemical burn to eye.
Cut, burn, or bruise to eye.

EMERGENCY ACTION
1. Flush with lots of clean water if chemicals are burning the eye. Remove contact lenses if chemicals are in the eye.
2. Cover injured eye with clean, moist bandage. Do not put pressure on a cut eye. Do not place eye back in socket.
3. Cover injured eye with a protective cup if an object is embedded in the eye. This will help prevent motion of the object.
4. Apply a roller bandage over BOTH eyes.
5. Keep victim face up. Immobilize head.
6. Treat for shock, if necessary.
7. **GET IMMEDIATE MEDICAL AID.**

TECHNIQUES

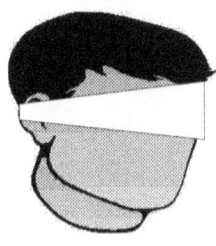

Cover both eyes with roller bandage.

ANIMAL BITES

SYMPTOMS   Puncture wounds to skin.   Cuts, lacerations to skin.   Bite can be from any animal; dog, rat, shark, human, etc.
EMERGENCY ACTION   1. **CHECK ABC's.**   2. Control any bleeding.   3. Wash wounds with soap and warm water.   4. Cover with thick dressing, applying firm pressure.   5. Immobilize injured part.   6. If severe injury, treat for shock, and administer oxygen.   7. Transport to medical facility or get medical aid.
TECHNIQUES   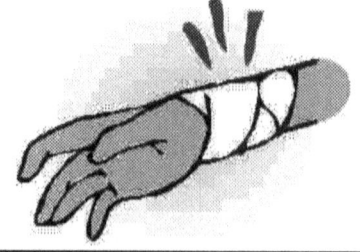 Wash, cover, and immobilize wound.

POISONING

SYMPTOMS
Nausea, vomiting, diarrhea, abdominal pain, cramps.
Slowed breathing and pulse.
Excessive salivation or sweating.
Stains, odors, or burns around the mouth.
Unconsciousness, convulsions.

EMERGENCY ACTION
1. **CHECK ABC's.**
2. Determine what poison was taken.
3. Induce vomiting, EXCEPT WHEN: victim is unconscious, poison is acid, lye, petroleum product, or if victim is having seizures or heart attack.
4. For acid ingestion, give milk of magnesia, milk, or antacids. For lye ingestion, give vinegar or citrus juice.
5. Treat for shock.
6. **GET IMMEDIATE MEDICAL AID, AND CONTACT POISON CONTROL CENTER.**

TECHNIQUES

Poison Control Center #: _____
or dial 911 on cell phone, or the Coast Guard on marine radio, channel 16.

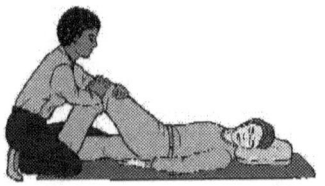

Determine what was ingested.
Treat for shock.

CARBON MONOXIDE

SYMPTOMS
Headache.
Dizziness, faintness.
Lethargy, stupor.
Unconsciousness.
Nausea or vomiting.
Lips may turn cherry-red or blue.

EMERGENCY ACTION
1. Get victim and yourself to area of fresh air immediately.
2. **CHECK ABC's.**
3. Administer oxygen, if available.
4. Keep victim inactive and quiet.
5. **GET IMMEDIATE MEDICAL AID.**

TECHNIQUES

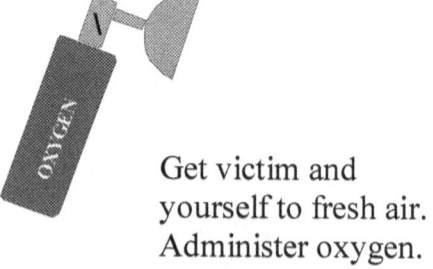

Get victim and yourself to fresh air. Administer oxygen.

SUDDEN ILLNESS

SYMPTOMS
Nausea, vomiting, or diarrhea.
Skin color changes.
Feeling dizzy, weak, or confused.
Difficulty seeing, breathing or talking.
Changes in consciousness.
Severe headache.
Seizure or paralysis.
Persistent pain.

EMERGENCY ACTION
1. **CHECK ABC's.**
2. Treat for shock.
3. Keep victim warm or cool as needed.
4. Contact nearest medical facility, and proceed as directed.
5. Victim may require immediate medical aid or transport.

TECHNIQUES

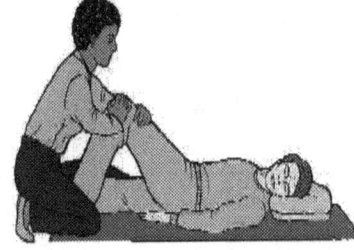

Keep victim warm or cool as needed.
Contact medical facility.

INTERNAL INJURY

SYMPTOMS
Swollen, bruised, tender, or hard areas of the abdomen.
Rapid, weak pulse.
Pale, bluish, moist skin.
Vomiting or coughing up blood.
Victim confused, faint, dizzy, or unconscious.
Excessive thirst.

EMERGENCY ACTION
1. **CHECK ABC's.**
2. Treat for shock.
3. Keep victim warm or cool as needed.
4. **GET IMMEDIATE MEDICAL AID.**

TECHNIQUES

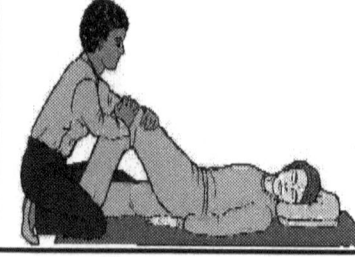

Treat for shock.
Keep victim warm or cool as needed.

SNAKE BITES

SYMPTOMS   One or two distinct puncture wounds.   Severe pain, burning at wound.   Swelling and discoloration at wound.
EMERGENCY ACTION   1. **CHECK ABC's.**   2. Have patient lay down and stay calm.   3. Keep bitten area below the heart, and immobilize the limb.   4. Remove jewelry from affected limb.   5. Apply a constricting band above the bite. **DO NOT** use a tourniquet. Leave the consticting band in place.   6. Treat for shock.   7. **GET IMMEDIATE MEDICAL AID.**   If possible, determine the type of snake.
TECHNIQUES   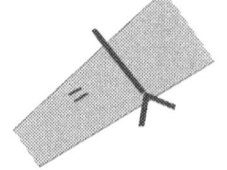 Apply a constricting band above the bite. Do not use tourniquet.

INSECT BITES AND STINGS

SYMPTOMS
Puncture marks or stinger in wound.
Red, swollen wound area.
Pain, burning, or stinging at wound area.
Nausea, vomiting, diarrhea.
Raised welt(s).
Allergic reactions including shock and unconsciousness.
EMERGENCY ACTION
1. **CHECK ABC's.**
2. Determine kind of insect involved.
3. Keep wound below heart.
4. Remove stinger by scraping it away with fingernail, credit card or knife. Do NOT squeeze the stinger with fingers.
5. Apply cold pack to area.
If victim shows symptoms of shock or adverse reaction:
6. Treat for shock.
7. Get medical aid.
TECHNIQUES

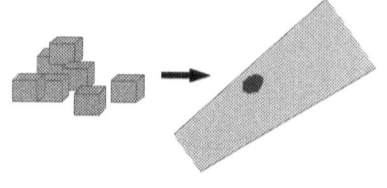

Apply cold pack.
Keep bite area below heart.

JELLYFISH STINGS

SYMPTOMS
Burning pain.
Swelling.
Stinging cells clinging to skin.
Shortness of breath, fainting.

EMERGENCY ACTION
1. **CHECK ABC's.**
2. Scrape off any stingers that may be sticking to the skin. Use dry sand if possible.
3. Apply alcohol, vinegar, or lemon juice to area.
4. If condition worsens, monitor for shock, and get immediate medical aid.

TECHNIQUES

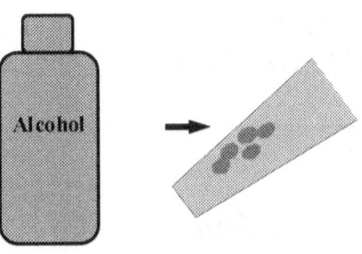

Remove stingers.
Apply alcohol, vinegar, or lemon juice.

HEAT STROKE

SYMPTOMS
Rapid, strong pulse and decreased blood pressure.
Deep, rapid breathing.
Body temperature between/around 105° - 110°.
Hot, dry, red skin.
Dry mouth.
Sudden collapse.
Muscular twitching.
Constricted pupils.
Headache, confusion.

EMERGENCY ACTION
1. **CHECK ABC's**.
2. Remove victim from heat source or direct sun.
3. Wet victim down with cold water.
4. Fan with cool air.
5. Convulsions or vomiting may follow cooling. Position victim for drainage.
6. **GET IMMEDIATE MEDICAL AID.**

TECHNIQUES

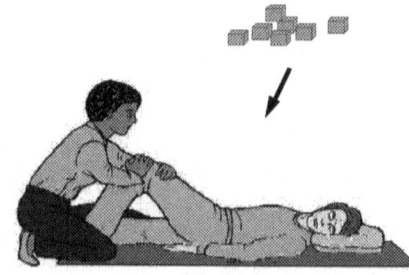

Position victim for drainage.
Fan with air or wet with cool water.

POISONOUS PLANTS

SYMPTOMS
Blisters on skin.
Skin rash.
Swelling.
Itching.
Pain.

EMERGENCY ACTION
1. Wash exposed areas with soap and water.
2. Apply cold packs to reduce swelling.
3. Apply Calamine lotion to area.
4. Consult doctor if conditions worsen.

TECHNIQUES

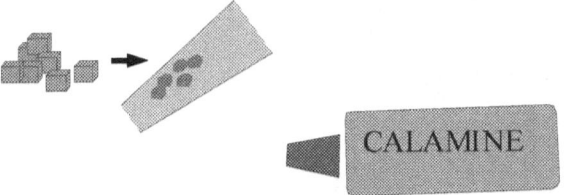

Apply cold pack.
Apply Calamine lotion.

HYPOTHERMIA

SYMPTOMS
Shivering.
Bluish skin.
Slow, slurred speech.
Memory lapses, incoherence, disorientation.
Stumbling, uncoordinated walk.
Apathy, drowsiness.
Dizziness, fainting, unconsciousness.

EMERGENCY ACTION
1. **CHECK ABC's.**
2. Remove wet clothing, and replace with dry clothing or blankets.
3. Add heat GRADUALLY and SLOWLY. Use any warm objects, including another person, that can safely be placed next to victim.
4. Give warm liquids only after shivering stops.
5. Transport to medical facility as soon as possible.

TECHNIQUES

Warm victim.
Give warm liquids only after shivering stops.

ASTHMA ATTACK

SYMPTOMS
Struggling to breathe.
Wheezing.
Rapid heartbeat.
Anxiety.

EMERGENCY ACTION
1. **CHECK ABC's.**
2. Position victim sitting, leaning forward.
3. Be prepared to clear possible airway obstruction, or use rescue breathing.
4. Assist victim with medication, inhaler.
5. Treat for shock, if necessary.
6. **GET IMMEDIATE MEDICAL AID,** if necessary.

TECHNIQUES

Seat victim leaning forward.
Monitor ABC's.

EPILEPTIC SEIZURE

SYMPTOMS
Victim may feel premonition of impending seizure.
Loss of consciousness.
Muscle spasms, convulsions.
Arched back during convulsions.
Frothing at mouth.
Loss of bladder or bowel control.
Attacks lasts 30 seconds to 5 minutes.

EMERGENCY ACTION
1. **CHECK ABC's.**
2. Protect victim from injury during convulsions; move away any dangerous objects. Do not restrain victim.
3. Protect victim from becoming a spectacle.
4. Position victim on his side to allow drainage of fluids, if necessary.
5. Loosen tight clothing.
6. Reorient victim after the seizure.
7. Allow victim to rest.
8. **If victim lapses into another seizure, GET IMMEDIATE MEDICAL AID.**

TECHNIQUES

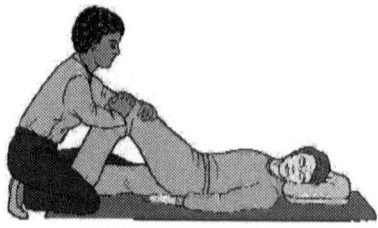

Move dangerous items away from victim.
Position for drainage, if necessary.

INSULIN SHOCK

SYMPTOMS   Dizziness, faintness, weakness.   Headache, irritability, apathy.   Tremors, convulsions.   Tingling in fingers and feet.   Pale, moist skin, and profuse sweating.   Drooling from mouth.   Shallow breathing and rapid pulse.
EMERGENCY ACTION   **1. CHECK ABC's.**   2. Ask victim if he is diabetic.   3. Give victim small amounts of sugar; from sugar packet, candy bar, non-diet soda pop. If victim is unconscious, rub sugar on tongue.   **4. GET IMMEDIATE MEDICAL AID.**
TECHNIQUES     Give small amounts of sugar.   Get immediate aid.

STROKE

SYMPTOMS
Severe headache.
Convulsions.
Paralysis or weakness on one or both sides of the body.
Decreased consciousness or mental ability, personality change.
Nausea or vomiting.
Inability to speak.
Pupils unequal in size, loss of vision.
Rapid, strong pulse.
Loss of bladder or bowel control.

EMERGENCY ACTION
1. **CHECK ABC's.**
2. Lay victim on his side, paralyzed side down, with head and shoulders raised.
3. Remove dentures or false teeth.
4. Keep victim warm or cool as needed.
5. Keep victim still and quiet. Do not give anything to eat or drink.
6. Comfort and reassure victim. Do not say anything to alarm victim.
7. **GET IMMEDIATE MEDICAL AID.**

TECHNIQUES

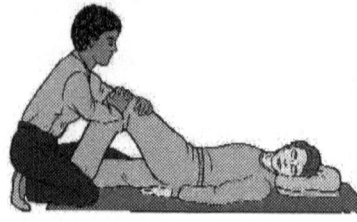

Lay victim with paralyzed side down. No food or drink.

CHILDBIRTH

SYMPTOMS
Contractions are 2 to 5 minutes apart.
Amniotic sac has ruptured (water has broken).
Needs to move bowels.
Mother feels the baby is ready to come out.
Crown of head or other part of baby is visible in vaginal opening.

EMERGENCY ACTION
1. If contractions are 5 minutes apart or more, transport to a medical facility. If contractions are 2 to 5 minutes apart, prepare to deliver child.
2. **CALL FOR IMMEDIATE MEDICAL AID.** Try to contact mother's physician.
3. Have mother lay on back, knees up and apart. Put clean materials underneath buttocks and floor area.
4. Instruct mother to take shallow, rapid breath.
5. Before baby's head emerges, make sure the membrane is broken. Break with fingernail if necessary.
(continued next page)

TECHNIQUES

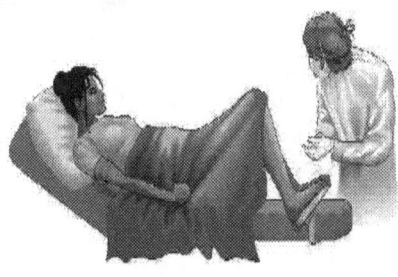

Lay on back, knees up and apart.
Break membrane, if necessary.

CHILDBIRTH, continued

EMERGENCY ACTION
6. As baby's head emerges, feel the neck for possible loop of umbilical chord. If present, slip it over the baby's head. If the cord is wrapped tightly around the baby's neck, and you cannot slip it off: clamp the cord in two places and cut the cord between the clamps. Then unwrap the cord.
7. Wipe out baby's nose and mouth with a clean cloth.
8. Support the baby with your hands as it emerges.
9. Rub the baby's back and flick the soles of its feet to stimulate breathing.
10. **If the baby does not start to breath within one minute, start CPR.**
11. Dry off the baby, and wrap in a blanket to keep warm.
12. Allow placenta to deliver. Place it in a plastic bag and save. The umbilical cord does not have to be cut.
13. If area between vagina and anus is torn and bleeding, treat as open wound.
14. Rub mother's uterus (belly) area until it is firm.
15. Immediately transport mother and baby to a medical facility.

TECHNIQUES

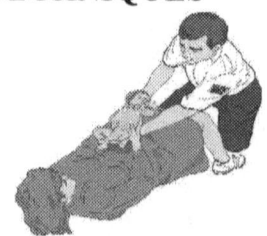

Wipe out baby's nose and mouth. Make sure baby starts to breath.

DIVING: DECOMPRESSION SICKNESS (THE BENDS)

SYMPTOMS   Symptoms can appear from 30 minutes to 24 hours after a dive.   Joint or limb pain, headache.   Numbness, tingling, paralysis, weakness.   Chest or abdominal pain.   Unconsciousness, fainting.   Dizziness, nausea, ringing in ears.   Unequal pupil size.   Loss of bladder or bowel control.   Staggering, slurred speech.
EMERGENCY ACTION   1. **CHECK ABC's**.   2. Lay the victim down flat.   3. Administer oxygen, if available.   4. Give fluids. Hydration is important.   5. **GET IMMEDIATE MEDICAL AID. CONTACT A DIVE PHYSICIAN. REQUEST TRANSPORT TO THE NEAREST HYPERBARIC CHAMBER.**
TECHNIQUES   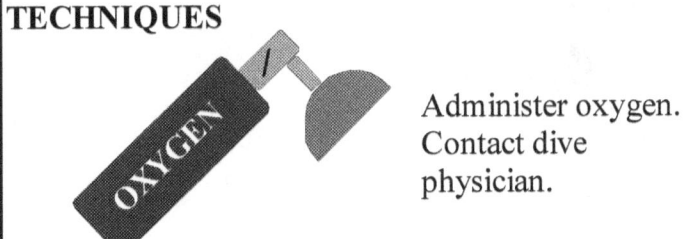 Administer oxygen. Contact dive physician.

DIVING: AIR EMBOLISM

SYMPTOMS   Symptoms tend to develop within minutes of the emergency.   Dizziness, disorientation.   Paralysis, weakness.   Convulsions.   Unconsciousness.   Chest pain, respiratory arrest.   Personality change.
EMERGENCY ACTION   1. **CHECK ABC's.**   2. Lay the victim down flat   3. Administer oxygen, if available.   4. Give fluids. Hydration is important.   5. **GET IMMEDIATE MEDICAL AID. CONTACT A DIVE PHYSICIAN. REQUEST TRANSPORT TO NEAREST HYPERBARIC CHAMBER.**
TECHNIQUES   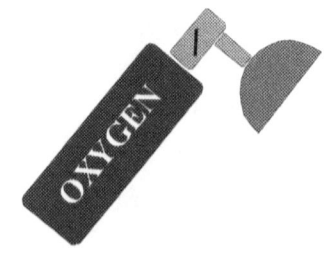 Administer oxygen. Contact dive physician.

DIVING: LUNG OVER-PRESSURE

SYMPTOMS
Pain in chest.
Rapid, shallow breathing.
Shortness of breath.
Difficulty breathing.
Faintness.
Bluish skin, lips, or fingernails.
Change in voice.

EMERGENCY ACTION
1. **CHECK ABC's**.
2. Administer oxygen, if available.
3. Closely monitor victim's condition.
4. Transport to a medical facility.
5. If condition worsens, get immediate medical attention. Contact a dive physician.

TECHNIQUES

Give oxygen. Monitor ABC's. Contact a dive physician.

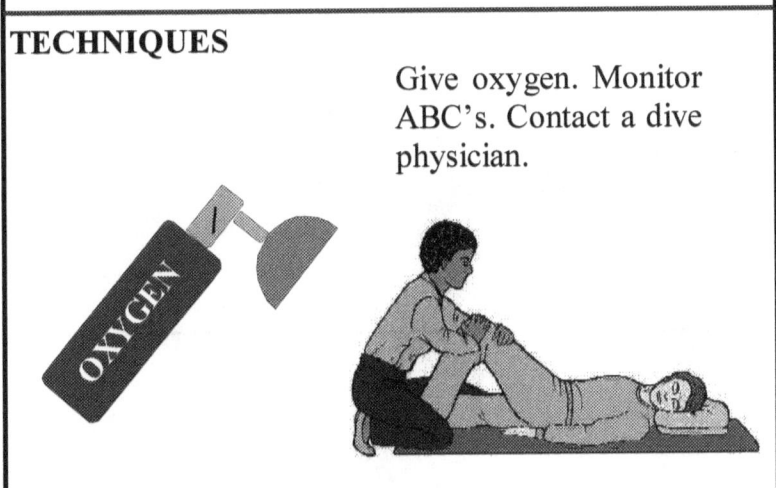

MOTION SICKNESS

SYMPTOMS
Nausea, vomiting.
Headache.
Dizziness.
Sweating.
Pale skin.

EMERGENCY ACTION
1. Move to area of fresh air, away from blowing engine exhaust.
2. Move to an area of the boat with the least amount of motion. This is usually the stern.
3. Keep eyes focused on the horizon.
4. Move as little as possible.
5. Give over-the-counter motion sickness medicine, if available.

TECHNIQUES

Keep eyes on horizon. Take available seasickness medication.

SUNBURN

SYMPTOMS
Red skin.
Blistering (may or may not be present).
Skin painful.
Skin may be warm to the touch.

EMERGENCY ACTION
1. Move victim to shaded area.
2. Do not break any blisters. If blisters will be rubbed by clothing, cover with clean dressings (bandages).
3. Apply cool, wet compresses to burned area.
4. Apply Calamine lotion only to mild sunburn.
5. Have victim take a cool bath or shower.
6. Give over-the-counter pain reliever like aspirin.

TECHNIQUES

Cool sunburned area.

Give pain reliever like aspirin.

Skipper's Handbook – Robert Grossman

FISHHOOK REMOVAL

SYMPTOMS
Fishhook embedded in skin.

EMERGENCY ACTION
1. Push the hook through the skin until the barb can be seen.
2. Using a wire cutter, cut off the barb or the shank of the hook, close to the skin.
3. Back out the unbarbed section of the hook by pulling gently.
4. Clean the wound and cover with a bandage.
5. To avoid possible infection, consult a physician.

TECHNIQUES

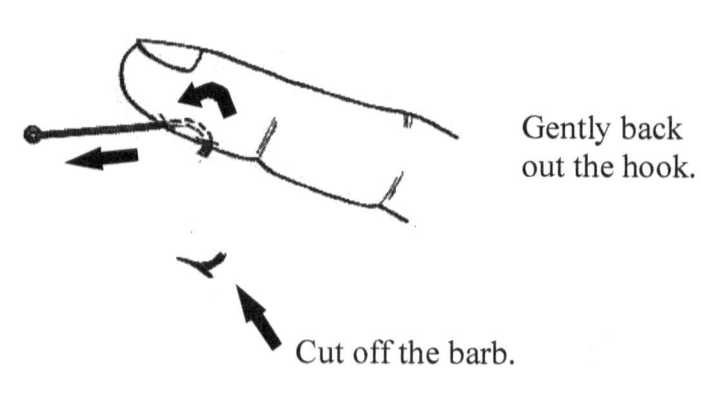

Gently back out the hook.

Cut off the barb.

SECTION 2
RULES OF THE ROAD

NAVIGATION RULES

Rights of Way: International and Inland.
For vessels within sight of one another.

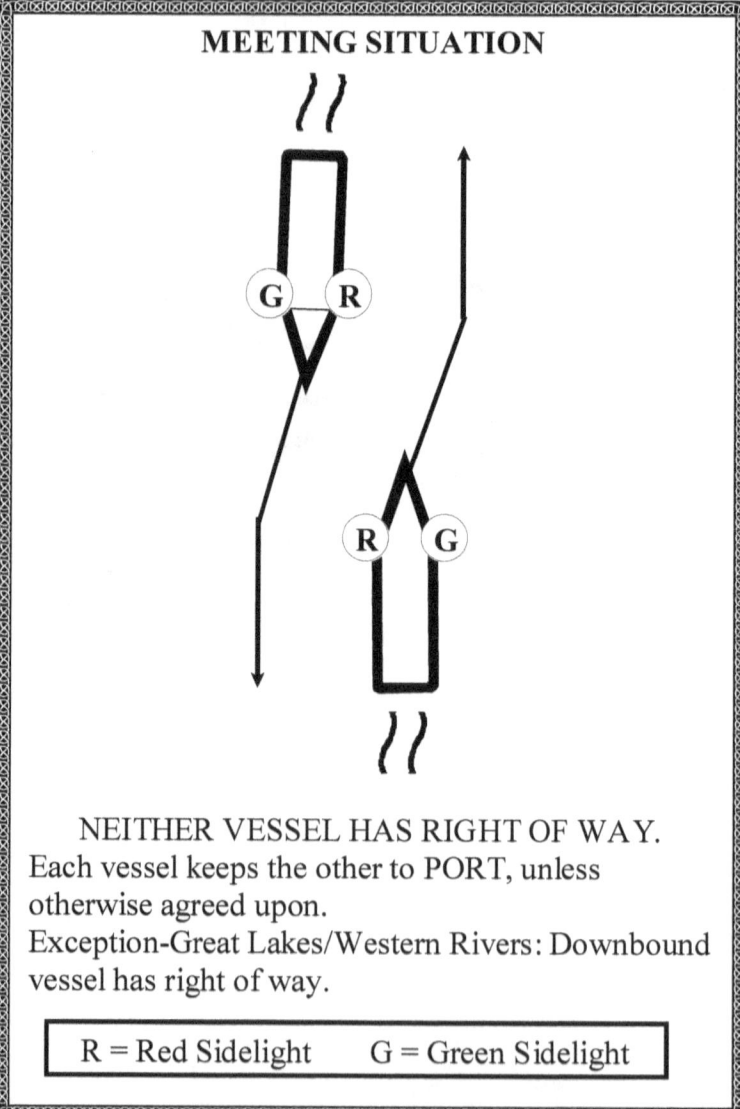

Rights of Way: International and Inland.
For vessels within sight of one another.

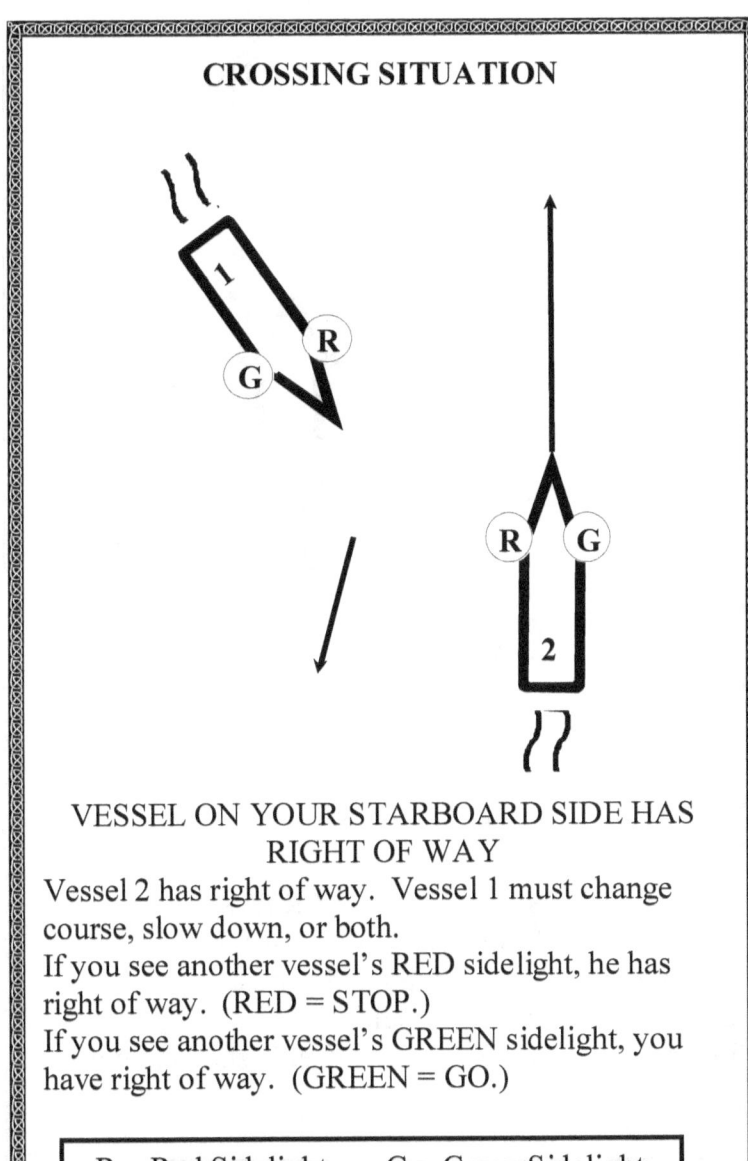

CROSSING SITUATION

VESSEL ON YOUR STARBOARD SIDE HAS RIGHT OF WAY

Vessel 2 has right of way. Vessel 1 must change course, slow down, or both.

If you see another vessel's RED sidelight, he has right of way. (RED = STOP.)

If you see another vessel's GREEN sidelight, you have right of way. (GREEN = GO.)

R = Red Sidelight   G = Green Sidelight

Rights of Way: International and Inland.
For vessels within sight of one another.

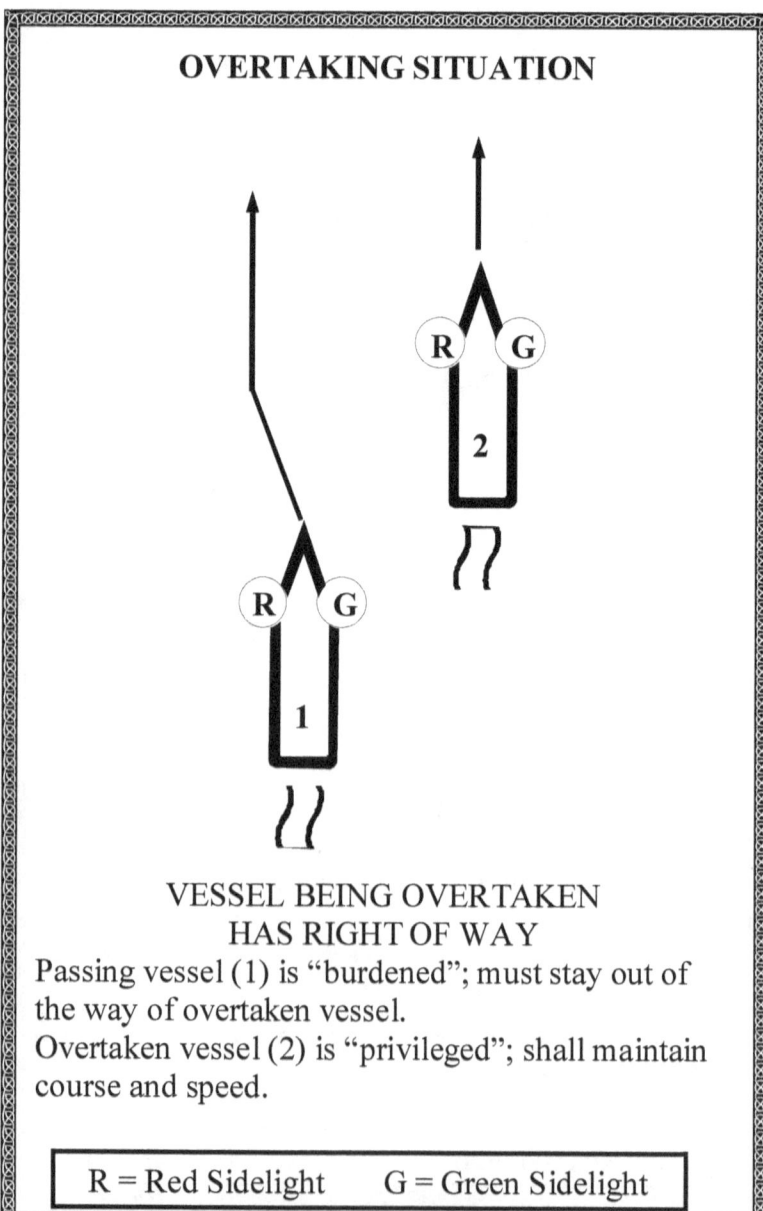

Rights of Way: International and Inland.
For vessels within sight of one another.

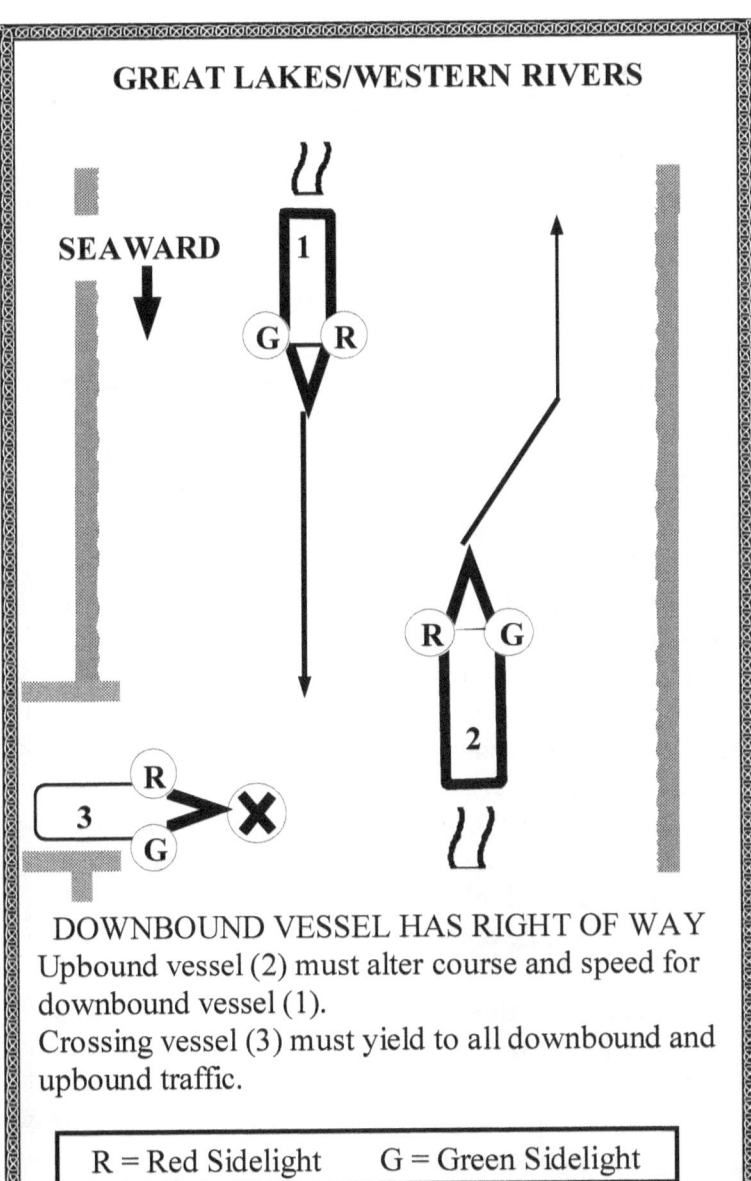

Hierarchy of Rights of Way

GENERAL VESSEL TRAFFIC:

1. **Vessel not under command.** Includes vessels adrift, vessels with mechanical failure, or other conditions that cause inability maneuver.

2. **Vessel restricted in ability to maneuver.** Includes vessels engaged in activities that limit maneuverability, such as towing, pushing, dredging, etc.

3. **Vessel engaged in fishing.** Vessels with lines out cannot maneuver as easily as other vessels.

4. **Sailing vessel.** Under sail only. If powered by sail and motor or motor only, then it has the same priority as a power-driven vessel.

5. **Power-driven vessel.** Regardless of size, power-driven vessels share the same (lowest) priory. This means that a 40 foot yacht does not have automatic right of way over a 20 foot runabout. Power-driven vessels must all obey the right-of-way rules for meeting, crossing and overtaking.

Each vessel on this list must yield right of way to vessel listed higher.

Note: A sailing vessel does not have the right of way if it overtakes a power-driven vessel.

Hierarchy of Rights of Way

VESSEL TRAFFIC IN NARROW CHANNELS:

1. **Vessel restricted in ability to maneuver.** Protects vessels that can safely navigate only within a narrow channel or fairway. Vessels restricted in maneuverability due to the nature of their work, such as towing or dredging, are secondary to vessels that can only maneuver within a channel or fairway. (Includes downbound vessels for Great Lakes and Western Rivers.)

2. **Sailing vessel.** Under sail only. If powered by sail and motor or motor only, then it has the same priority as a power-driven vessel.

3. **Power-driven vessel under 20 meters.**

4. **Vessel engaged in fishing.** Vessels with lines out cannot maneuver as easily as other vessels, but priority is given to through traffic.

5. **Vessel crossing channel.** Crossing vessels must wait for through traffic to clear.

Each vessel on this list must yield right of way to vessel listed higher.

Hierarchy of Rights of Way

ORDER AMONG SAILING VESSELS:

1. Vessel with the wind on its port side stays out of the way of the other vessel.

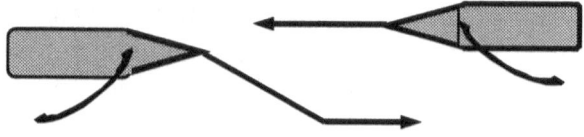

2. If the wind is on the same side for each vessel, the vessel that is to leeward has the right of way.

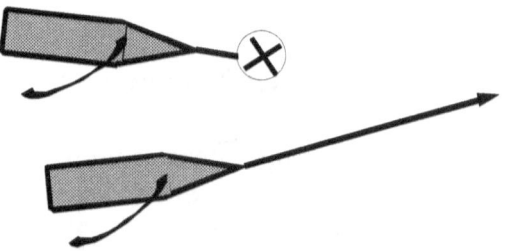

3. A vessel with the wind on its port side shall yield to a windward vessel, if it cannot be determined which side the other vessel carries the wind.

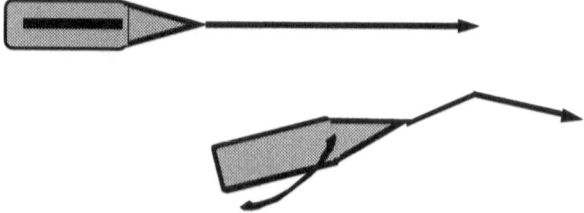

SKIPPER'S RESPONSIBILITIES

1. Good Seamanship Rule: You must take action to avoid a collision. You must comply with the Navigation Rules or take some other action as necessary to avoid a collision. Applies to skipper, vessel owner, crew, and vessel.

2. Prudential Rule: If immediate danger cannot be avoided when following the Navigation Rules, then take some other positive action. A departure from the Rules may be taken when both vessels must act to avoid a collision, and when collision will result if action is not taken.

3. Lookouts: Every vessel must have an alert lookout while underway, to warn of any risk of collision or other danger. The observer can be the skipper or helmsman, as long as he has no other responsibilities that would distract him from observing. The use of radar, autopilot, or other equipment does not replace an observer.

4. Collision Avoidance: Many vessel operators do not know the rules of the road. You must be prepared to take action to avoid a collision, if necessary.

SKIPPER'S RESPONSIBILITIES

5. Obvious Action: Any action taken to avoid a collision must be obvious, and readily apparent to the other vessel. Avoid small or gradual changes in course or speed; make them pronounced enough so that there is no mistaking your intentions.

6. Overtaking: Any vessel overtaking (passing) another vessel must keep out of the way of the overtaken vessel.

7. Sound Signals: Use the appropriate sound signals whenever required. Contact the other skipper on the radio, when necessary, to reach an agreement for crossing, passing, or overtaking.

8. Traffic Schemes: Many ports and other congested waterways have regulated traffic schemes that may control the movement of your vessel or others.

9. Right of Way: It is the Skipper's responsibility to know who has the right of way in any given situation. Even if you have the right of way, yielding is always a better option than endangering your vessel or crew.

10. Safety: Your are responsible for the safety of your crew and passengers. You are obligated to take action as necessary to avoid injury or accident to anyone aboard. Being unfamiliar with navigational rules or with vessel handling techniques does not lessen your responsibilities as a skipper.

U.S. AIDS TO NAVIGATION

Buoys and markers on navigable waters except Western Rivers and Intracoastal Waterway.

Port Side: Green buoys, cans, and daymarks with **odd** numbers.	Returning from sea, or traveling upstream.	**Starboard Side: Red** buoys, nuns, and daymarks with **even** numbers.
Lighted Buoy		Lighted Buoy
Can		Nun
Daymark	Keep the **RED** buoys on your **RIGHT** when **RETURNING** from seaward.	Daymark

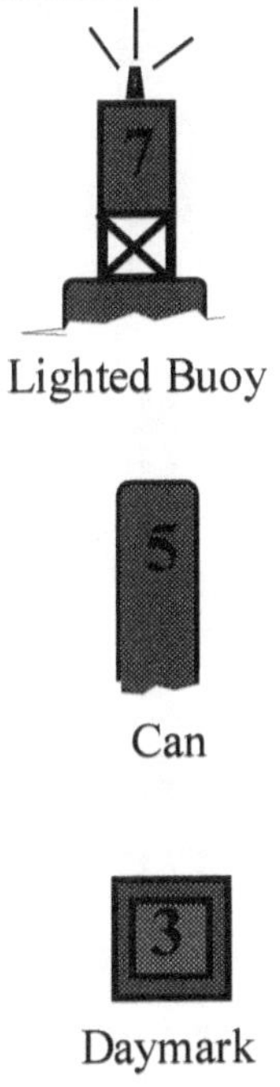

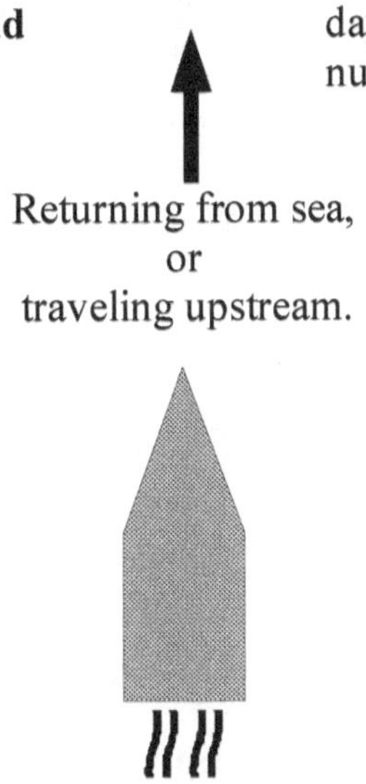

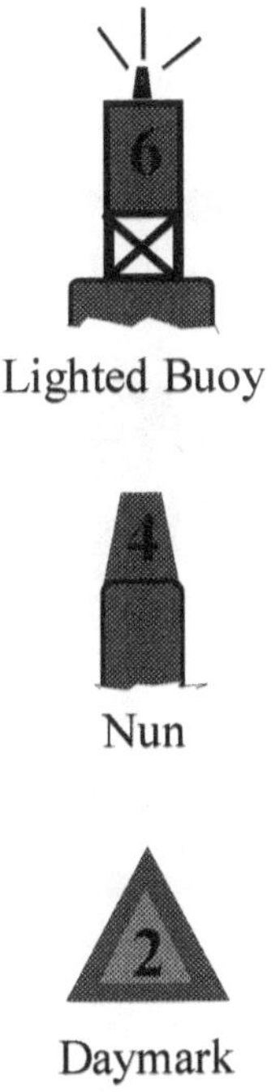

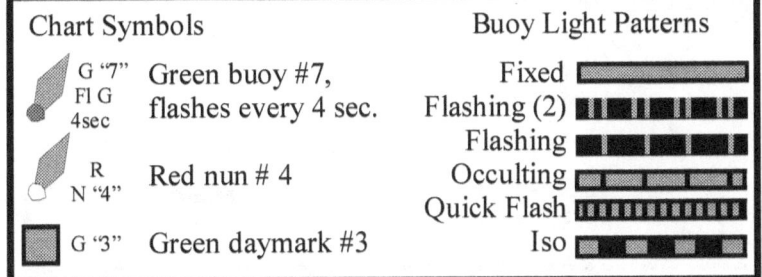

Chart Symbols
- G "7" Fl G 4sec — Green buoy #7, flashes every 4 sec.
- R N "4" — Red nun # 4
- G "3" — Green daymark #3

Buoy Light Patterns
- Fixed
- Flashing (2)
- Flashing
- Occulting
- Quick Flash
- Iso

Buoys and markers on navigable waters except Western Rivers and Intracoastal Waterway.

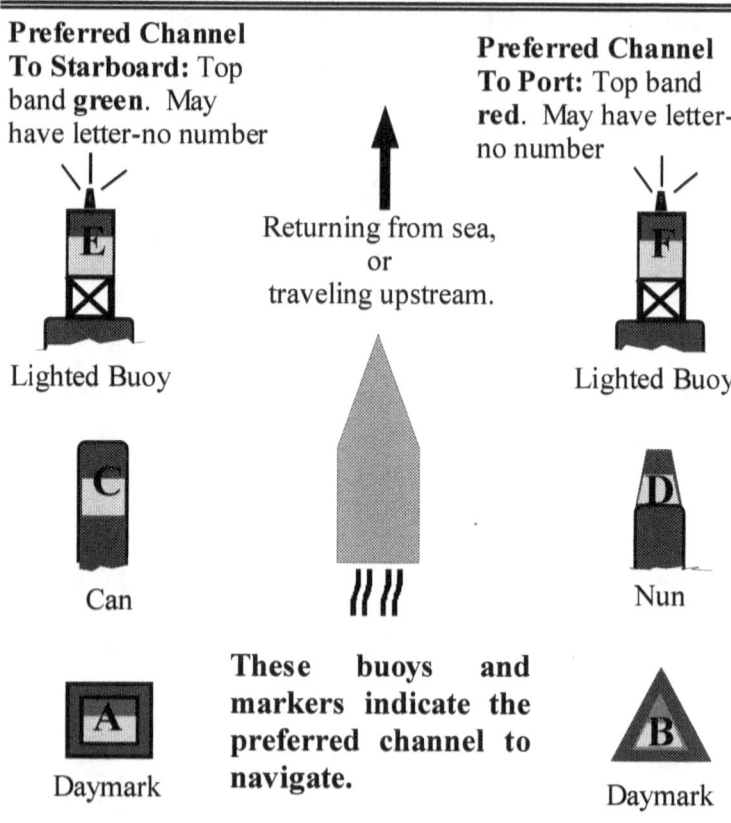

Preferred Channel To Starboard: Top band **green**. May have letter-no number

Lighted Buoy

Can

Daymark

Returning from sea, or traveling upstream.

These buoys and markers indicate the preferred channel to navigate.

Preferred Channel To Port: Top band **red**. May have letter-no number

Lighted Buoy

Nun

Daymark

Chart Symbols

GR"E" Fl 2+1G — Green-over-Red buoy "E", flashes 2 + 1 green

RG N "D" — Red-over-Green nun "D"

GR "A" — Green-over-Red daymark "A"

Buoy Light Pattern
Flashing (2 + 1)

Buoys and markers on navigable waters except Western Rivers and Intracoastal Waterway.

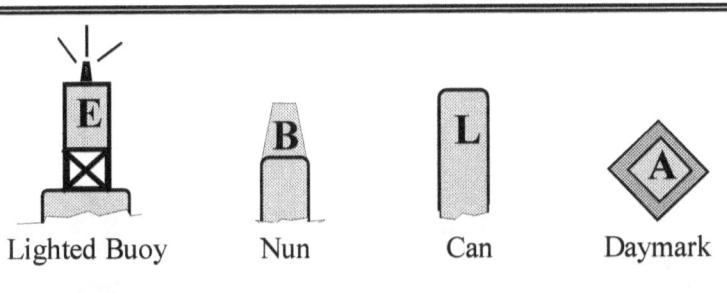

Lighted Buoy   Nun   Can   Daymark

Special Marks: Usually yellow, may be lettered. Placed appropriate for its position in the waterway, and the direction of buoyage.

Range Daymarks   Daymarks can be red, green, or black. Informational or regulatory only.

Danger   Exclusion Area Do Not Enter   Restricted Area

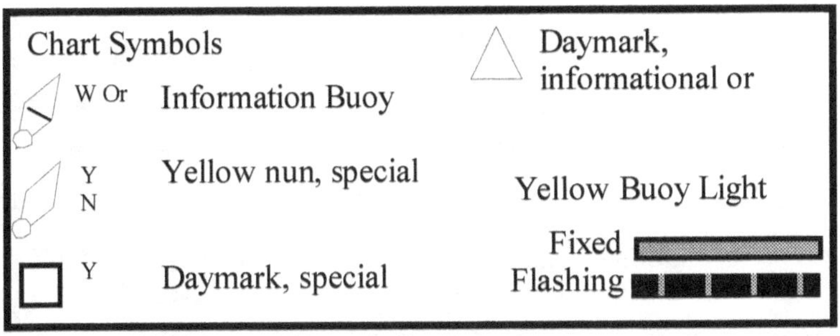

Chart Symbols		
W Or	Information Buoy	△ Daymark, informational or
Y N	Yellow nun, special	Yellow Buoy Light
Y	Daymark, special	Fixed ▬▬▬▬ Flashing ▪▪▪▪▪

Buoys and markers on Western Rivers.

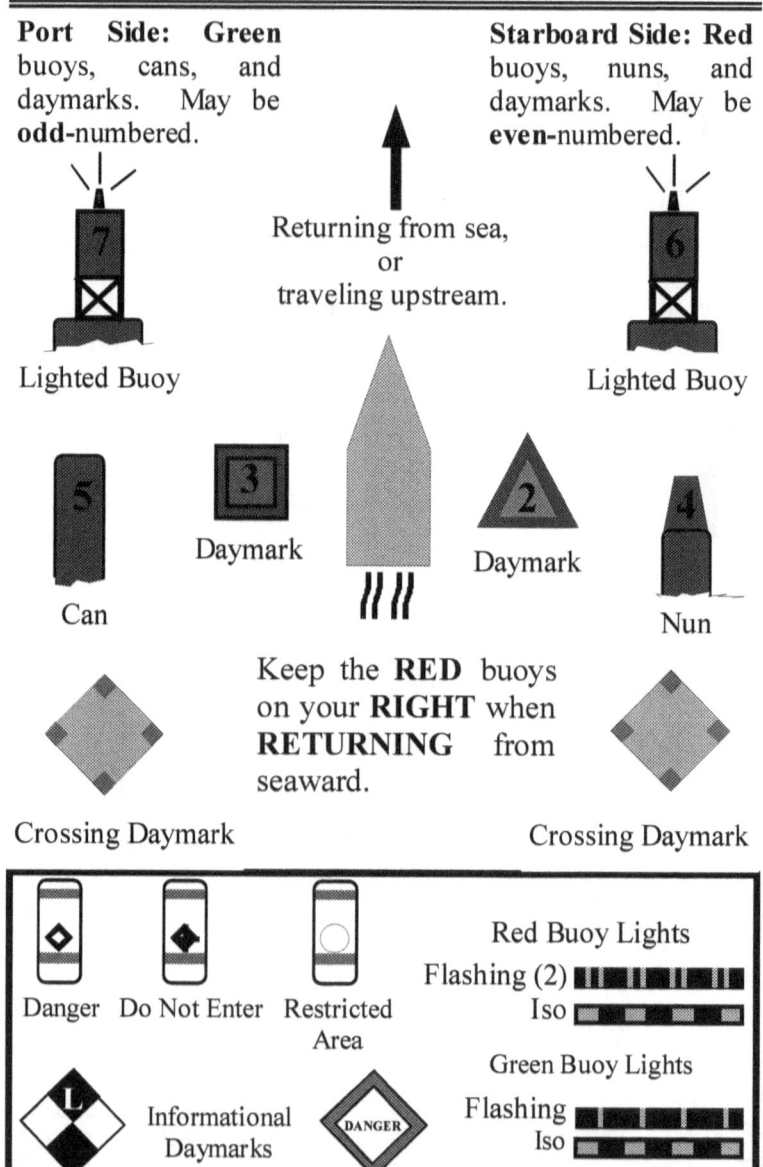

Buoys and markers on Western Rivers.

Preferred Channel To Starboard: Top band **green**.

Preferred Channel To Port: Top band **red**.

↑ Returning from sea, or traveling upstream.

Lighted Buoy

Lighted Buoy

Can

Nun

Daymark

These buoys and markers indicate the preferred channel to navigate.

Daymark

Chart Symbols

- GR Fl 2+1G — Green-over-Red buoy, flashes 2 + 1 green
- RG N — Red-over-Green nun
- GR — Green-over-Red daymark

Buoy Light Pattern
Flashing (2 + 1)

Buoys and markers on the Intracoastal Waterway.

Port Side: Green buoys, cans, and daymarks with **odd** numbers.

Starboard Side: Red buoys, nuns, and daymarks with **even** numbers.

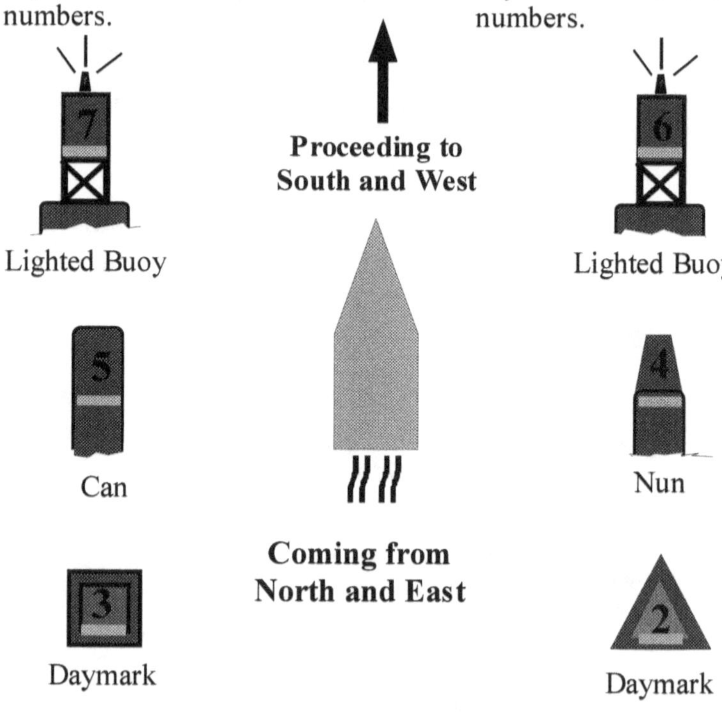

Proceeding to South and West

Lighted Buoy (7) Lighted Buoy (6)

Can (5) Nun (4)

Coming from North and East

Daymark (3) Daymark (2)

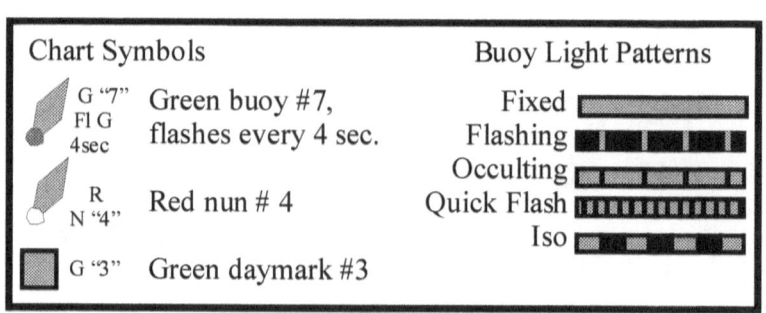

Chart Symbols

- G "7" Fl G 4sec — Green buoy #7, flashes every 4 sec.
- R N "4" — Red nun # 4
- G "3" — Green daymark #3

Buoy Light Patterns

- Fixed
- Flashing
- Occulting
- Quick Flash
- Iso

Skipper's Handbook – Robert Grossman

Buoys and markers on Intracoastal Waterway.

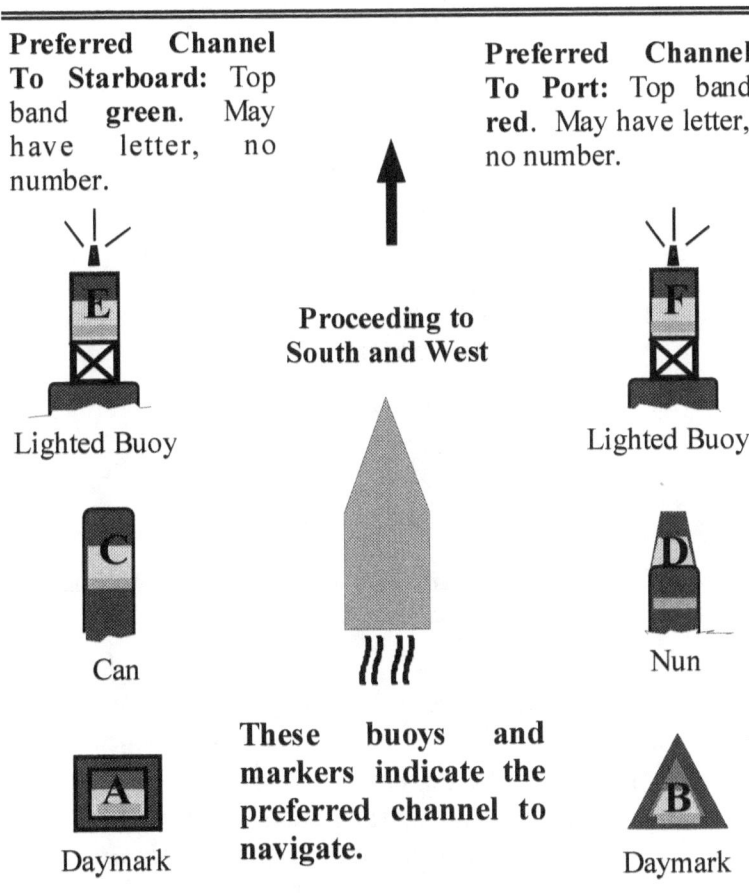

Preferred Channel To Starboard: Top band **green**. May have letter, no number.

Lighted Buoy

Can

Daymark

Preferred Channel To Port: Top band **red**. May have letter, no number.

Lighted Buoy

Nun

Daymark

Proceeding to South and West

These buoys and markers indicate the preferred channel to navigate.

Chart Symbols

GR"E" Fl 2+1G — Green-over-Red buoy "E", flashes 2 + 1 green

RG N"D" — Red-over-Green nun "D"

GR "A" — Green-over-Red daymark "A"

Buoy Light Pattern Flashing (2 + 1)

Buoys and markers on Intracoastal Waterway.

Lighted Buoy   Spherical Mark   Daymark

Safe Water Marks: Red and white, may be lettered. Shows areas of water that are safe to navigate.

Range Daymarks   Daymarks can be red, green, or black. Informational or regulatory only.

When following the Intracoastal Waterway from New Jersey through Texas, a " r " mark appearing on a navigation aid should be kept to starboard, and a □ mark appearing on a navigation aid should be kept to port. This applies despite the color of the navigation aid.

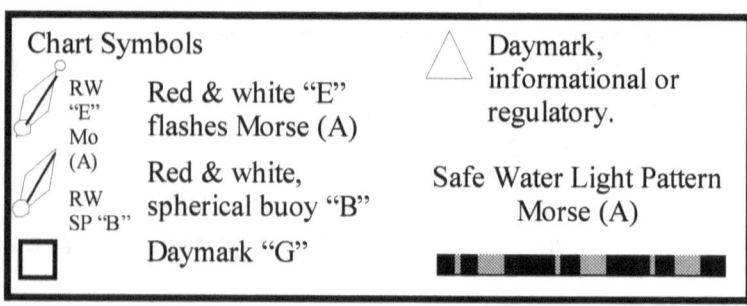

Skipper's Handbook – Robert Grossman

Uniform State Waterway Marking System: Buoys and markers in channels, rivers, and lakes.

Port Side: Black with odd numbers. Shape of buoys may vary.		Starboard Side: Red with even numbers. Shape of buoys may vary.
 Port	 Keep the **RED** buoys on your **RIGHT** when **R E T U R N I N G** upstream..	 Starboard
 Black-topped white buoy: Boat should pass to North or East of the buoy. May show quick-flashing white light.	 Red and white vertical-striped buoy: Do not pass between this buoy and the nearest shore.	 Red-topped white buoy: Boat should pass to South or West of the buoy. May show quick-flashing white light.
 **DANGER:** Nature of warning is described within.	 **Boats Keep Out:** Area is off-limits to vessel traffic.	 Regulated Area: Contains instructions.

NAVIGATION LIGHTS

Inland Waters
As seen from an oncoming vessel at night.

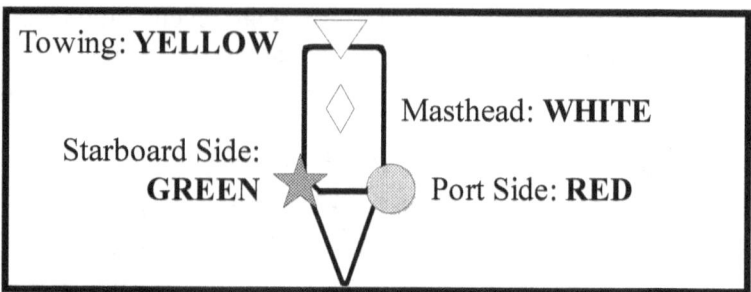

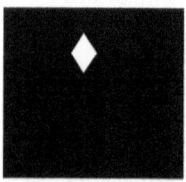
At Anchor: under 50 m. Not required for vessels under 7 m if anchored where other vessels do not normally navigate.

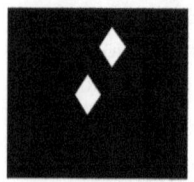
At Anchor: 50 m and over.

Power-Driven Vessel: under 50 m, making way. Power-driven vessels under 7 m and whose maximum speed is less than 7 knots, need only one white all-round light.

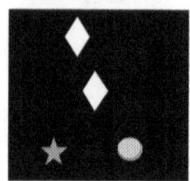
Power-Driven Vessel: 50 m and over, making way.

INLAND WATERS
As seen from an oncoming vessel at night.

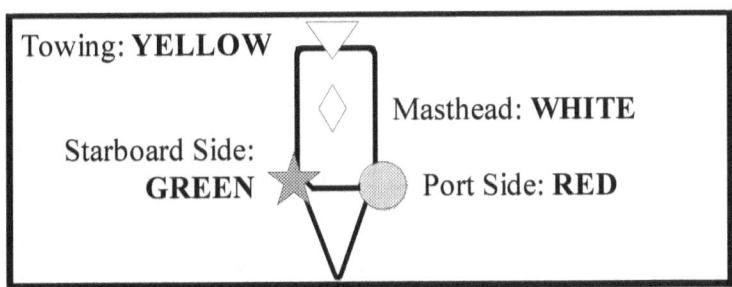

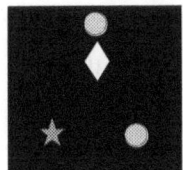
Engaged in Fishing: making way.

Engaged in Fishing: at anchor or not making way.

Fishing by Trawling: making way. No sidelights if not making way or anchored. If over 50 m, it will carry a white masthead light over other lights.

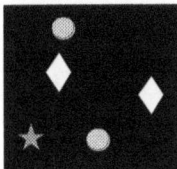
Fishing with Gear: gear extends out over 150 m to side of vessel. The extra all-round white light will be on the side where the gear is an obstruction.

INLAND WATERS
As seen from an oncoming vessel at night.

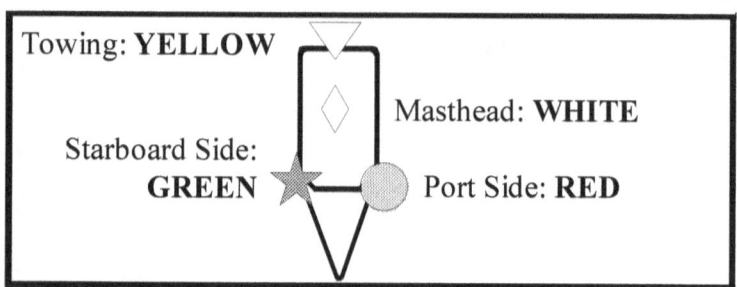

Vessel Under Sail: over 7 m. Also, vessel being towed. Sailing vessel under 7 m needs only hand-held white light.

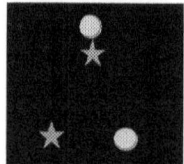
Vessel Under Sail: optional lights. Not allowed if sidelights and sternlight are combined into one lantern at top of mast.

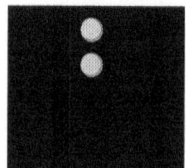
Not Under Command: not making way. Vessels under 12 m are exempt.

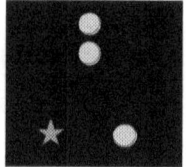
Not Under Command: making way. Vessels under 12 m are exempt.

INLAND WATERS
As seen from an oncoming vessel at night.

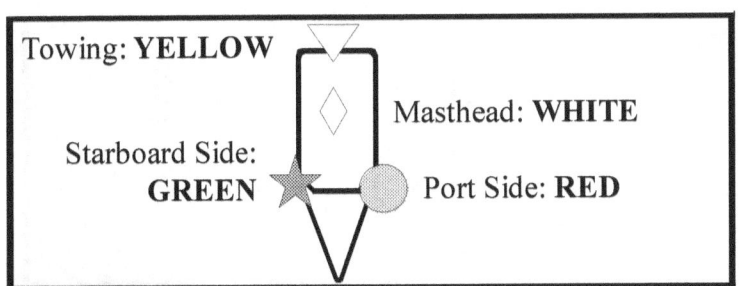

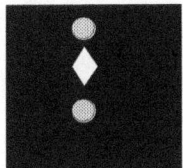

Restricted Maneuverability: not making way. Vessels under 12 m are exempt.

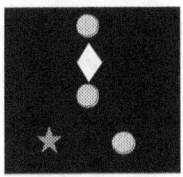

Restricted Maneuverability: making way. Will have extra masthead white light if 50 m or over. Vessels under 12 m are exempt.

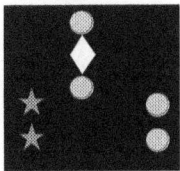

Restricted Maneuverability: obstruction/dredging. All-round red lights mark side of obstruction. All-round green lights mark clear side. Vessels under 12 m are exempt.

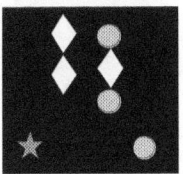

Restricted Maneuverability: while towing. The red-white-red lights can be added when the towing vessel is unable to deviate from its course. Vessels under 12 m are exempt.

Skipper's Handbook – Robert Grossman

INLAND WATERS
As seen from an oncoming vessel at night.

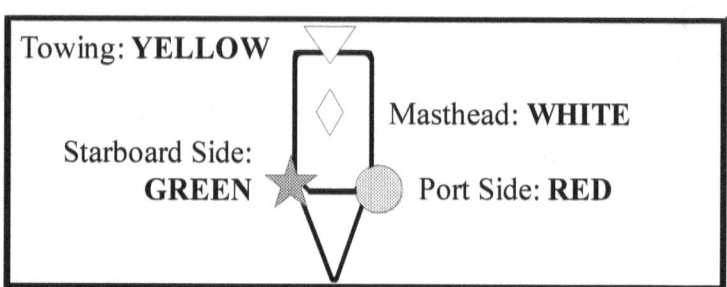

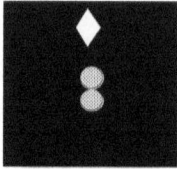

Vessel Aground: under 50 m. Add second masthead light if 50 m or over. Vessels under 12 m need only display anchor light.

Vessel Being Towed. Towed astern or alongside. Must also have stern light.

Towing Astern: tow length 200 m or less astern, tow vessel under 50 m. Add a white masthead light if tow vessel is 50 m or over.

Towing Astern: tow length over 200 m astern, tow vessel under 50 m. Add a white masthead light if tow vessel is 50 m or over.

INLAND WATERS
As seen from an oncoming vessel at night.

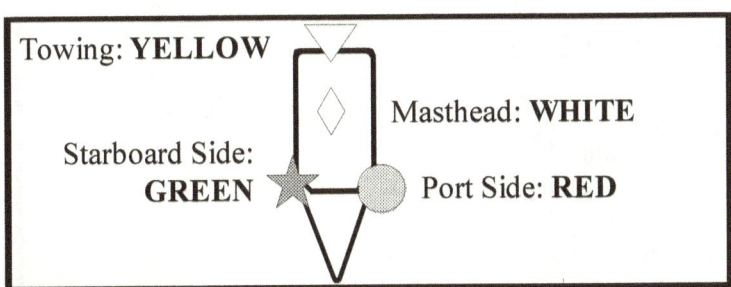

Towing: **YELLOW**
Masthead: **WHITE**
Starboard Side: **GREEN**
Port Side: **RED**

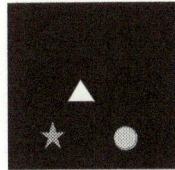

Vessel Being Pushed. Yellow light flashes at 50-70 times per minute, and must have visibility arc of 180° - 225°.

Tug-Barge: composite unit. Has same lights as single power-driven vessel, making way.

Pilot Vessel: on pilotage duty.

Power-Driven Vessel: Great Lakes. Carries an all-round white light instead of a second masthead light and sternlight.

Skipper's Handbook – Robert Grossman

INLAND WATERS
As seen from an oncoming vessel at night.

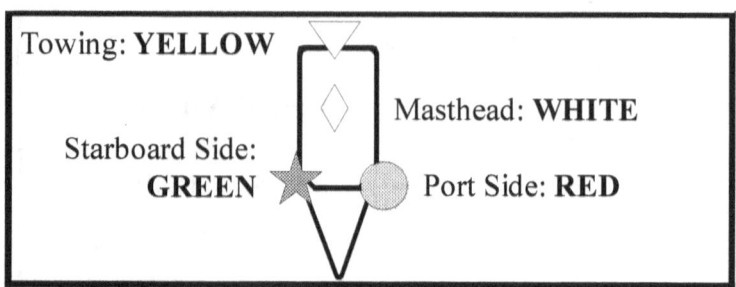

Towing By Pushing Ahead: under 50 m. (Excluding Western Rivers*.) Green, yellow, red at bottom are on barge. Yellow flashes. Add masthead white light if tow vessel is 50 m or more.

Towing By Pushing Ahead: Western Rivers*. Green, yellow, red at bottom are on barge. Yellow flashes.

Towing Alongside: tow vessel under 50 m. (Excluding Western Rivers*.) Green and red at left are on barge. Add white masthead light if tow vessel is 50 m or more.

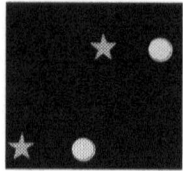

Towing Alongside: Western Rivers*. Green, red at left are on barge.

INLAND WATERS
As seen from an oncoming vessel at night.

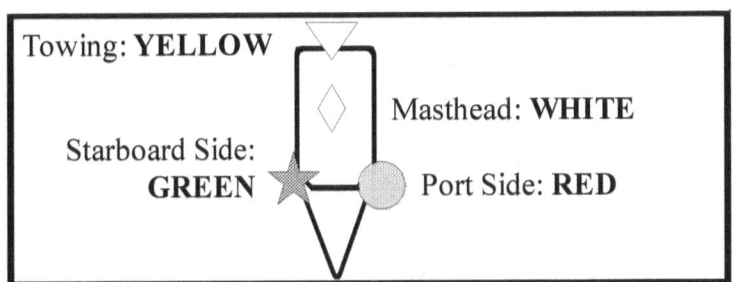

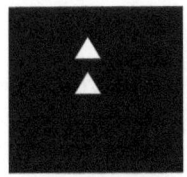
Towing By Pushing Ahead: stern view. All Inland Waters, including Western Rivers*.

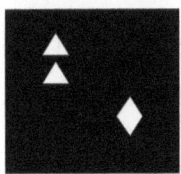
Towing Alongside: stern view. All Inland Waters, including Western Rivers*.
White light is the sternlight of the barge.

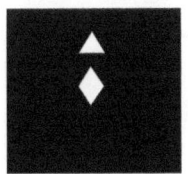
Towing Astern: stern view.

Mineclearance Vessel: under 50 m. Keep clear. Dangerous to approach within 1000 m. Add second masthead light if 50 m or over.

INLAND WATERS

As seen from an oncoming vessel at night.

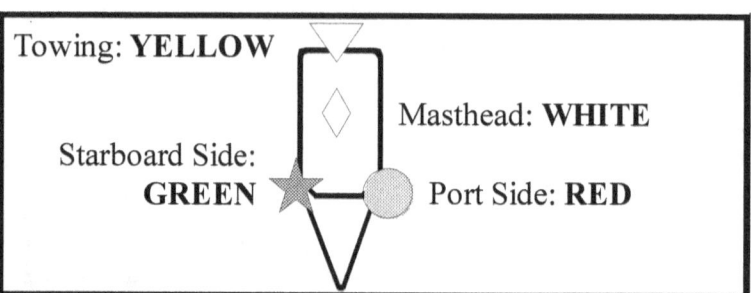

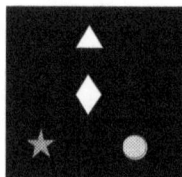

Air Cushion Vessel. When in non-displacement mode, all-round yellow light flashes at least 120 times per minute.

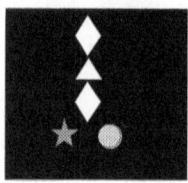

Submarine. All-round yellow light flashes three times (1 sec. each), then off for 3 seconds.

ARCS OF VISIBILITY

Masthead lights: 225°, toward the bow.
Starboard sidelight: 112.5°, from front to side.
Port sidelight: 112.5°, from front to side.
Anchor light: 360°, visible all around.
Towing light: 135°, toward the stern.
Special identity lights: 360°, visible all around.
* **Western Rivers** above the Huey P. Long bridge on the Mississippi River, or waters specified by the Secretary.

INTERNATIONAL WATERS
As seen from an oncoming vessel at night.

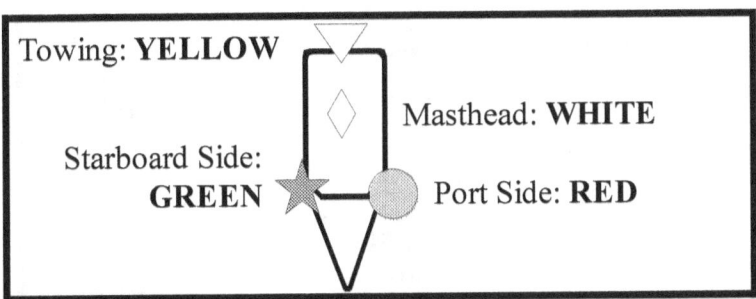

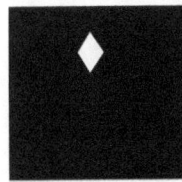

At Anchor: under 50 m. Not required for vessels under 7 m if anchored where other vessels do not normally navigate.

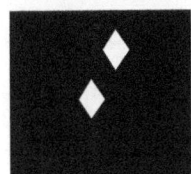

At Anchor: 50 m and over.

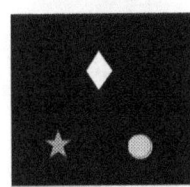

Power-Driven Vessel: under 50 m, making way. Power-driven vessels under 7 m and whose maximum speed is less than 7 knots, need only one white all-round light.

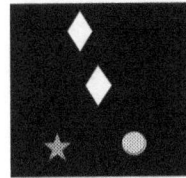

Power-Driven Vessel: 50 m and over, making way.

INTERNATIONAL WATERS
As seen from an oncoming vessel at night.

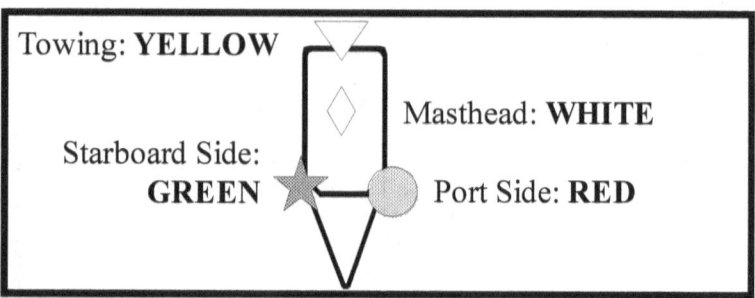

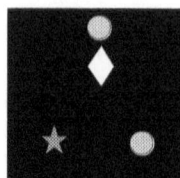

Engaged in Fishing: making way.

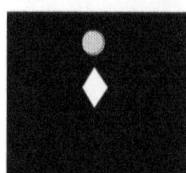

Engaged in Fishing: at anchor or not making way.

Fishing by Trawling: making way. No sidelights if not making way or anchored. If over 50 m, it will carry a white masthead light over other lights.

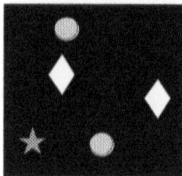

Fishing with Gear: gear extends out over 150 m to side of vessel. The extra all-round white light will be on the side where the gear is an obstruction.

INTERNATIONAL WATERS
As seen from an oncoming vessel at night.

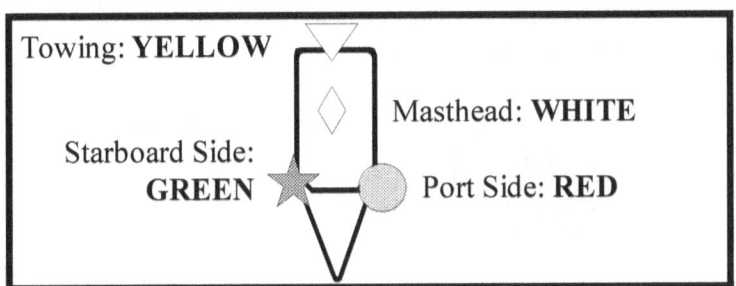

Vessel Under Sail: over 7 m. Also, vessel being towed. Sailing vessel under 7 m needs only hand-held white light.

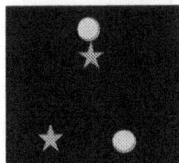

Vessel Under Sail: optional lights. Not allowed if sidelights and sternlight are combined into one lantern at top of mast.

Not Under Command: not making way. Vessels under 12 m are exempt.

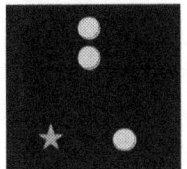

Not Under Command: making way. Vessels under 12 m are exempt.

Skipper's Handbook – Robert Grossman

INTERNATIONAL WATERS
As seen from an oncoming vessel at night.

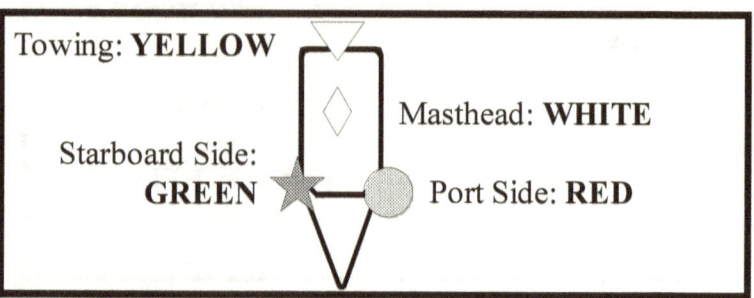

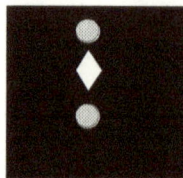
Restricted Maneuverability: not making way. Vessels under 12 m are exempt.

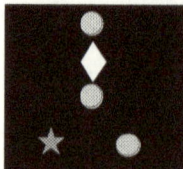
Restricted Maneuverability: making way. Will have extra masthead white light if 50 m or over. Vessels under 12 m are exempt.

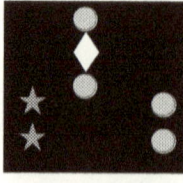
Restricted Maneuverability: obstruction/dredging. All-round red lights mark side of obstruction. All-round green lights mark clear side. Vessels under 12 m are exempt.

Restricted Maneuverability: while towing. The red-white-red lights can be added when the towing vessel is unable to deviate from its course. Vessels under 12 m are exempt.

INTERNATIONAL WATERS
As seen from an oncoming vessel at night.

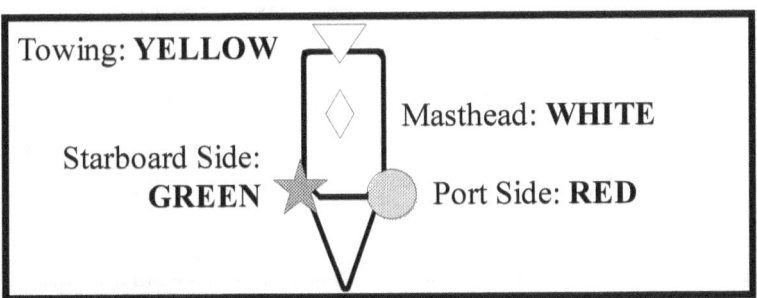

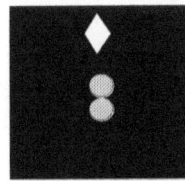

Vessel Aground: under 50 m. Add second masthead light if 50 m or over. Vessels under 12 m need only display anchor light.

Vessel Being Towed. Towed astern or alongside. Must also have sternlight.

Towing Astern: tow length 200 m or less astern, tow vessel under 50 m. Add a white masthead light if tow vessel is 50 m or over.

Towing Astern: tow length over 200 m astern, tow vessel under 50 m. Add a white masthead light if tow vessel is 50 m or over.

INTERNATIONAL WATERS
As seen from an oncoming vessel at night.

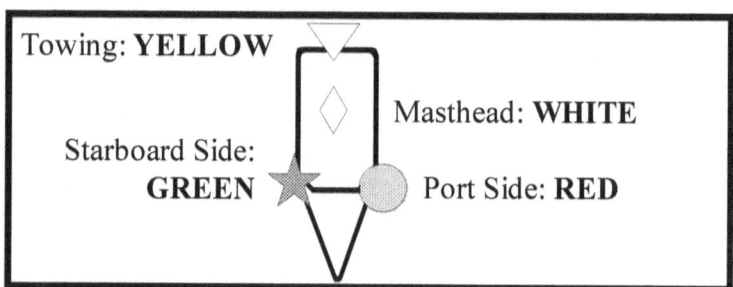

Vessel Being Pushed. No sternlight required.

Tug-Barge: composite unit. Has same lights as single power-driven vessel, making way.

Pilot Vessel: on pilotage duty.

Constrained by Draft: making way
Add second masthead light if 50 m or over.

INTERNATIONAL WATERS
As seen from an oncoming vessel at night.

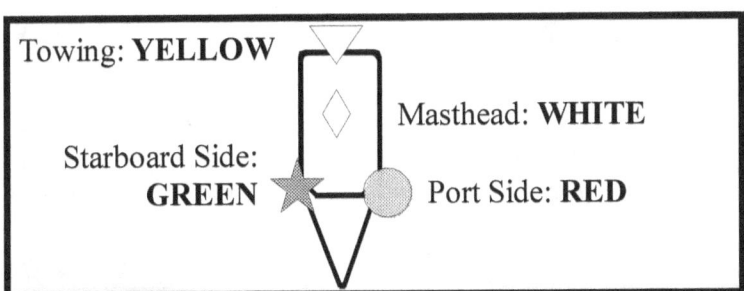

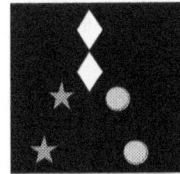
Towing By Pushing Ahead: under 50 m. Green and red lights at bottom are on the barge.

Towing By Pushing Ahead: 50 m and over. Green and red at bottom are on barge.

Towing Alongside: under 50 m. Green and red at left are on barge.

Towing Alongside: 50 m and over. Green and red at left are on barge.

INTERNATIONAL WATERS
As seen from an oncoming vessel at night.

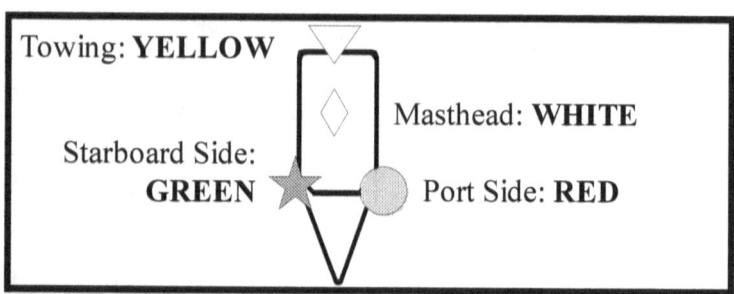

Towing By Pushing Ahead: stern view.

Towing Alongside: stern view. Light on lower right is the sternlight of the barge.

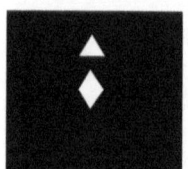

Towing Astern: stern view.

Mineclearance Vessel: under 50 m. Keep clear. Dangerous to approach within 1000 m. Add second masthead light if 50 m or over.

Skipper's Handbook – Robert Grossman

INTERNATIONAL WATERS
As seen from an oncoming vessel at night.

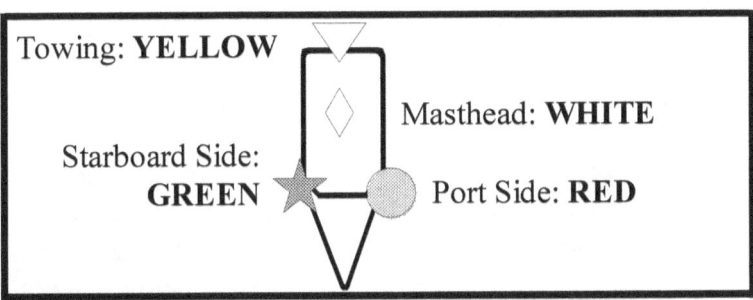

Towing: **YELLOW**

Masthead: **WHITE**

Starboard Side: **GREEN**

Port Side: **RED**

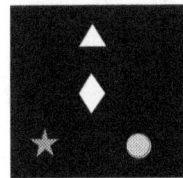

Air Cushion Vessel. When in non-displacement mode, all-round yellow light flashes at least 120 times per minute.

Submarine. All-round yellow light flashes three times (1 sec. each), then off for 3 seconds.

ARCS OF VISIBILITY

Masthead lights: 225°, toward the bow.
Starboard sidelight: 112.5°, from front to side.
Port sidelight: 112.5°, from front to side.
Anchor light: 360°, visible all around.
Towing light: 135°, toward the stern.
Special identity lights: 360°, visible all around.

DAYSHAPES

International and Inland Waters
Vessels are required to display dayshapes during daylight hours. Vessels under 12 meters are not required to display dayshapes, except for vessels engaged in diving. Vessels engaged in diving must display either the code flag alpha or the ball-diamond-ball dayshape. Vessels under 20 meters are not required to display a dayshape when anchored in a special anchorage area. Vessels under 7 meters are not required to show anchor lights or dayshapes unless they are in or near an area where other vessels normally navigate, such as a channel or fairway.

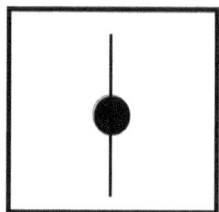

Vessel at Anchor.

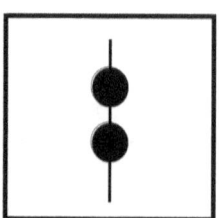

Not Under Command: making way or not making way.

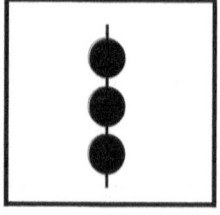

Vessel Aground.

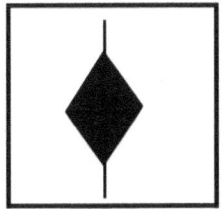 **Towing Astern or Vessel Being Towed:** tow length over 200 m.

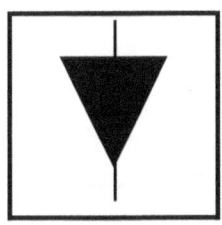 **Sailing Vessel:** under sail and power.

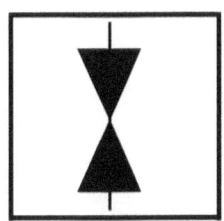 **Engaged in Fishing:** making way or not making way.

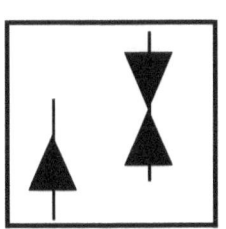 **Engaged in Fishing:** gear out more than 150 m from vessel. Cone at the left marks the side where obstruction exists.

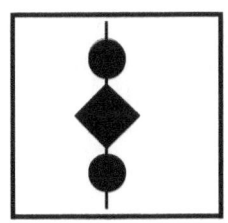 **Restricted Maneuverability.** Also: engaged in towing where vessel cannot deviate from course.

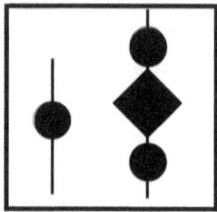

Restricted Maneuverability: at anchor.

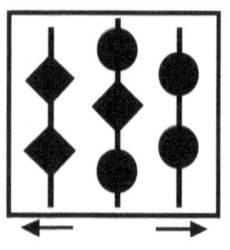

Restricted Maneuverability: Dredging. Balls are on side of obstruction. Diamonds indicate the safe side to navigate.

← SAFE   → DANGER

Constrained By Draft: International Rules Only.

Blue and white "Alpha" flag.

Diving Operations In Progress. A rigid flag replica should be displayed only on vessels whose size makes it impractical to exhibit the Restricted Maneuverability Dayshapes.

SOUND SIGNALS

Inland Waters
The following sound signals are used when you are within sight of another vessel, and will meet or pass within 1/2 mile of the other vessel.

▬ Prolonged blast (5 sec)　　■ Short blast (1 sec)

Situation or Intent	Sound Signal	Answer Signal
"Warning", "Danger", or "I disagree with your intent".	■ ■ ■ ■ ■	None
Leaving a dock or berth.	▬	None
Approaching a bend or blind curve in a channel or fairway, where other vessels may be obscured.	▬	▬ Acknowledgment
"My engines are in reverse", even if the vessel is moving forward.	■ ■ ■	None

Inland Waters

■▬▬ Prolonged blast (5 sec)   ■ Short blast (1 sec)

Situation or Intent	Sound Signal	Answer Signal
Meeting / Crossing: "I intend to leave you on my PORT side".	■	■ Agreement ■ ■ ■ ■ ■ Danger or Disagree
Meeting / Crossing: "I intend to leave you on my STARBOARD side".	■ ■	■ ■ Agreement ■ ■ ■ ■ ■ Danger or Disagree

Inland Waters

▬ Prolonged blast (5 sec)   ■ Short blast (1 sec)

Situation or Intent	Sound Signal	Answer Signal
Overtaking another vessel in a narrow channel or fairway: "I intend to pass you on your STARBOARD side".	■	■ Agreement ■■■■■ Danger or Disagree
Overtaking another vessel in a narrow channel or fairway: "I intend to pass you on your PORT side".	■■	■■ Agreement ■■■■■ Danger or Disagree

Additional Rules - Inland Waters

You must have visual contact with other vessel and be within ½ mile of each other when using sound signals, except when approaching a blind curve in a channel or fairway, or when leaving a dock or berth.

Certain sound signals may be supplemented by flashing an all-round white or yellow light, visible at a minimum of 2 miles and synchronized with the sound signals:

"I intend to leave you on my PORT side"- 1 flash lasting 1 second, "I intend to leave you on my STARBOARD side" -2 flashes, lasting 1 second each, "I am operating astern propulsion"- 3 flashes lasting 1 second each, "Danger" or disagreement response to being overtaken by another vessel - 5 short, rapid flashes.

You may establish a meeting, crossing, or overtaking agreement with the other vessel by using the marine radio, instead of using sound signals. If unable to contact and agree by radio, then sound signals must be used.

If whistles are fitted on a vessel more than 100 meters apart, then only one whistle shall be used for these sound signals.

Skipper's Handbook – Robert Grossman

SOUND SIGNALS

International Waters
The following sound signals are used when you are within sight of another vessel, and will meet or pass within 1/2 mile of the other vessel.

▬ Prolonged blast (5 sec)   ▪ Short blast (1 sec)

Situation or Intent	Sound Signal	Answer Signal
"Warning", "Danger", or "I disagree with your intent".	▪▪▪▪▪	None
Approaching a bend or blind curve in a channel or fairway, where other vessels may be obscured.	▬	▬ Acknowledgment
"My engines are in reverse", even if the vessel is moving forward.	▪▪▪	None

International Waters

■ Prolonged blast (5 sec)   ▪ Short blast (1 sec)

Situation or Intent	Sound Signal	Answer Signal
Meeting / Crossing: "I am altering my course to STARBOARD".	▪	No Agreement signal, or ▪▪▪▪▪ Danger or Disagree
Meeting / Crossing: "I am altering my course to PORT".	▪▪	No agreement signal, or ▪▪▪▪▪ Danger or Disagree

101

International Waters

▬ Prolonged blast (5 sec)   ■ Short blast (1 sec)

Situation or Intent	Sound Signal	Answer Signal
Overtaking another vessel in a narrow channel or fairway: "I intend to pass you on your STARBOARD side".	▬ ▬ ■	▬ ■ ▬ ■ Agreement or ■ ■ ■ ■ ■ Danger or Disagree
Overtaking another vessel in a narrow channel or fairway: "I intend to pass you on your PORT side".	▬ ▬ ■ ■	▬ ■ ▬ ■ Agreement or ■ ■ ■ ■ ■ Danger or Disagree

Additional Rules - International Waters

You must have visual contact with other vessel and be within ½ mile of each other when using sound signals, except when approaching a blind curve in a channel or fairway.

Certain sound signals may be supplemented by flashing an all-round white light, visible at a minimum of 5 miles and synchronized with the sound signals:

"I am altering course to STARBOARD"- 1 flash lasting one 1 second, "I am altering course to PORT" 2 flashes, lasting 1 second each, "I am operating astern propulsion" 3 flashes lasting 1 second each, "Danger" or disagreement response to being overtaken by another vessel - 5 short, rapid flashes.

You may establish a meeting, crossing, or overtaking agreement with the other vessel by using the marine radio, instead of using sound signals. If unable to contact and agree by radio, then sound signals must be used.

If whistles are fitted on a vessel more than 100 meters apart, then only one whistle shall be used for these sound signals.

SOUND SIGNALS
Restricted Visibility, International and Inland

Sound Signals
Vessels are required to produce sound signals during periods of restricted visibility. This can occur any time, day or night, when conditions limit one's ability to see clearly. Fog, heavy rain, snow, thick haze, smoke, blowing sea foam, and darkness are typical examples of conditions that may restrict visibility. The use of radar does not release a skipper from using proper sound signals.

Speed
In addition to sound signals, skippers are obligated to navigate at a speed no faster than visibility conditions allow. This means that a vessel must be able to avoid a collision (by turning or stopping) within the distance that the danger is sighted. It may be necessary to proceed at no more than a dead crawl.

Signaling Other Craft
If it is necessary to attract the attention of another vessel, you may make sound or light signals that cannot be mistaken for the signals above. You may point your searchlight in the direction of danger. You may not use any signals in such a way that will embarrass another vessel.

Signaling Devices
Sound signals used during restricted visibility consist of whistles, bells, and gongs. Vessels under 12 m are only required to carry some efficient means of producing sound. "Annex III" specifies equipment requirements.

SOUND SIGNALS

Restricted Visibity, Inland Waters

▬ Prolonged blast (5 sec)   ■ Short blast (1 sec)

Vessel Situation	Sound Signal	Repetition
Any vessel under 12 m.	Not required to give signals as above, but must make some efficient sound signal.	Repeat signal every 2 minutes.
Power-driven, making way.	▬	Repeat signal every 2 minutes.
Power-driven, not making way.	▬ ▬	Repeat signal every 2 minutes.
Towing or pushing ahead.	▬ ■ ■	Repeat signal every 2 minutes.
Engaged in fishing.	▬ ■ ■	Repeat signal every 2 minutes.

SOUND SIGNALS

Restricted Visibility, Inland Waters

▬ Prolonged blast (5 sec)   ■ Short blast (1 sec)

Vessel Situation	Sound Signal	Repetition
Restricted maneuverability.	▬ ■ ■	Repeat signal every 2 minutes.
Sailing vessel.	▬ ■ ■	Repeat signal every 2 minutes.
Vessel not under command.	▬ ■ ■	Repeat signal every 2 minutes.
Manned vessel being towed.	▬ ■ ■ ■	Repeat signal every 2 minutes.
Vessels under 20m, barges, scows, etc., anchored in a special anchorage area.	No signal required.	No signal required.
Vessel at anchor, under 100 m.	Bell (5 sec), may also sound: ■ ▬ ■	Repeat signal every 1 minute.

SOUND SIGNALS

Restricted Visibity, Inland Waters

▬ Prolonged blast (5 sec)   ■ Short blast (1 sec)

Vessel Situation	Sound Signal	Repetition
Vessel at anchor, over 100 m.	Bell (5 sec) fore + Gong (5 sec) aft, may also sound: ■ ▬ ■	Repeat signal every 1 minute.
Vessel aground, under 100 m.	Bell (3 taps) + Bell (ring 5 sec) + Bell (3 taps) may also sound: ■ ▬ ■	Repeat signal every 1 minute.
Vessel aground, over 100 m.	Bell (3 taps) + Bell (ring 5 sec) + Gong (5 sec) + Bell (3 taps) may also sound: ■ ▬ ■	Repeat signal every 1 minute.
Vessel engaged in pilotage duty.	In addition to signals as needed above, may sound identity signal: ■ ■ ■ ■	Repeat signal every 1 minute.

SOUND SIGNALS

Restricted Visibity, International Waters

▬ Prolonged blast (5 sec)   ▪ Short blast (1 sec)

Vessel Situation	Sound Signal	Repetition
Any vessel under 12 m.	Not required to give signals as above, but must make some efficient sound signal.	Repeat signal every 2 minutes.
Power-driven, making way.	▬	Repeat signal every 2 minutes.
Power-driven, not making way.	▬ ▬	Repeat signal every 2 minutes.
Towing or pushing ahead.	▬ ▪ ▪	Repeat signal every 2 minutes.
Engaged in fishing.	▬ ▪ ▪	Repeat signal every 2 minutes.

SOUND SIGNALS

Restricted Visibity, International Waters

▭ Prolonged blast (5 sec)   ▪ Short blast (1 sec)

Vessel Situation	Sound Signal	Repetition
Restricted maneuverability.	▭ ▪ ▪	Repeat signal every 2 minutes.
Sailing vessel.	▭ ▪ ▪	Repeat signal every 2 minutes.
Vessel not under command.	▭ ▪ ▪	Repeat signal every 2 minutes.
Manned vessel being towed.	▭ ▪ ▪ ▪	Repeat signal every 2 minutes.
Vessel constrained by draft.	▭ ▪ ▪	Repeat signal every 2 minutes.
Vessel at anchor, under 100 m.	Bell (5 sec), may also sound: ▪ ▭ ▪	Repeat signal every 1 minute.

SOUND SIGNALS

Restricted Visibility, International Waters

▬ Prolonged blast (5 sec)   ■ Short blast (1 sec)

Vessel Situation	Sound Signal	Repetition
Vessel at anchor, over 100 m.	Bell (5 sec) fore + Gong (5 sec) aft, may also sound: ■ ▬ ■	Repeat signal every 1 minute.
Vessel aground, under 100 m.	Bell (3 taps) + Bell (ring 5 sec) + Bell (3 taps) may also sound: ■ ▬ ■	Repeat signal every 1 minute.
Vessel aground, over 100 m.	Bell (3 taps) + Bell (ring 5 sec) + Gong (5 sec) + Bell (3 taps) may also sound: ■ ▬ ■	Repeat signal every 1 minute.
Vessel engaged in pilotage duty.	In addition to signals as needed above, may sound identity signal: ■ ■ ■ ■	Repeat signal every 1 minute.

DISTRESS SIGNALS

For Inland and International Waters: Use the following signals if your vessel is in distress or you require assistance.

1. Red star flares, fired one at a time, into the air.

2. Parachute flair fired into the air.

3. Vessel's fog horn sounding continuously.

4. Black ball and square on orange background.

5. Square Flag and Ball.

6. Code flags: November Charlie.

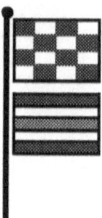

7. Call "Mayday, Mayday, Mayday" on marine radio.

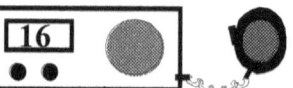

8. Wave arms up and down.

9. Smoke signal, handheld or in the water.

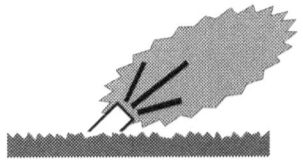

10. Signal from EPIRB (Emergency Position Indicating Radio Beacon).

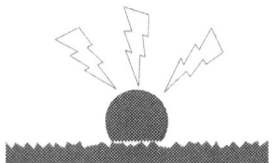

11. Dye marker of any color on the water.

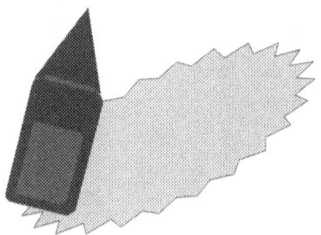

12. Gunshots, fired at intervals of one minute.

13. Alarms from radiotelegraph or radiotelephone, or SOS.

14. Flames on a vessel.

(Note: Do not start a fire on board to attract attention. Use other methods first.)

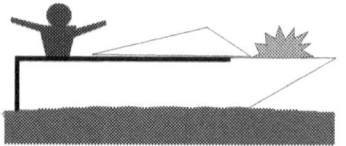

15. INLAND ONLY: A high intensity white light that flashes at regular intervals from 50 to 70 times per minute.

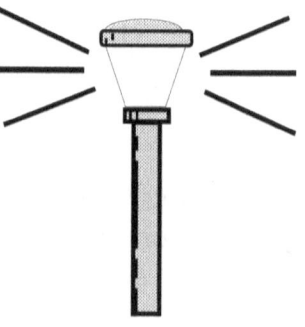

Skipper's Handbook – Robert Grossman

SECTION 3
NAVIGATION

COMPASS

Reading your Compass

Compasses on recreational boats are typically front-reading, which must only be viewed from the front. As seen from the top, its card is reversed. A top-reading compass may be found on larger vessels. With all compasses, your heading is indicated by the lubber's line. Make sure you know how many degrees are indicated by the marks on your compass card. Each compass is different.

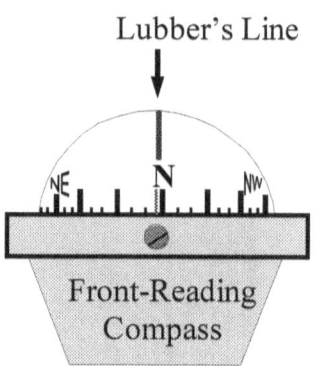

Front-Reading Compass

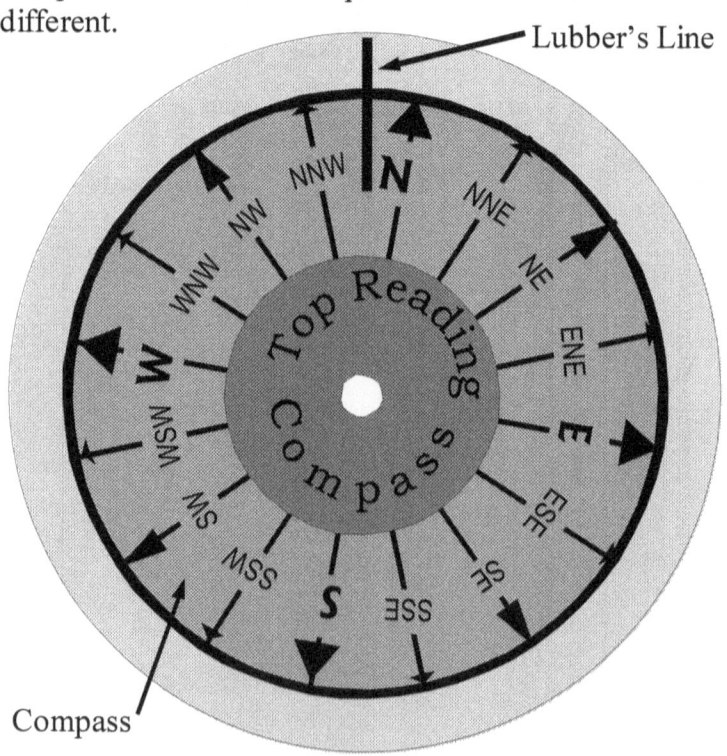

Compass

Conversion of Compass Points to Degrees

Direction	Points	Degrees
North to **East**	N N by E NNE NE by N NE NE by E ENE E by N	0°00' 11°15' 22°30' 33°45' 45°00' 56°15' 67°30' 78°45'
East to **South**	E E by S ESE SE by E SE SE by S SSE S by E	90°00' 101°15' 112°30' 123°45' 135°00' 146°15' 157°30' 168°45'
South to **West**	S S by W SSW SW by S SW SW by W WSW W by S	180°00' 191°15' 202°30' 213°45' 225°00' 236°15' 247°30' 258°45'
West to **North**	W W by N WNW NW by W NW NW by N NNW N by W	270°00' 281°15' 292°30' 303°45' 315°00' 326°15' 337°30' 348°45'

Skipper's Handbook – Robert Grossman

Compass Variation

The direction of the north pole from your position is called **TRUE NORTH**. The card (or needle) on your compass is not attracted to true north, but rather to an area in northern Canada known as **MAGNETIC NORTH**. Depending on where you are located, Magnetic North may be located to the east, to the west, or right in line with the North Pole. The angle between Magnetic North and True North is called **VARIATION**.

The position of Magnetic North moves slowly over time, so local variation changes slightly from year to year. In the western United States, the compass card is deflected to the east, giving an east variation. In the eastern United States, the compass card is deflected to the west, giving a west variation.

The amount of east or west variation is given on nautical charts, as well as most topographic maps. Look at the center of the compass rose nearest your vessel's position. The variation and annual adjustment are shown at the center of the compass rose. The annual adjustment tells you to add or subtract a certain amount to the variation for each year after the map's print date. Since navigation by compass is dependent upon accuracy, always account for the annual change in variation before calculating your heading or position. Not correcting for variation can throw you significantly off course.

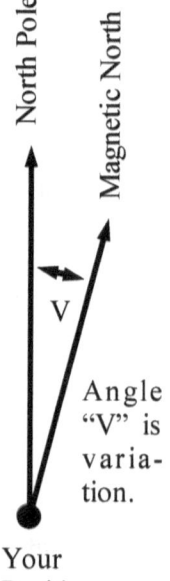

Angle "V" is variation.

Your Position

Deviation and Deviation Tables

Your compass is affected by magnetic fields around it. Engine blocks, metal tanks, audio speakers, electronic equipment, and other metallic or magnetized objects may deflect the compass card (or needle) away from Magnetic North. This deflection is called **deviation**.

Deviation changes with the heading of your vessel. For example, consider a marine radio sitting just starboard of the compass. When heading North, the compass card may be deflected 6° to the east, resulting in a deviation of 6E. When heading East, the compass card may not be deflected at all, resulting in 0 deviation.

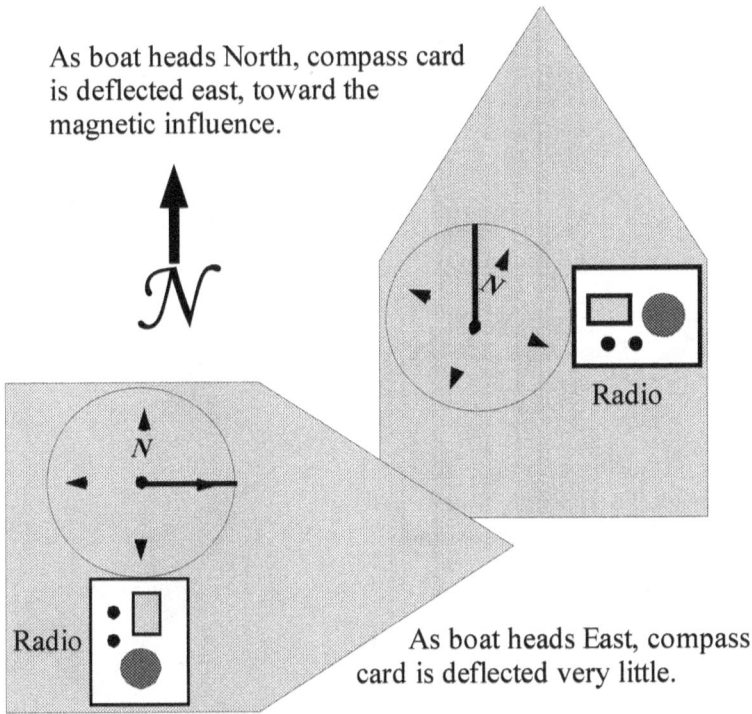

As boat heads North, compass card is deflected east, toward the magnetic influence.

As boat heads East, compass card is deflected very little.

Not correcting for deviation can throw you significantly off course. Maintaining a deviation table is important to accurate navigation. Since a vessel's deviation settings may change whenever metallic equipment is added, removed, or repositioned, the deviation table should be revised periodically.

Creating a Deviation Table
1. Facing foreward on your vessel, line up two distant fixed objects that form a range in a known **magnetic** direction. You will find the **magnetic** direction from the compass rose on your nautical chart.
2. Position your vessel in line (fore and aft) as exactly as possible with that range.
3. Note your **compass** heading and record it next to the magnetic heading on your deviation table.

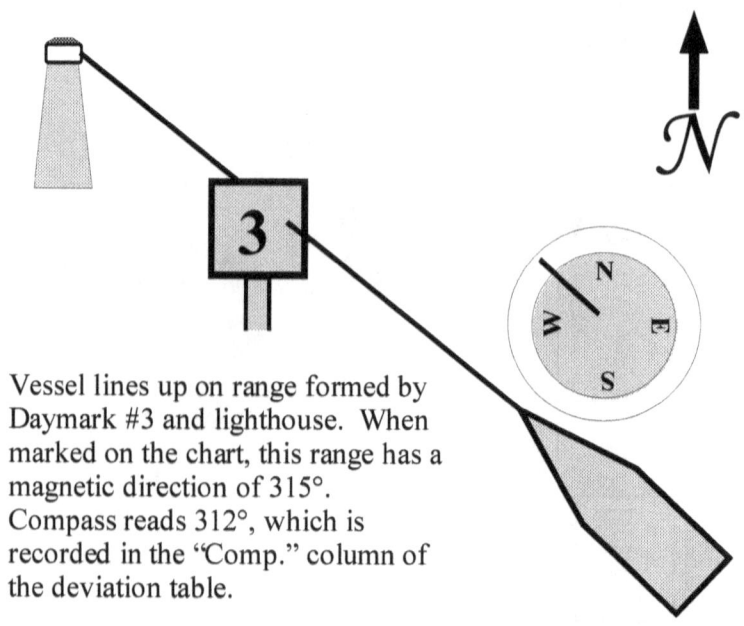

Vessel lines up on range formed by Daymark #3 and lighthouse. When marked on the chart, this range has a magnetic direction of 315°.
Compass reads 312°, which is recorded in the "Comp." column of the deviation table.

4. On your deviation table, record the difference, to the nearest degree, between the magnetic heading and the compass heading.

5. If the **compass** heading is **less** than the **magnetic** heading, then the deviation is **East**.

If the **compass** heading is **more** than the **magnetic** heading, then the deviation is **West**.

REMEMBER: COMPASS LEAST, ERROR EAST

DEVIATION TABLE					
Vessel Name: **Papa's Pride**			Table Date: **6-24-00**			
Mag.	Comp.	Dev.	Mag.	Comp.	Dev.
000°			180°		
015°			195°		
030°			210°		
045°			225°		
060°			240°		
075°			255°		
090°			270°		
105°			285°		
120°			300°		
135°			315°	**312**	**3E**
150°			330°		
165°			345°		

Mag. = Magmetic Comp.= Compass Dev.= Deviation

6. Line up on a new range of a different known **magnetic** heading, and repeat this process. Do this for as many of the magnetic headings on the deviation table as you can.

DEVIATION WORKSHEET						
Vessel Name:			Table Date:		
Mag.	Comp.	Dev.	Mag.	Comp.	Dev.
000°	**004**	**4W**	180°	**179**	**1E**
015°			195°	**194**	**1E**
030°	**037**	**7W**	210°		
045°	**049**	**4W**	225°	**223**	**2E**
060°	**062**	**2W**	240°		
075°			255°		
090°			270°	**266**	**4E**
105°			285°		
120°	**122**	**2W**	300°	**298**	**2E**
135°	**135**	**0**	315°	**312**	**3E**
150°			330°		
165°	**163**	**2E**	345°	**346**	**1W**

Mag. = Magmetic Comp.= Compass Dev.= Deviation

Photocopy and use the deviation table below. Not correcting for deviation can throw you significantly off course.

DEVIATION TABLE						
Vessel Name:				Table Date:		
Mag.	Comp.	Dev.	Mag.	Comp.	Dev.	
000°			180°			
015°			195°			
030°			210°			
045°			225°			
060°			240°			
075°			255°			
090°			270°			
105°			285°			
120°			300°			
135°			315°			
150°			330°			
165°			345°			

Mag. = Magmetic Comp.= Compass Dev.= Deviation

DEVIATION MUST BE EAST OR WEST

- If the COMPASS heading is LESS than the MAGNETIC heading, the deviation is EAST.
- If the COMPASS heading is MORE than the MAGNETIC heading, the deviation is WEST.

Remember: Compass Least, Error East.

Skipper's Handbook – Robert Grossman

COMPASS CONVERSION DIAGRAM

In order to navigate with your compass accurately, you must be able to convert between TRUE COURSE, MAGNETIC HEADING, and COMPASS HEADING. True course is the direction you are traveling relative to the north pole. Magnetic Heading is the direction you are traveling relative to the magnetic pole, which is some distance from the north pole, and which slowly changes position. Compass heading is the direction indicated on your compass. Only TRUE directions are drawn on a chart.

The Compass Conversion Diagram corrects for **variation** and **deviation.** Variation is the difference in direction between the north pole and the magnetic pole. Deviation is the deflection of your compass needle caused by the effect of metal objects around it. Fill in and solve the Compass Conversion Diagram to find your true direction, magnetic heading, or your compass heading, depending on what you need to accomplish.

A completed Compass Conversion Diagram.

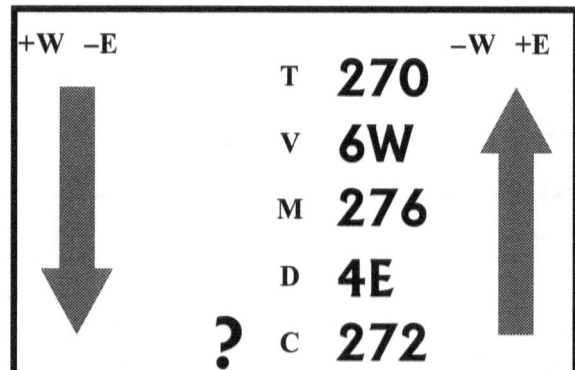

Conversion Diagram Instructions

1. Put a question mark next to the value you are trying to find. For example, if you know the True Course and want to find the compass heading you should steer, put a question mark by the "C".

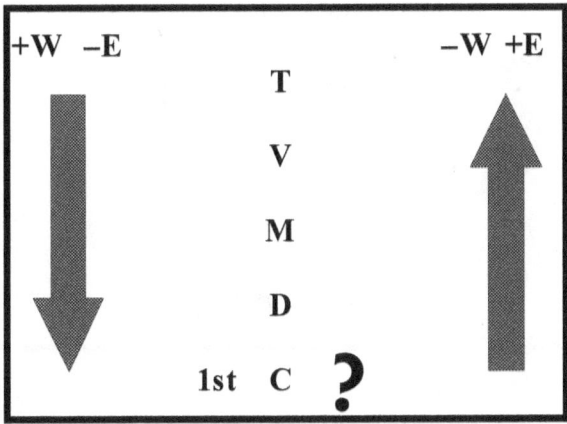

2. Fill in the heading that you already know. If you know the True Course is 270, and you are looking for the compass heading to steer, write 270 next to the "T".

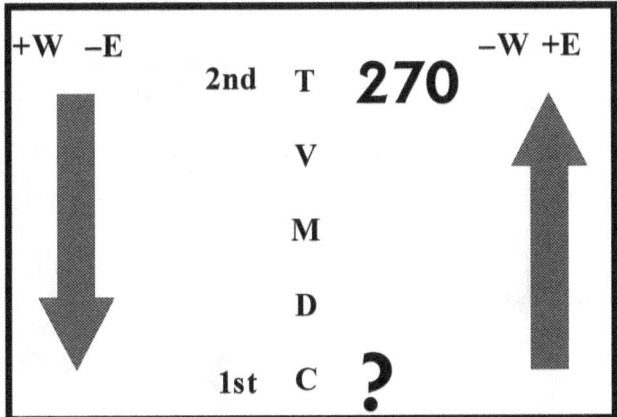

3. Look at the center of the compass rose nearest your location on the nautical chart. Write down the Variation (after adjustment of any annual change) next to the "**V**". Variation must be in degrees East or West.

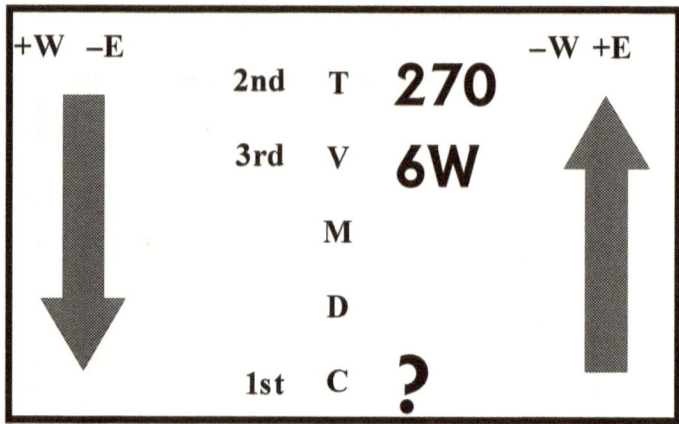

4. Look up the deviation from your Deviation Table. Use the value found closest to your True Heading. Record it next to the "**D**". Deviation must be in degrees East or West.

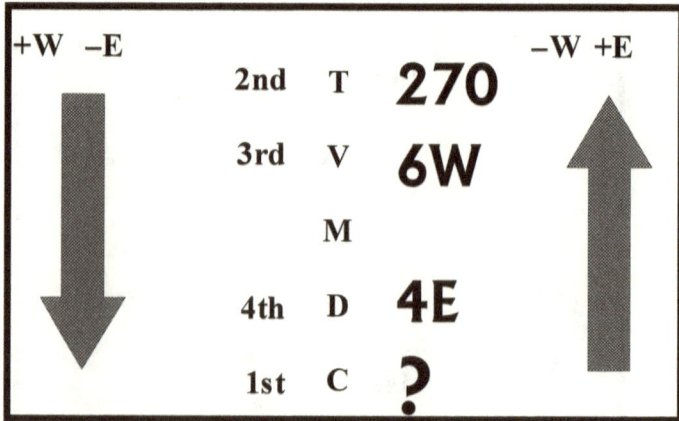

5. Add or subtract values as directed on the Diagram. West values are added moving down the diagram, and are subtracted moving up. East values are subtracted moving down the diagram, and are added moving up. In this example, we know that 270 is our true heading. Add Variation of 6W (west is added going down) to get a Magnetic Heading of 276. Subtract Variation of 4E (east is subtracted going down) to get the answer of Compass Heading 272.

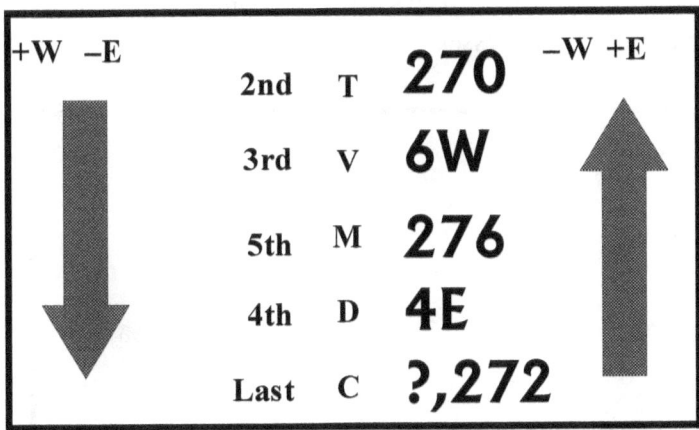

By starting with the known values, you can solve for any unknown variable on the diagram. It is imperative to make corrections for variation and deviation whenever navigating by compass. Remember:

T = TRUE COURSE
V = VARIATION
M = MAGNETIC HEADING
D = DEVIATION

Add west down.
Subtract west up.
Add east up.
Subtract east down.

Compass Conversion Diagram

Copy the Compass Conversion Diagram below. Use it to correct for **deviation** and **variation** while navigating. First, enter known values on the diagram. Then solve the unknown values to find True direction, Magnetic heading, or Compass heading. Not correcting for deviation or variation can put you significantly off course. Maintain an up-to-date deviation table for your vessel, and keep it handy. Update your deviation table whenever metallic or electronic equipment is added or moved on your vessel.

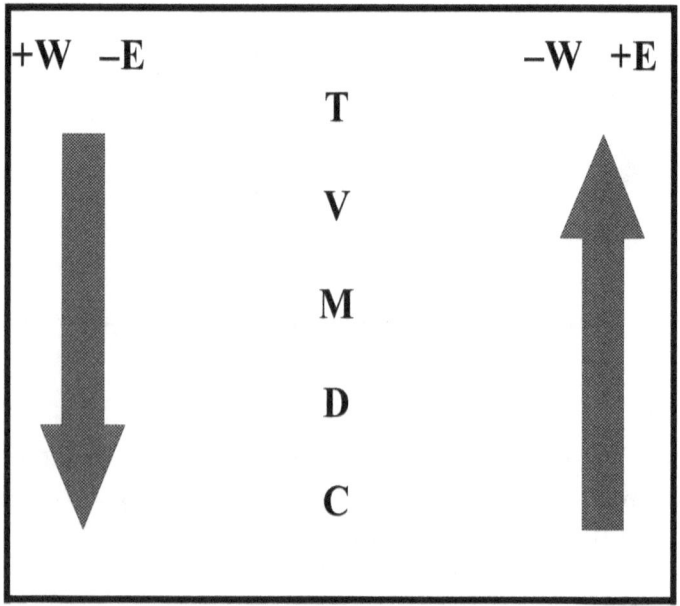

Add west moving down.
Subtract west moving up.
Add east moving up.
Subtract east moving down.

NAUTICAL CHARTS

A complete guide to all of the symbols used on nautical charts can be found in "Chart No. 1", published by the National Oceanic and Atmospheric Administration. It is not actually a chart, but rather a small book. "Chart No. 1" can be purchased from most marine supply dealers, or directly from the NOAA. Go to "www.noaa.gov" for the NOAA main webpage. For direct ordering of nautical charts, go to "http://chartmaker.ncd.noaa.gov".

There are hundreds of different symbols that may appear on nautical charts. Many of these symbols may never be encountered on your local chart. Several important types of symbols will appear on just about every chart, some of which are shown below.

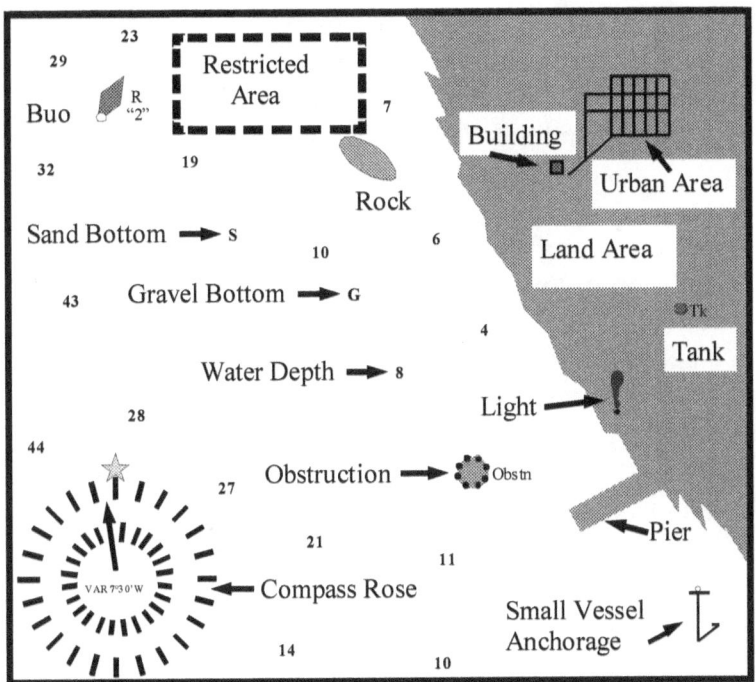

DEAD RECKONING

Dead reckoning is used to determine your **approximate** position on a nautical chart. It can also be used to find distance traveled, time to reach a destination, or vessel speed. Dead reckoning is a necessary skill when navigating by compass. It is also used to double-check your position when navigating by GPS, or when your GPS is not functioning.

Rules
The rules for dead reckoning remain the same, whether you are trying to determine position, speed, distance, or time:
1. Plot only **True** courses on a chart.
2. Starting point is a well-determined fix.
3. Effects of current are ignored.
4. Use the 24 hour clock for time.
5. Keep all measurement units the same.
6. Bearings are recorded as three numerals: 37° = 037.
7. Accuracy and neatness are essential.

Tools
Dead reckoning involves plotting lines and symbols directly onto a nautical chart. Several simple tools are required:
1. Nautical charts, for the areas you will be navigating.
2. Compass, either vessel-mounted or handheld.
3. Parallel rules.
4. Dividers.
5. Pencils and erasers.

Parallel Rules   Dividers

Symbols
Several symbols and abbreviations are commonly plotted on charts for dead reckoning:

⊙ = Fix from a known point
• = DR position
S = Speed
T = True (course)
C = Course
D = Distance

Equations
Just one equation, expressed three different ways, can be used to find the answers to dead reckoning problems.

> Distance = Speed x Time
> Speed = Distance / Time
> Time = Distance / Speed

Units of measurement must be kept the same throughout the equation. If speed is measured in miles per hour, then distance should be in statute miles. Time units are best expressed in hundreds of an hour, rather than in minutes. Written in the equation, 1 hour 45 minutes would appear as 1.75 hr. Unit conversions are provided below.

Ex: A vessel travels at 12 knots for 1 hour 30 minutes. How far does the vessels go?
Distance = 12 kn x 1.5 hr = 18 naut. mi.

Conversions
1 knot = 1.15 mph = 1.852 km/h
1 naut. mi. = 1.15 mi. = 1.852 km
1 mi. = 0.87 naut. mi. = 1.609 km
Convert minutes to tenths of an hour: 1 min = 0.0166 hr.

24 Hour Clock

The 24 hour clock is used whenever the time is recorded on a chart, and for all time calculations. Using the 24 hour clock will make time calculations much easier.

All times are given as four digits, so 3:35 p.m. is recorded as 1535 hours (hrs) on the chart. One minute before midnight is 2359 hrs. To find the amount of time taken to travel between two points on a chart, subtract the departure time from the arrival time. Remember the first two digits are hours, and the second two digits are minutes.

Ex. 1: Arrive Pier   0915 hrs
        Depart Pirate's Point 0805 hrs
        Running Time   =   01'10" (or 1 hr 10 min)

Ex. 2: Arrive Buoy "7"   1406 hrs
        Depart Dock   1025 hrs
        Running Time   =   03'41" (or 3 hrs 41 min)

In this example, think of 1406 hrs as 13 hours and 66 minutes, by "borrowing" 60 minutes from the 14 hours. That makes possible subtracting 25 minutes in the "depart time" from 6 minutes in the "arrive time".

Ex. 3: Arrive Bass Isle Pier 0225 hrs, 29 July
        Depart Shark Reef   2158 hrs, 28 July
        Running Time   =   04'27" (or 41 hr 27 min)

In this case, "borrow" 24 hours from the 29th of July (making it the 28th of July) and add it to the 0225 time, giving a "time" of 2625. Do the same for the minutes as shown above. Your adjusted equation will look like this:

        Arrive Bass Isle Pier 2585 hrs, 28 July
        Depart Shark Reef   2158 hrs, 28 July
        Running Time   =   04'27"

Skipper's Handbook – Robert Grossman

24 HOUR CLOCK			
12 Hour Time	24 Hour Time	12 Hour Time	24 Hour Time
Midnight	0000	Noon	1200
1 am	0100	1 p.m.	1300
2 am	0200	2 p.m.	1400
3 am	0300	3 p.m.	1500
4 am	0400	4 p.m.	1600
5 am	0500	5 p.m.	1700
6 am	0600	6 p.m.	1800
7 am	0700	7 p.m.	1900
8 am	0800	8 p.m.	2000
9 am	0900	9 p.m.	2100
10 am	1000	10 p.m.	2200
11 am	1100	11 p.m.	2300

Compass Rose

The compass rose found on a nautical chart allows the navigator a convenient way to align parallel rules to True bearings.

Magnetic North is given on the inner ring of the rose, and True North is given on the outer ring. If there is more than one compass rose on your chart, use the one closest to your vessel's position.

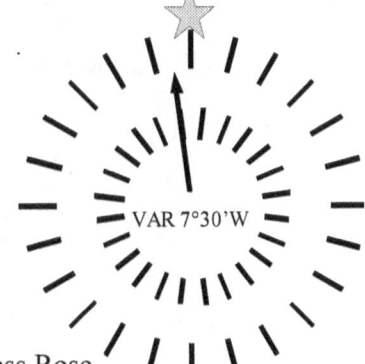

Compass Rose

Finding Your Position

1. Start from a well-determined fix. If you are sitting off of Channel Buoy #6, draw a ⊙ symbol at that place on your chart. This is your starting position.
2. Determine your direction of travel. Take your **Compass** course and convert it to **True** course by using the Compass Conversion Diagram (provided in this section).
3. Put your **parallel rules** on the **compass rose** nearest your starting position on the chart. Align the rules to the **True** course on the rose, then "walk" the rules over to your ⊙.
4. With the parallel rules in this position, draw a **Dead Reckoned line** from your ⊙, in the direction of the True course.
5. Write the True course over the DR line (Ex: **190 T**), and write your speed below the DR line (Ex: **S - 15**).
6. Find the **distance** traveled. Use the equation:

Distance = Speed x Time.

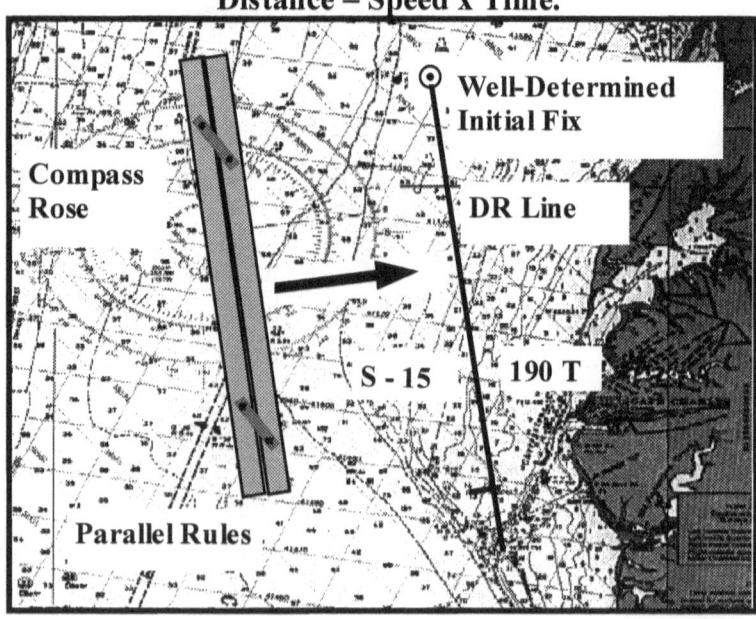

Ex: If you traveled on the course 190T at 15 knots for 15 minutes, what distance was traveled?
Distance equals 0.25 hr x 15 knots = 3.75 nautical miles.

7. Open the **dividers** to a length on the mileage scale equal to the distance traveled. The scale can be found at the top or bottom of the chart. With one point of the dividers on the ⊙ point, mark the distance traveled on the DR line. With a distance like 3.75 n mi, set the dividers to 3 n mi, and make a small mark at 3 miles on the DR line. Then reset the dividers to 0.75 n mi, and finish marking the distance. If the distance is much longer than the scale, choose a suitable fraction of the distance, and "walk" the dividers along the DR line.

8. Mark this point with a semi-circle. **This is your dead-reckoned position.**

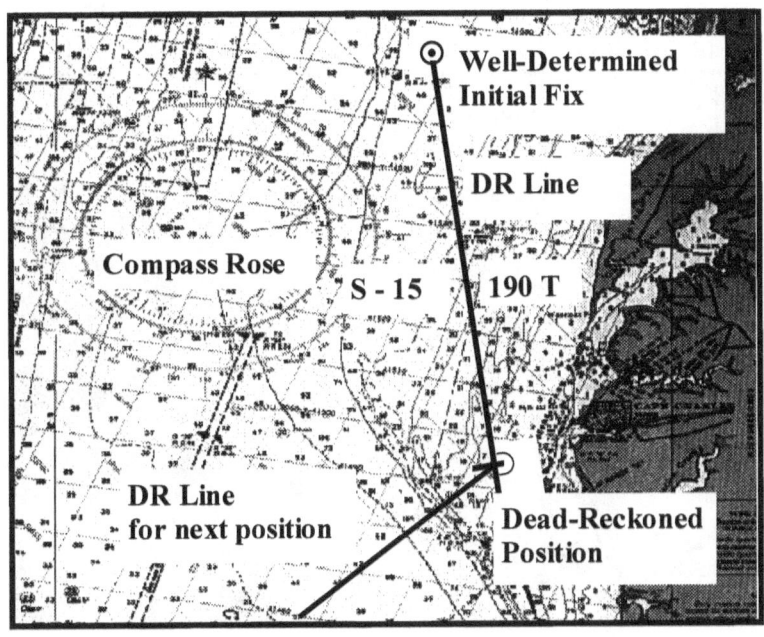

Finding Distance Traveled or Vessel Speed

1. Start from a well-determined fix. If you are sitting off of Channel Buoy #6, draw a ⊙ symbol at that place on your chart. This is your starting position. Mark your departure time next to the ⊙.

2. Mark your destination point on the chart (or find your DR position). Mark your arrival time at the destination point on the chart.

3. Connect the starting position and destination point with a **DR line**. Mark the True Course above the DR line.

4. Find the distance between these points. Using the mileage scale at the top of the chart, open the **dividers** to the nearest whole mile that is equal to or less than the length of the DR line. If the DR line is very long, open the dividers to a suitable fraction of the distance, and "walk" the dividers along the DR line. Any leftover segment of the DR line can be measured by adjusting the dividers to the length of the segment, and measuring it on the mileage scale. Mark the distance below the DR.

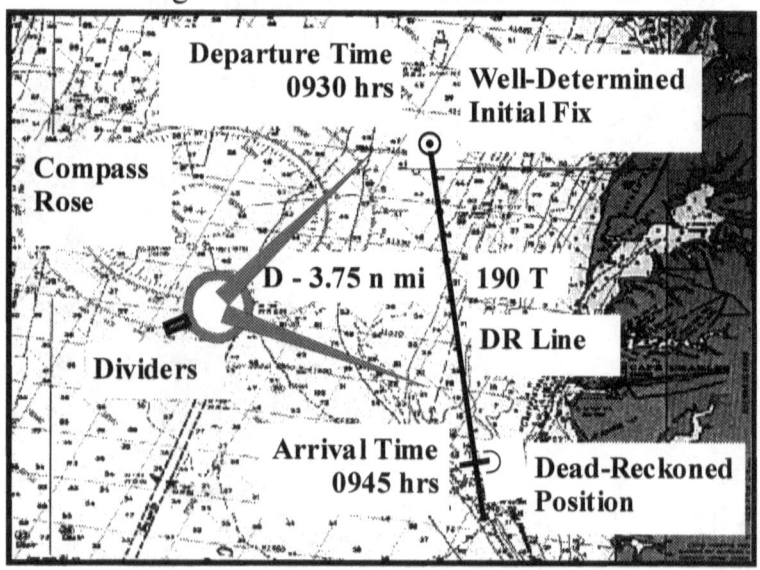

5. Find your vessel **speed**. Use the equation:
   Speed = Distance/Time.
In this equation, Time is the amount of time it took to go from the starting position to the destination point.

Ex: If you departed Pirate Point at 0930 hrs, arrived at Pier #3 at 0945 hrs, and traveled 3.75 n mi, what was the speed of the vessel?
Convert time to tenths: 15 minutes = 0.25 hour, then apply the equation: Speed = 3.75 n mi/0.25 hr = 15 knots

6. Write the speed next to the distance on the DR line.
7. Repeat for each new destination or change in speed.

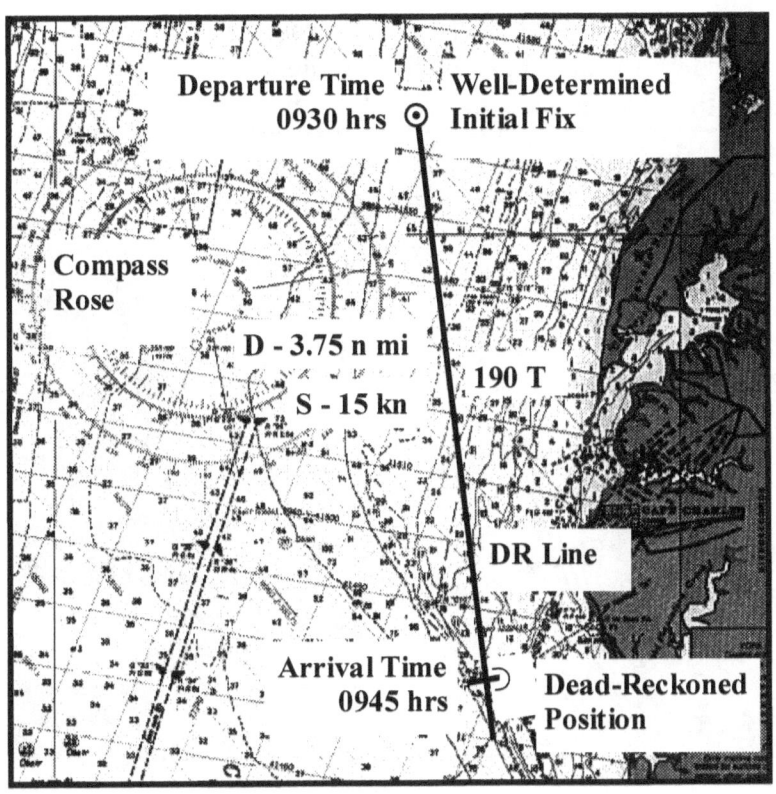

Finding Time Needed To Reach Destination

1. Start from a well-determined fix. If you are sitting off of Channel Buoy #6, draw a ⊙ symbol at that place on your chart. This is your starting position. Mark your starting time next to the ⊙.

2. Mark your destination point on the chart.

3. Connect the starting position and destination point with a **DR line**. Mark the True Course above the DR line.

4. Find the distance between these points. Using the mileage scale at the top of the chart, open the **dividers** to the nearest whole mile that is equal to or less than the length of the DR line. If the DR line is very long, open the dividers to a suitable fraction of the distance, and "walk" the dividers along the DR line. Any leftover segment of the DR line can be measured by adjusting the dividers to the length of the segment, and measuring it on the mileage scale. Mark the distance below the DR.

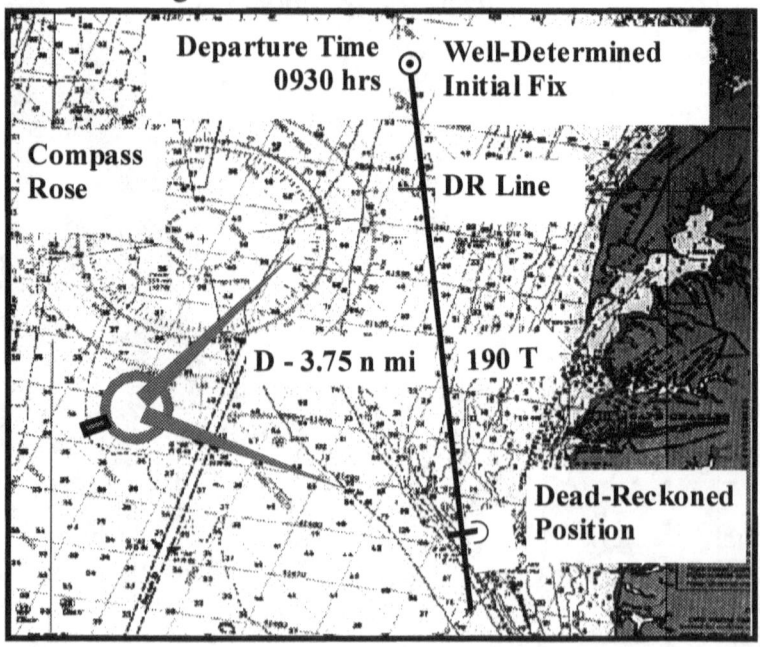

5. Write the speed next to the distance on the DR line.
6. Solve for **Time** needed to travel the distance. Use the equation **Time = Distance/Speed.**

Ex: If you traveled on the course 190T at 15 knots, and went 3.75 miles, how much time did it take?
Time = 3.75 n mi/15 kn = 0.25 hours. Convert 0.25 hours back to minutes (0.25 hr x 60 min/hr = 15 min). Since the departure time was 0930 hrs, the arrival time is 15 minutes later, 0945 hrs.

7. Repeat this process for each new destination or change in speed.

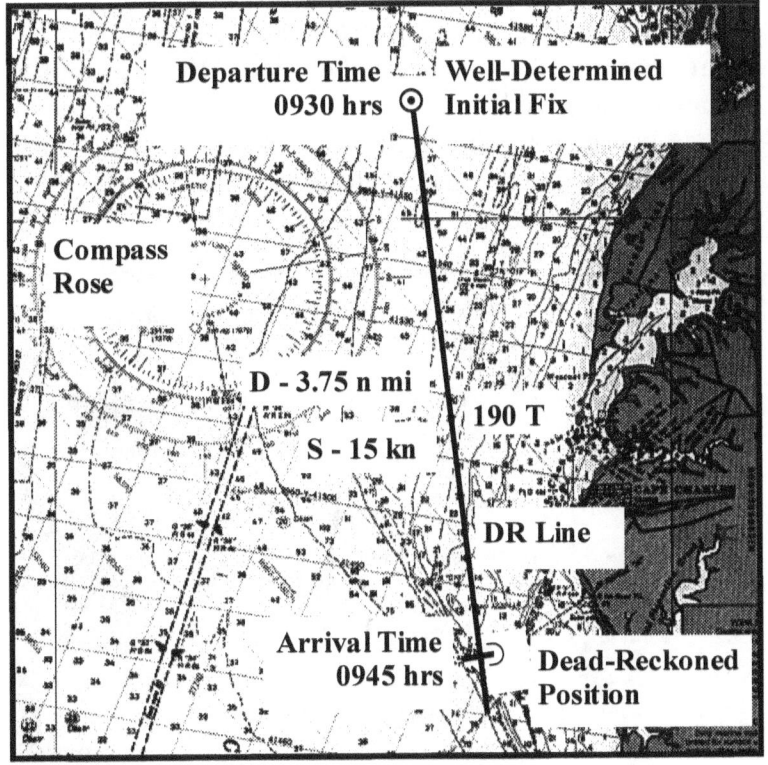

Set and Drift

Wind, waves, current, and tidal action (collectively called "current") all influence the course and speed of a vessel. Determining the set and drift will allow for the correction of these discrepancies when using dead reckoning techniques. These methods can also be used to find a course to steer that will compensate for the effects of current, and allow more accurate navigation to your chosen destination.

Definitions: Set - The True direction that the current is moving toward.
Drift - Speed of the current in knots.

To find set and drift:
1. Plot your dead-reckoned position on the nautical chart, marking the initial fix, DR line, DR fix, course, distance, and speed.
2. Use bearings to obtain an exact fix on your position. Your exact position can be confirmed by GPS, LORAN, or visual landmarks, such as a numbered buoy.

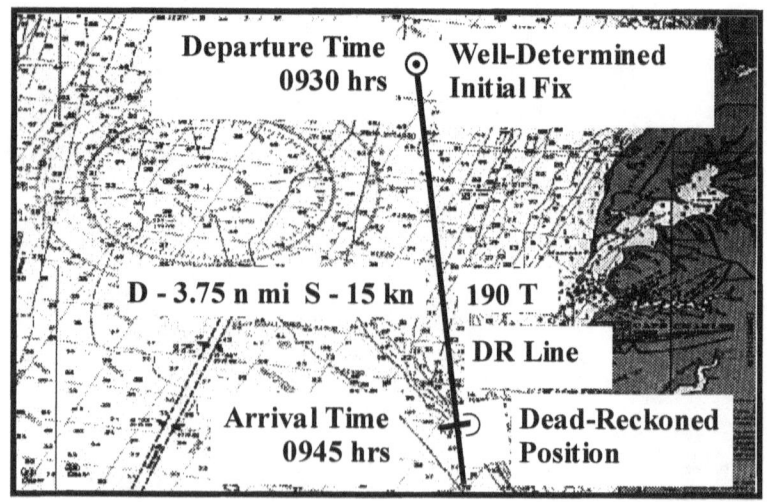

3. Mark the exact fix with a ⊙ on the chart, and note the time.
4. Using the parallel rules, draw a dashed line from your DR fix to the exact fix.
5. "Walk" the parallel rules to the compass rose nearest the exact fix to determine the **True** direction of the current. This is the SET.
6. Open the dividers so that one point is on the DR fix and the other on the exact fix. Then, hold the dividers next to the mileage scale at the top of the chart, to give the distance between the DR fix and the exact fix.
7. Use this distance in the equation:
   Speed = Distance / Time
to find the drift (speed of the current).

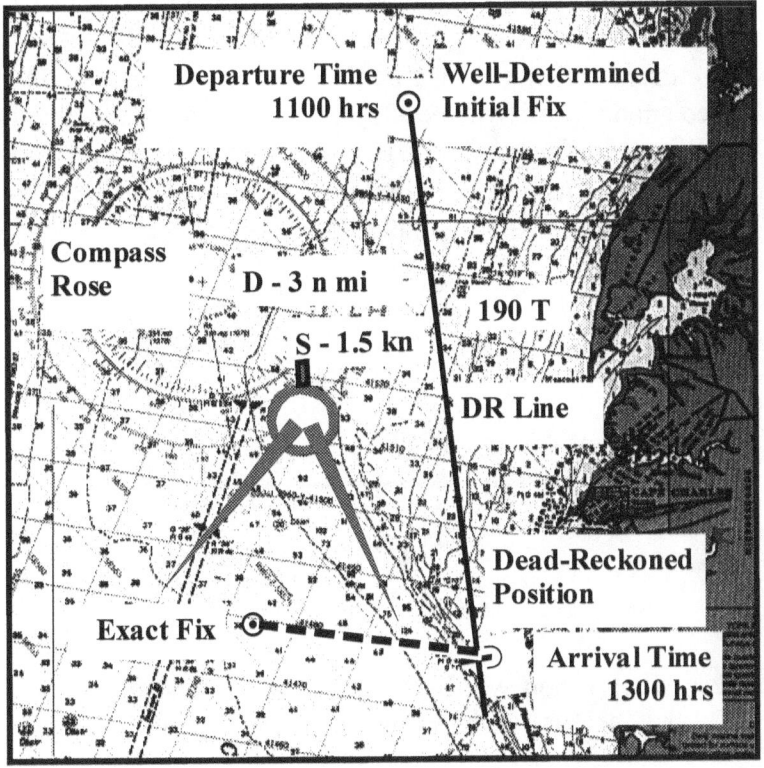

Ex: Your vessel departs Pirate's Cove (initial fix) at 1100 hrs, and arrives near Shark Reef (DR fix) at 1300 hrs. You determine the distance between the DR fix and your exact fix to be 3 nautical miles. What is the drift?

Since travel time is the difference between departure time (1100 hrs) and arrival time (1300 hrs), the trip took 2 hours. During this time, the current pushed the vessel 3 nautical miles from the DR fix. The speed of the current (drift) = 3 n mi/2 hrs = 1.5 knots. This is the DRIFT.

Course and Speed Made Good

The "course made good" is the True direction that a vessel actually travels, including the effects of the current. The "speed made good" is the actual speed that the vessel travels along its route, including the effects of the current. If a vessel travels against the current, the speed made good will be slower than what is indicated on the vessel's gauges. If a vessel travels with the current, the speed made good will be faster than what is indicated on the vessel's gauges.

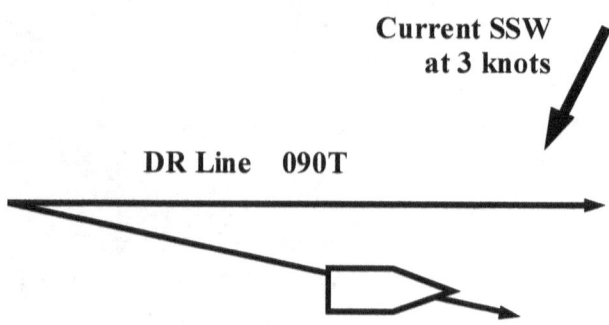

Vessel's position will be different than indicated on the DR line, because of the effects of current.

To find course and speed made good:
1. Plot your dead-reckoned position on the nautical chart, marking the initial fix, DR line, DR fix, exact fix, course, distance, and speed.
2. Determine set and drift. Record information on chart.
3. Draw a dashed line on the chart from the initial fix to the exact fix. This is the "course made good" line, and should be labeled on the chart.
4. Line up the parallel rules with the course made good line. Walk the parallel rules to the nearest compass rose on the chart. Read the outer ring of the compass rose to give the True course made good.

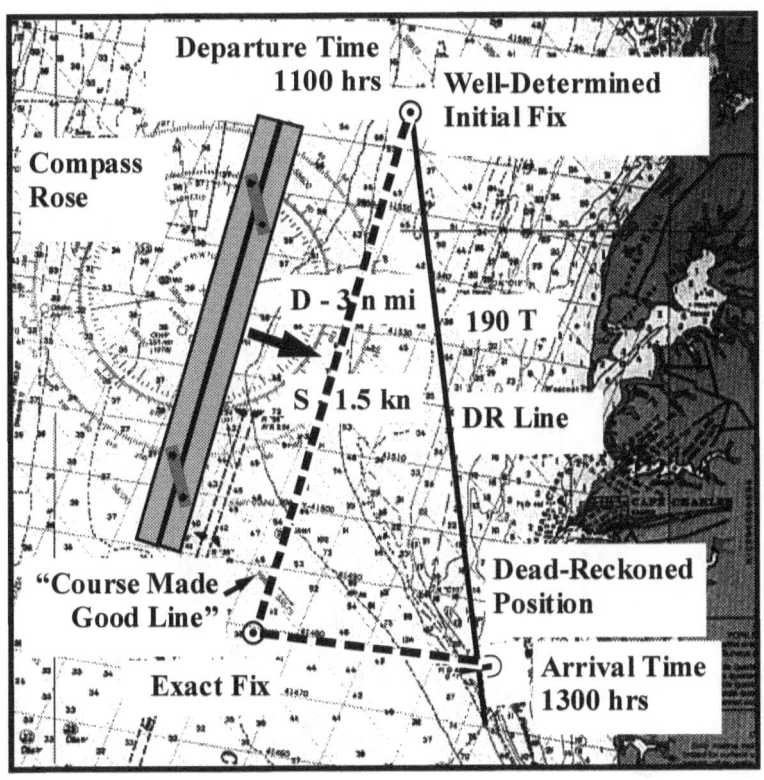

5. Using the dividers, measure the distance of the course made good line. This is the distance the vessel actually traveled.

6. Solve for "speed made good" by using the equation:

Speed = Distance/Time.

In this equation, Speed is the speed made good, and Distance is the distance traveled along the course made good line.

Ex: Your vessel departs Pirate's Cove (initial fix) at 1100 hrs, and arrives near Shark Reef (DR fix) at 1300 hrs. The course made good line has a distance of 4 n mi. What is the speed made good?

Since travel time is the difference between departure time (1100 hrs) and arrival time (1300 hrs), the trip took 2 hours. During this time, the vessel traveled 4 n mi (along the course made good line). The speed made good = 4 n mi/2 hrs = 2 knots.

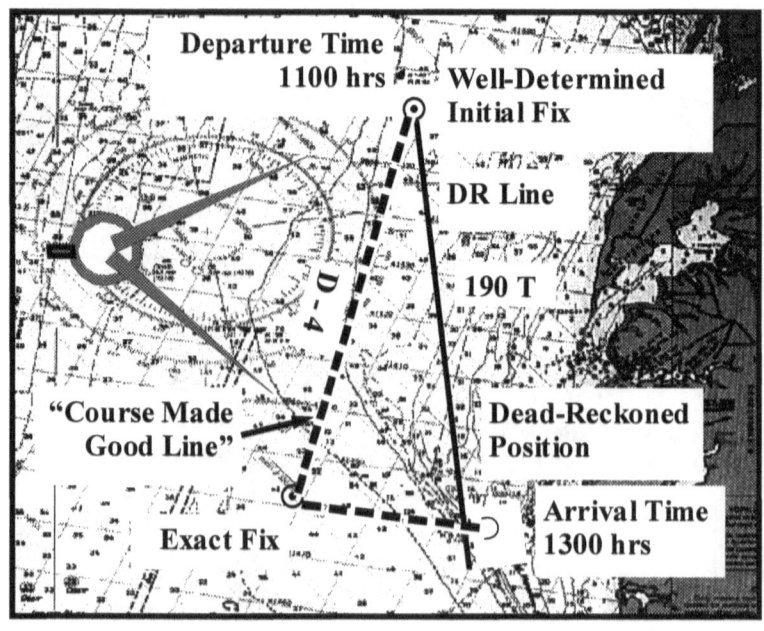

Finding Estimated Position Using Set and Drift

Wind, waves, current, and tidal action all influence the course and speed of your vessel. Compensating for Set and Drift greatly increases the accuracy of navigation by dead reckoning.

When the SET and DRIFT are known before departure, use the following technique to determine your "Estimated Position":
1. Plot your dead-reckoned position on a chart, marking the initial fix, DR line, DR fix, course, distance, and speed.
2. Using the compass rose nearest your DR fix, line up the parallel rules with the True direction of the SET. Remember that Set is the True direction the current flows. True direction will be found on the outer ring of the compass rose.

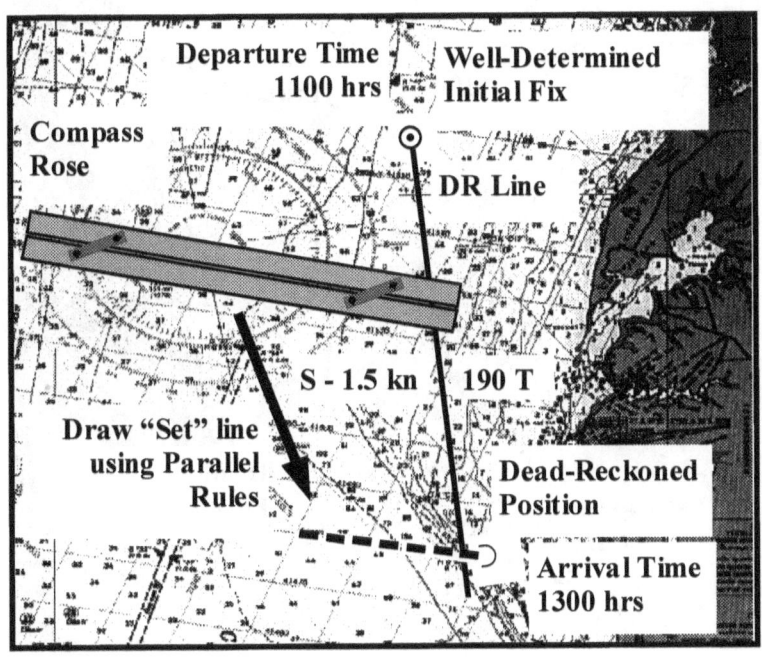

3. Walk the parallel rules over to the DR fix, and draw a dashed line from your DR fix, in the direction of the current.

4. Find the **Distance** along the Set line to your Estimated Position. In this case, Distance represents how far the current has pushed the vessel from the DR Fix. Use the equation:

Distance = Speed x Time.

In this equation, Speed is the drift, and Time is measured in hours, from Initial Fix to DR fix. See the example under "Set and Drift" section.

5. Set the dividers to this distance, using the mileage scale at the top of the chart.

6. Use the dividers to mark this distance from the DR Fix along the Set line. This new point is your ESTIMATED POSITION.

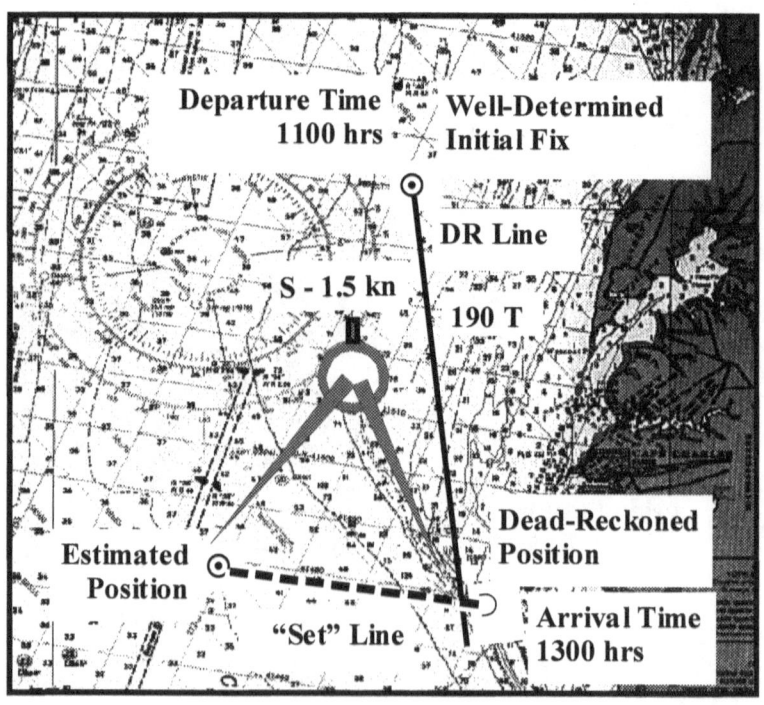

Finding Course To Steer

The "Course To Steer" is the True direction a vessel must take to reach an intended destination, while including the effects of set and drift. For example, if the destination is ahead at 090T, the vessel speed is 15 knots, the set is 200T, and the drift is 3 knots, what course should the vessel steer to reach its intended destination? This problem can be answered by using the compass rose on the nautical chart.

To find the Course To Steer:
1. From the center of the compass rose on your chart, draw a line in the direction you want to make good. In the example above, the course made good is 090T.
2. Draw a dashed line from the center of the compass rose, in the direction of the current set. In the example above the set is 200T. This is called a "set line".
3. On the set line, measure the distance the current will move in one hour. In this case, the drift is 3 knots, so the current will move 3 n mi in one hour. Using the dividers, mark this distance on the set line.

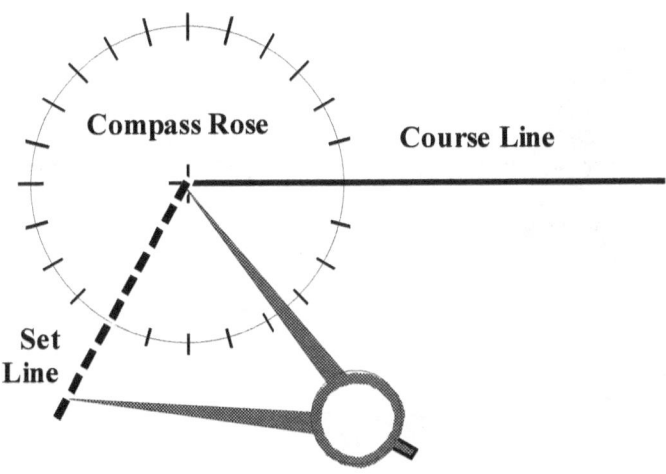

To fix your position with bearings:
1. Plot your course on a chart with a DR Line from your initial fix. The example below shows a DR Line bearing 270T.
2. Using a hand-held compass or your vessel's compass, take a bearing to a fixed landmark. If using the vessel's compass, point the boat straight at the fixed landmark before reading the compass. The example below shows the tower bearing 320T from your vessel. Remember to convert all bearings to True, before plotting on the chart.
3. Using the compass rose nearest your position on the chart, line up the parallel rules with the bearing taken on the landmark.
4. Walk the parallel rules over to the landmark. Draw a line from the landmark to the vicinity of your DR Line.

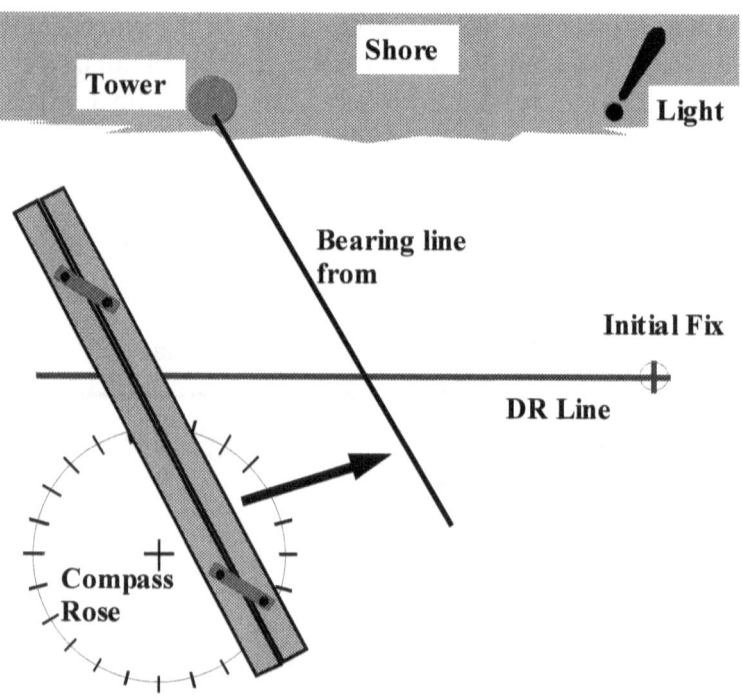

4. Determine the distance your vessel will travel in one hour. In this case, speed is 15 knots, so you will travel 15 nautical miles in one hour. Set your dividers to this distance.

5. With one point of the dividers on the mark made on the set line, bring the other point to the course line. Mark that point.

6. Line up the parallel rules with the marks on the course line and the set line.

7. Walk the parallel rules to the center of the compass rose, and read the True Course on the outside ring. This is your COURSE TO STEER.

The course to steer is not drawn on the chart.

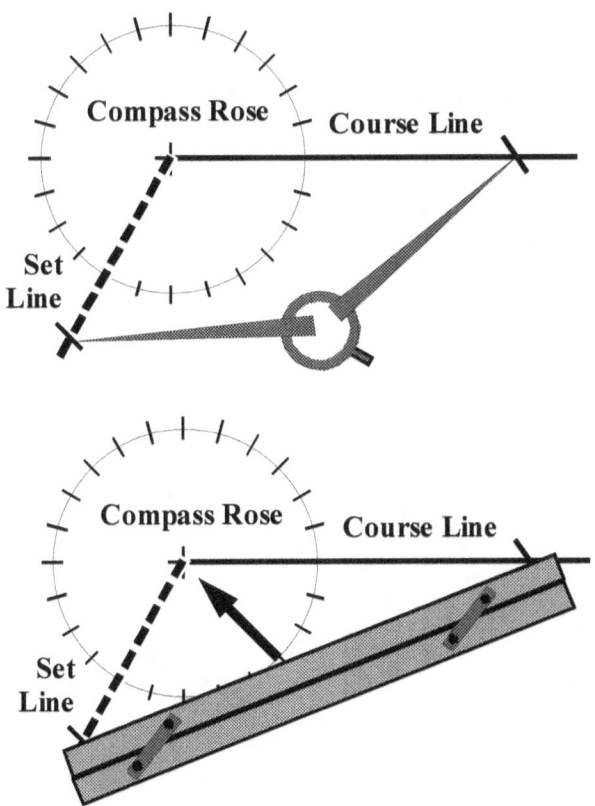

Speed Made Good, Alternate Method

In determining the Course To Steer, lines were drawn on the compass rose. The same diagram can be used to find the Speed Made Good. Remember that Speed Made Good is the speed that the vessel actually travels over the water, after compensating for set and drift.

Using the same input for Course To Steer, determine the Speed Made Good:
1. Start with a completed "Course To Steer" diagram.
2. Adjust the dividers to the length of the course line, from the center of the compass rose out to the mark. The length of this line represents the distance traveled in one hour.
3. Measure this length on the mileage scale printed on the chart. This is your SPEED MADE GOOD.

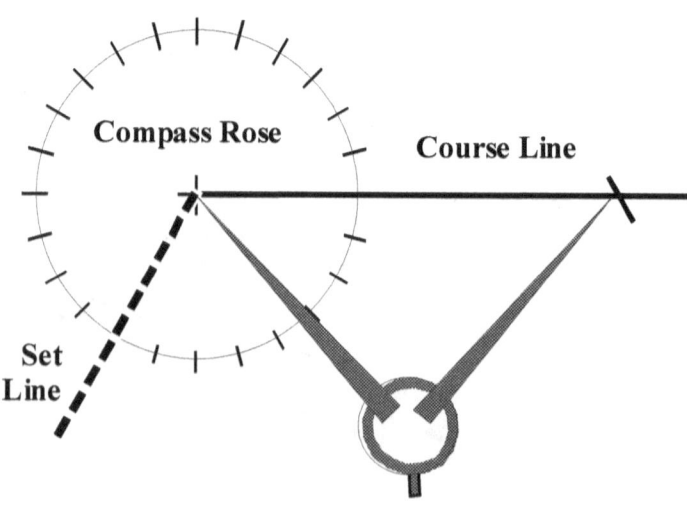

Fixing Your Position Using Bearings

You can obtain a fix on your position by drawing **bearing lines** on a nautical chart. A **bearing** is the True direction from an observer's vessel to a particular object. The object can be a buoy, lighthouse, mountain peak, or even another vessel. A bearing line is a line drawn on a nautical chart, from the observer's vessel to an object. A fix is obtained at the point where two or more bearing lines intersect.

Rules for plotting bearing lines:

1. Before plotting bearing lines on a chart, convert Compass or Magnetic bearings to True, using a Compass Conversion Diagram.
2. A minimum of two bearing lines are required to determine a fix. Three bearing lines will give a more accurate fix than two. A single bearing line intersecting a DR line is not a fix.
3. If two bearings are taken, the fix will be most accurate if the bearing lines intersect at or near a 90° angle. If three bearings are taken, the fix will be most accurate if the bearing lines intersect at or near 60° angles.
4. Three bearing lines may not intersect at a single point, forming a small triangle instead. Your fix will be in the center of the triangle. The smaller the triangle, the more accurate the fix.
5. If the bearing fix is unreasonably far from your DR Line (or a Dead Reckoned fix), you may have plotted incorrectly, or failed to convert all bearings to TRUE before plotting on the chart.
6. The more accurate your compass work, the more accurate your fix.

5. Choose another landmark, and take a bearing to it. The example below shows the second landmark marked as "Light".
6. With the parallel rules, walk the new bearing from the compass rose to the landmark.
7. Draw a line from the second landmark to where it intersects the first bearing line.
8. A third bearing line will increase the accuracy of the fix.

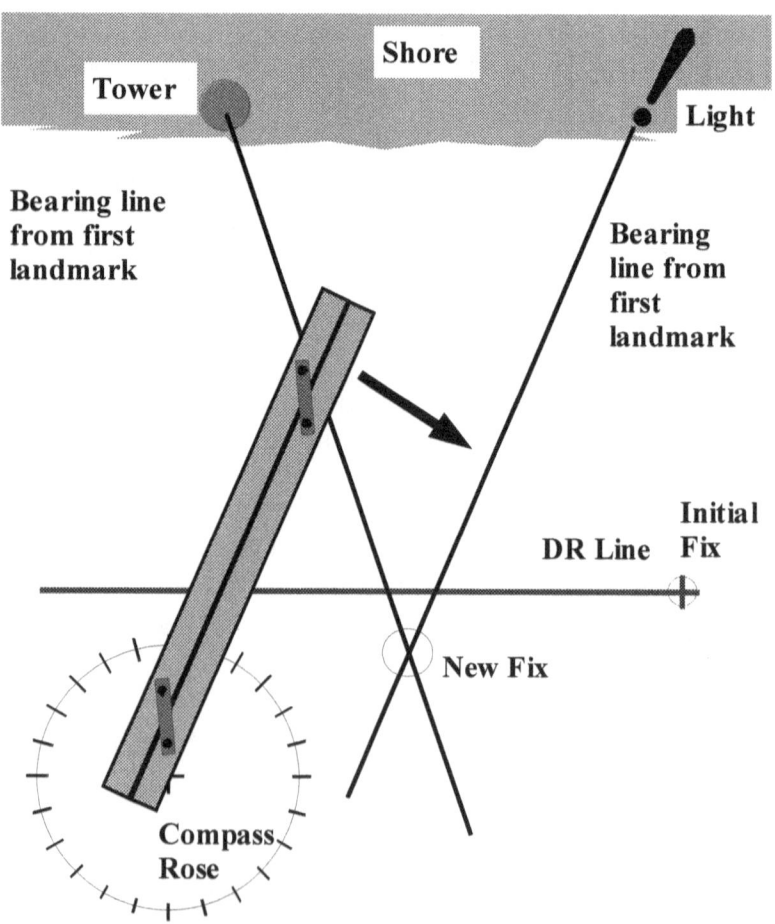

Skipper's Handbook – Robert Grossman

SECTION 4
BOAT HANDLING

EMERGENCIES

Person Overboard:
1. If the person in the water is close to the boat, kill the engine or move the stern away from the person.
2. Throw the person a flotation device, with a line attached.
3. Have a crew member watch the overboard person and continually point to him.
4. If you cannot see the person, mark the spot with a life preserver, or other floating object.
5. If not nearby, turn the boat around to retrace your course. Try to approach the person heading into the wind or waves.
6. When the person is located, get a flotation device to him immediately. Tie a line to the flotation device, and secure the other end to the boat.
7. Pull the person over to the boat, using the line attached to the flotation device.
8. Help the person get back aboard. Making sure the engine is off, board the person from the stern.
9. If the person is not immediately rescued, call for help on the marine radio. Say "Pan-Pan, Pan-Pan, Pan-Pan..." before the message (not "Mayday").
10. Do not give up the search.

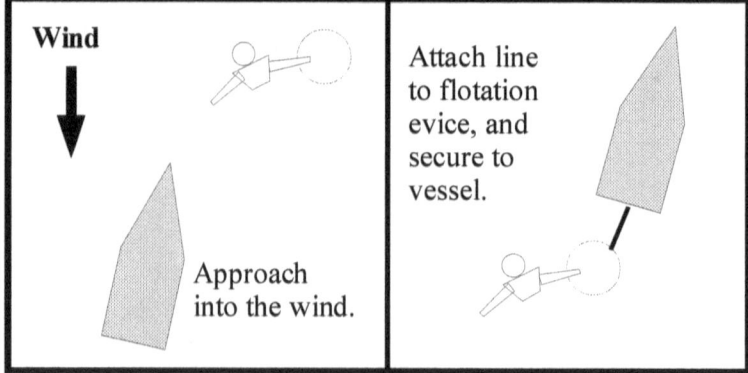

Taking On Water:

1. If you have just had a collision, **check for injuries to passengers and crew.**
2. Switch on electric bilge pumps.
3. Locate the source of the leak. Common locations are the drain plug, seacocks (through-hull fittings), and engine coolant drains.
4. Have the crew start bailing with buckets, cooking pots, hand pumps, or other means.
5. Patch the leaking area. Use anything at your disposal; blankets, pillows, clothes, duct tape.
6. Wedge the patch into place using a boathook, a paddle, or a ski.
7. Have everyone put on personal flotation devices.
8. Head for the nearest marina or docks. Keep the bilge as free from water as possible, so that rising water does not kill the engine or short out the electronics.
9. If necessary, you can beach the vessel so that it does not sink.
10. Call for assistance, if needed. Do not use "Mayday" unless your boat is in immediate danger of sinking.

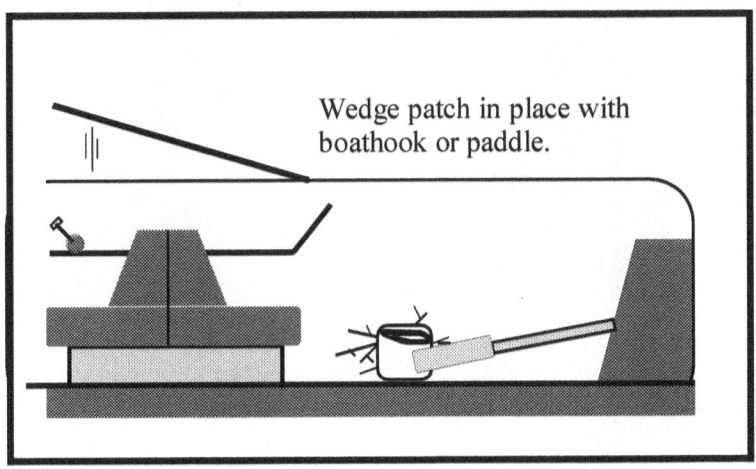

Wedge patch in place with boathook or paddle.

Towing:

1. **Towing can be dangerous.** You or your crew can be injured if the towline parts, or if a cleat pulls free. Your vessel also may be damaged.
2. Use only double-braided nylon line. It absorbs shock.
3. Toss the line to the disabled vessel. If the line cannot be tossed to the other vessel because of distance or sea conditions, float the towline to the disabled boat using a flotation device.
4. On the tow boat, the towline should be made fast as far forward as possible. It is best to use a bridle around both boats to distribute the strain.
5. Tow slowly.
6. The length of the towline should be such that both vessels travel together in the troughs or on the crests of the waves.
7. Be ready to cast off or cut the line if necessary.
8. **Never fend off another boat using hands or feet.**
9. You are not obligated to save someone's boat.

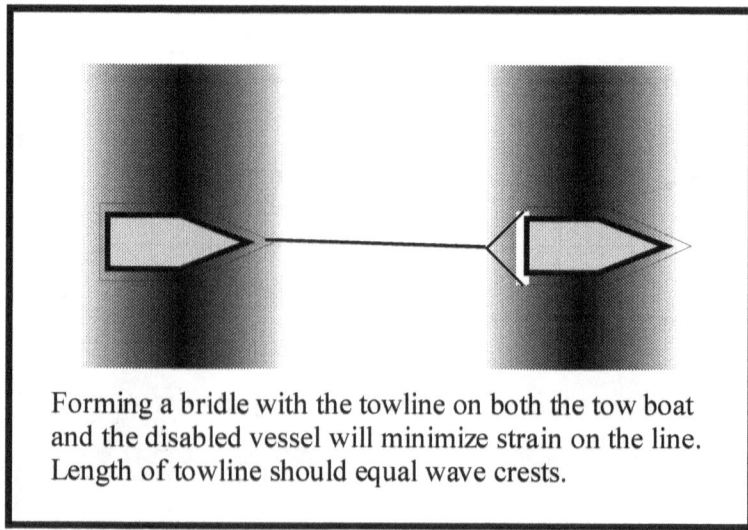

Forming a bridle with the towline on both the tow boat and the disabled vessel will minimize strain on the line. Length of towline should equal wave crests.

Vessel Aground:
1. Shut off the engine. Running the engine while stuck can force sand and rocks to be sucked up into the engine.
2. Tilt up the outdrive unit and inspect the propeller for damage.
3. Rock the boat back and forth while a crew member pushes off.
4. Remove passengers, crew, and extra weight to help lift and float the vessel.
5. Set out an anchor in the direction that you came from. The anchor can be floated out on a flotation cushion and then dropped into position. Set the anchor, and with the line tight, fasten to a cleat. The tight anchor line will help pull you off.
6. Have another boat go back and forth nearby. Its wake can help lift you off. As your boat rises on the wake, pull against the anchor.
7. If unsuccessful, have another boat pull you off. Use a bridle as shown below.

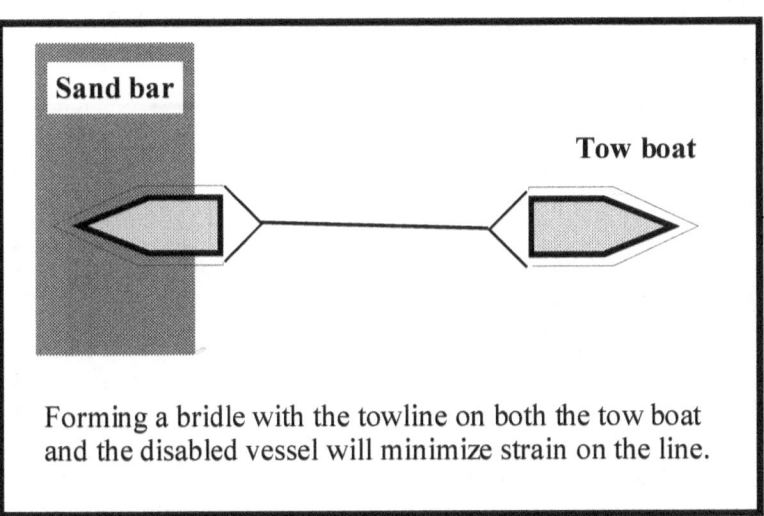

Forming a bridle with the towline on both the tow boat and the disabled vessel will minimize strain on the line.

BOAT HANDLING BASICS

Propellers

Propellers are produced in hundreds of configurations for use in many different applications. The more important variables of propeller design include:

1. Right hand vs. left hand. Most single screw boats are fitted with a right hand propeller, which rotates clockwise. Left hand propellers rotate counterclockwise. A left hand propeller is frequently fitted next to a right hand propeller on twin engine craft.

2. Pitch. Pitch is the angle the propeller blade forms with the hub. It is measured in inches, which is the theoretical distance the propeller would travel through the water. A properly pitched propeller allows the engine to operate within optimal RPMs, at full throttle. Fitting a vessel with a lower pitched (flatter) propeller will increase engine RPMs. This may be preferable for a good "hole shot" when pulling water-skiers, or when boating at high altitude lakes. A higher pitched propeller will lower engine RPMs, which will provide higher top end speeds. Many engines are damaged or worn out prematurely because improperly pitched propellers.

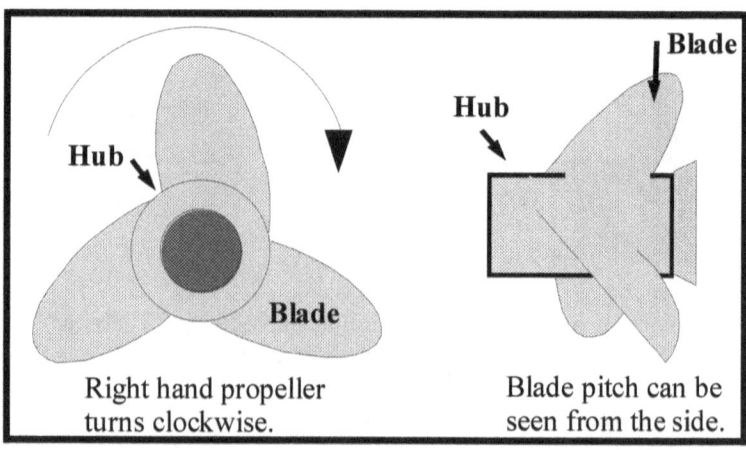

Right hand propeller turns clockwise.

Blade pitch can be seen from the side.

3. Diameter. This is the diameter of the circle formed by a rotating propeller. The diameter needs to be properly sized to optimize engine performance.

4. Number of Blades. As the number of blades increases, efficiency decreases. However, more blades produce less vibration. For most recreational boats, three-bladed propellers offer the best compromise.

5. Style. Propellers are designed in many different styles to perform varying functions. A race boat propeller may be designed to run partially submerged at high RPMs. A propeller on a fishing trawler may be designed to run fully submerged at low RPMs. Choose a propeller best suited to your intended use, hull and engine design.

6. Material. Propellers are most commonly manufactured out of bronze, stainless steel, or aluminum. Aluminum propellers are the least expensive, but flex more under strain, reducing efficiency. Stainless steel and bronze propellers are very strong, but can be expensive.

Always keep an extra propeller on board in case the one in use becomes damaged. Despite its strength, a propeller can be easily broken or damaged if it contacts any hard object, or is run aground while rotating.

For many trailerable boats, it may be useful to have available several propellers of different pitch. One propeller might be used for cruising, another for water-skiing, and another for use at higher altitudes.

Propeller Diameter

A race propeller may run partly submerged.

Cavitation

A propeller moves by creating lower pressure on the back sides of its blades. As the propeller is drawn toward the lower pressure, the boat is carried with it. Water boils at 212°F at normal (sea level) pressure. At much lower pressures, water can boil at low temperatures, even 50° or 60°F. If a propeller blade creates sufficiently lower pressures, water can boil and create small bubbles of water vapor along part of the blade. As these bubbles collapse, the can release enough energy to burn the blade material. These burns look like small pits on a propeller blade. This process is called cavitation.

When cavitation occurs, the boat's performance will decline significantly. The propeller will also be damaged. Cavitation can be caused by using a damaged, improperly pitched, or poorly designed propeller.

Ventilation

Ventilation occurs when surface air or exhaust gases mix with the blade area, causing the engine to over-rev. Thrust is lost during ventilation, and the engine can be severely damaged by the momentary high RPMs. Ventilation will also cause cavitation burns to a propeller. Ventilation damage can be minimized by proper boat handling. A product such as an anti-ventilation plate, a hydrofoil, or an engine RPM limiter can also help.

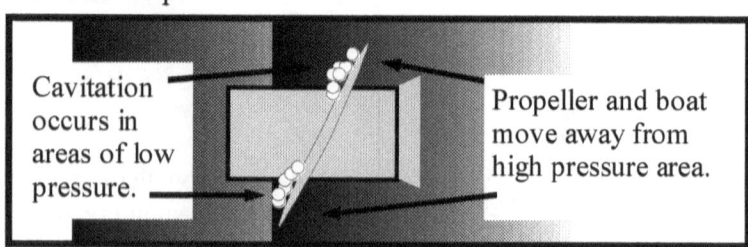

Cavitation occurs in areas of low pressure.

Propeller and boat move away from high pressure area.

Trim

Trim is the side-to-side or fore-and-aft angle that a vessel floats in the water. Vessels will perform poorly and may become unstable if not properly trimmed. Power boats may be equipped with manual or power trim adjustment controls of the outdrive unit, or be equipped with trim tabs. Uneven lateral trim results in a port or starboard list. Fore and aft trim are discussed below.

Trimming up lifts the bow up and out of the water. It reduces drag, since less of the boat is in the water. Trimming up also increases speed and increases the engine RPMs. A vessel should be trimmed up when running at cruising and planing speeds on calm water, when running full throttle, and when running in the same direction of a light chop. Trim up after the boat accelerates from a stop.

Trimming too far up can cause "porpoising", where the bow bounces up and down. Trimming too far up can also result in boat instability and loss of control.

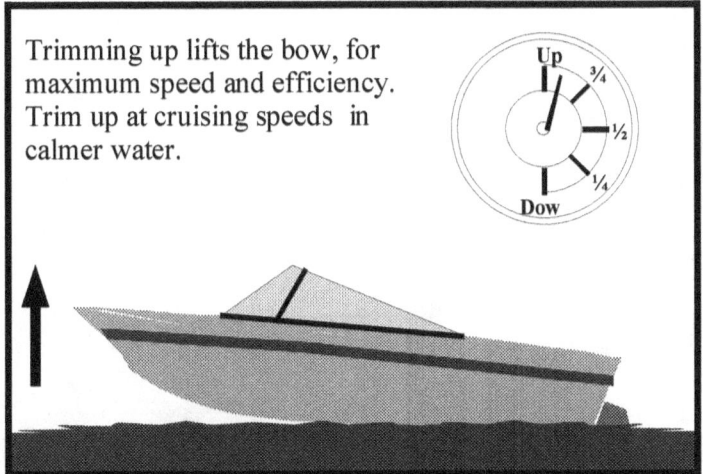

Trimming up lifts the bow, for maximum speed and efficiency. Trim up at cruising speeds in calmer water.

Trimming down pushes the bow down into the water. This increases the effective power, since the thrust is directed more forward, rather than upward. Drag is also increased, reducing both top-end speed and engine RPMs. Since the propeller is lower in the water, the bow will not rise as sharply during acceleration from a stop. When trimmed down during sharp turns, the propeller is less prone to ventilation. The boat hull is more stable through sharp turns, will not lose power, and will not "skip" across the water.

Trim down when approaching a sharp turn, such as when picking up a fallen water-skier. Keep the trim all the way down when accelerating from a stop. Once on plane, the trim can be brought back up. When the water gets rough, or when moving against choppy waves, trimming down will smooth out the ride.

Trimming too far down while cruising will increase strain on the engine, and greatly reduce efficiency.

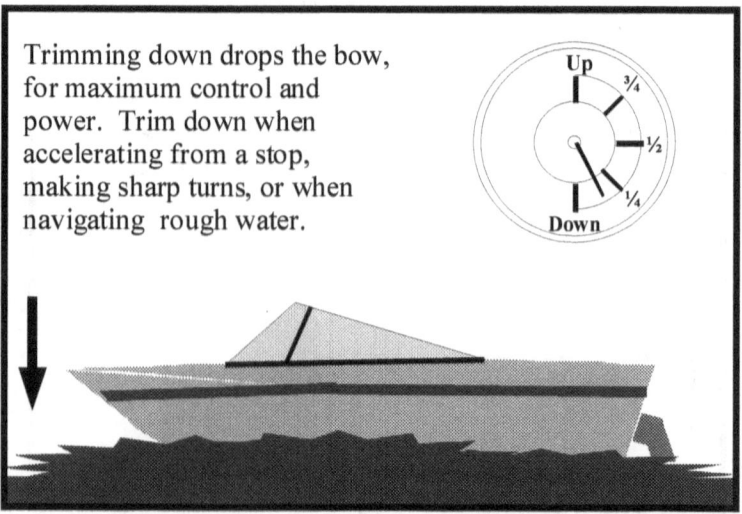

Trimming down drops the bow, for maximum control and power. Trim down when accelerating from a stop, making sharp turns, or when navigating rough water.

Blade Thrust

Because of the relative angle that water travels past rotating propeller blades, the thrust generated on the descending side of the propeller is often different than that generated on the ascending side. For a right-handed propeller moving ahead, the result is that the bow tends to turn to port. When backing, the stern tends to go to port.

These principles can be used to a skipper's advantage when maneuvering a vessel. For example, by reversing the engine when approaching a dock, the stern can be gently "walked" sideways, bringing the boat broadside to the dock.

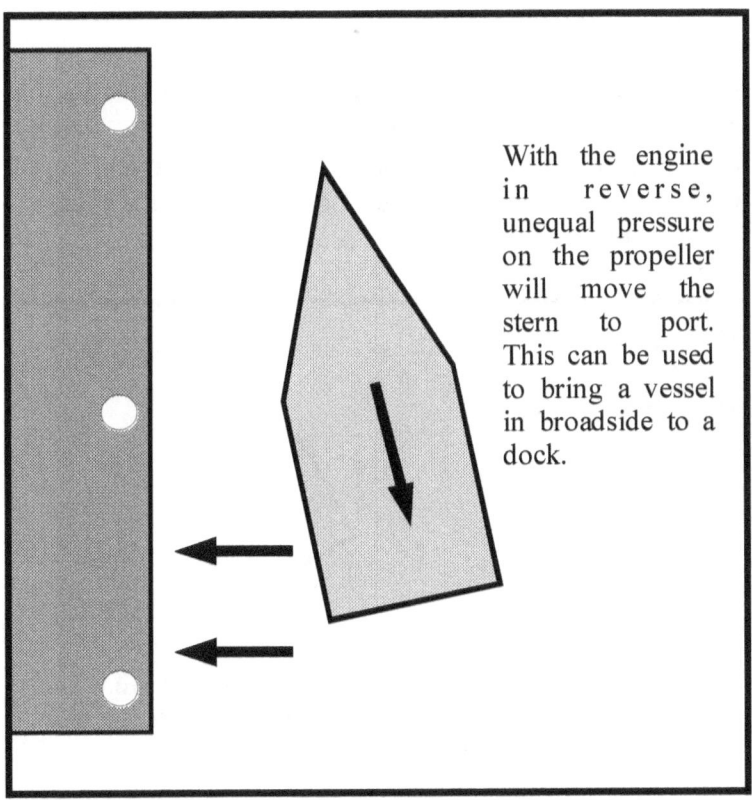

With the engine in reverse, unequal pressure on the propeller will move the stern to port. This can be used to bring a vessel in broadside to a dock.

Turning

One reason that boat handling can be so challenging is that boats do not steer the same way as automobiles. Whether rear-wheel, front-wheel, or all-wheel drive, cars are always steered from the front. Boats work in the opposite way. Watercraft, no matter the size, are propelled and steered from the rear.

Turning an automobile is intuitive and takes little planning. When the steering wheel is turned, the front of the car points in the desired direction, and the rest of the car follows. This motion describes a single arc, as the rear wheels follow the front. When turning a boat, the stern moves away from the desired direction. The bow of the boat travels along a smaller arc than the stern.

Because a boat turns by swinging its stern out to the side, the skipper must always be aware of nearby obstacles that might impede the outward movement of the stern. An obstacle might be a dock, another vessel, or a nearby swimmer.

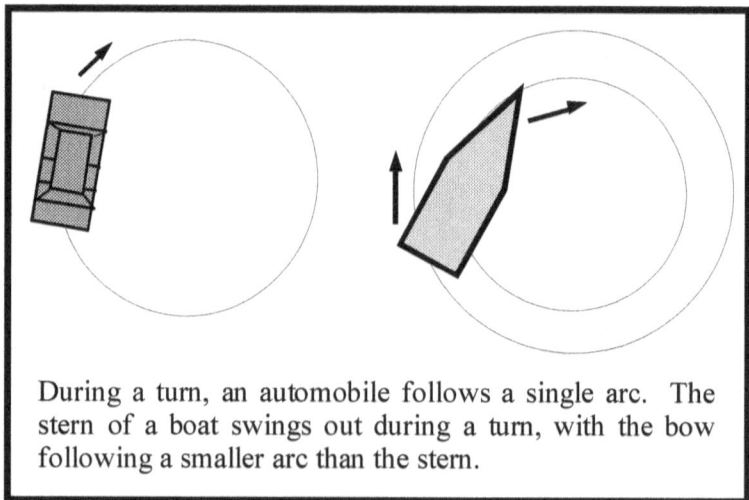

During a turn, an automobile follows a single arc. The stern of a boat swings out during a turn, with the bow following a smaller arc than the stern.

General Steering Characteristics

Although no two vessels handle exactly alike, there are several characteristics that most vessels share. Awareness of these characteristics will increase boat handling proficiency. The discussion below assumes that a vessel is turning a right-handed propeller:

1. Engaging forward gear from a dead stop will cause the stern to swing out to starboard.
2. Engaging reverse gear from a dead stop will throw the stern to port. When backing, a vessel will tend to go to port despite rudder angle.
3. Headway has better control than sternway.
4. Always approach docks or other vessels slowly. If reverse gear cannot be engaged or the engine stalls, a collision could result.
5. Power vessels have little steering or stopping ability when not propelled in forward or reverse gear.
6. Planing-hull vessels tend not to track straight when in displacement mode.
7. Port and starboard reactions are reversed for left-hand propellers.

Brakes

Unlike an automobile, a boat has no brakes. There are three ways to stop a boat:

1. Decelerate or "coast" until the friction of the water finally slows the vessel to a stop. The stopping distance can be quite long, as the inertia of the vessel will carry it forward. Heavier vessels have greater inertia.
2. Put the engine in reverse. The action of the propeller will slow the vessel more quickly, and allows a more controlled, calculated stop.
3. Collide with something. This is the least-preferred method.

Dock Lines

Correct selection and use of docklines will assist in many maneuvers, and protect a vessel from damage caused by wakes, rough water and storms. Although rope can be made of many different materials, nylon is best suited for docklines. Since nylon stretches, it absorbs shock well. Shock absorption is necessary to evenly distribute the strain when under load. This will prevent the vessel's cleats from pulling free. Nylon is also durable, inexpensive, and can be made with a soft texture.

Laid lines are formed with three twisted strands. It can be used as anchor line, tow line, and dock line. Twisted line is strong, and is abrasion and snag resistant.

Braided line typically has an inner braided core surrounded by a braided sheath. This line is smooth, easy to handle, and will not kink. Braided line will not chafe as easy as twisted line, making it the best choice for dock line.

Proper length and diameter of dock lines is proportional to the size of the vessel. Length should equal about 2/3 the length of the vessel. Recommended minimum line diameter is shown on the chart below.

Minimum Line Diameter	
Vessel Length	Line Size
Under 20'	3/8"
20' - 30'	1/2"
30' - 40'	5/8"
Over 40'	3/4"

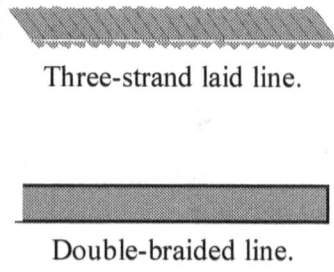

Three-strand laid line.

Double-braided line.

The number and placement of lines used when tying up to a dock is determined by the size of the vessel, how long the vessel will be docked, the weather conditions, and the sea conditions. One line fore and one line aft may be sufficient to hold a 24' boat docked for a couple of hours on a calm day. On a windy day, four lines might be more appropriate. Setting out fenders will help protect the boat from the ravages of wind, waves, and wakes.

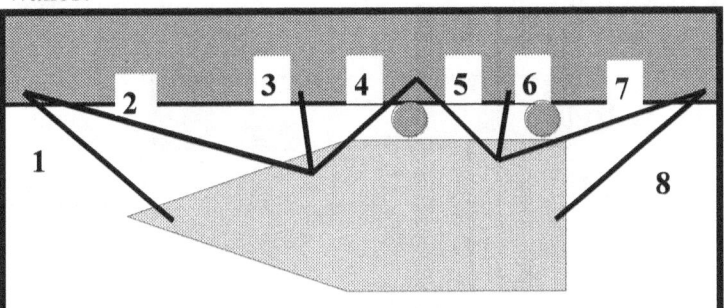

1. Bow line
2. Forward bow spring
3. Forward (bow) breast
4. After bow spring
5. Forward quarter spring
6. After (quarter) breast
7. After quarter spring
8. Stern line

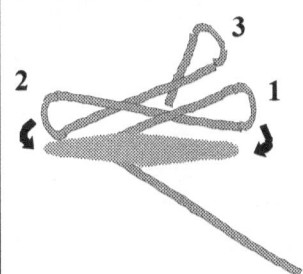

Tying to a Cleat: Loop figure-eights around the cleat with the end of the line. Three or four turns are all that is needed.

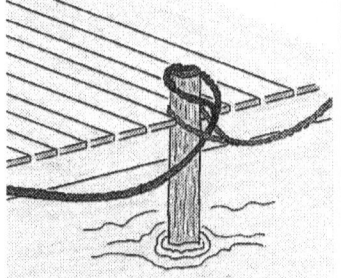

Sharing a Pile or Cleat: If a pile or cleat already has a line on it, slip your line through the eye of the existing line, then over the cleat.

Leaving Dock Into Wind Or Current, Or Leaving A Crowded Dock:

1. Secure a forward quarter spring line to the dock.
2. Set out a fender near the cleat on the boat where the spring line is attached.
3. With the rudder turned into the dock, back against the spring line. The bow of the boat will swing out from the dock.
4. Release the dock line, and pull forward, away from the dock.

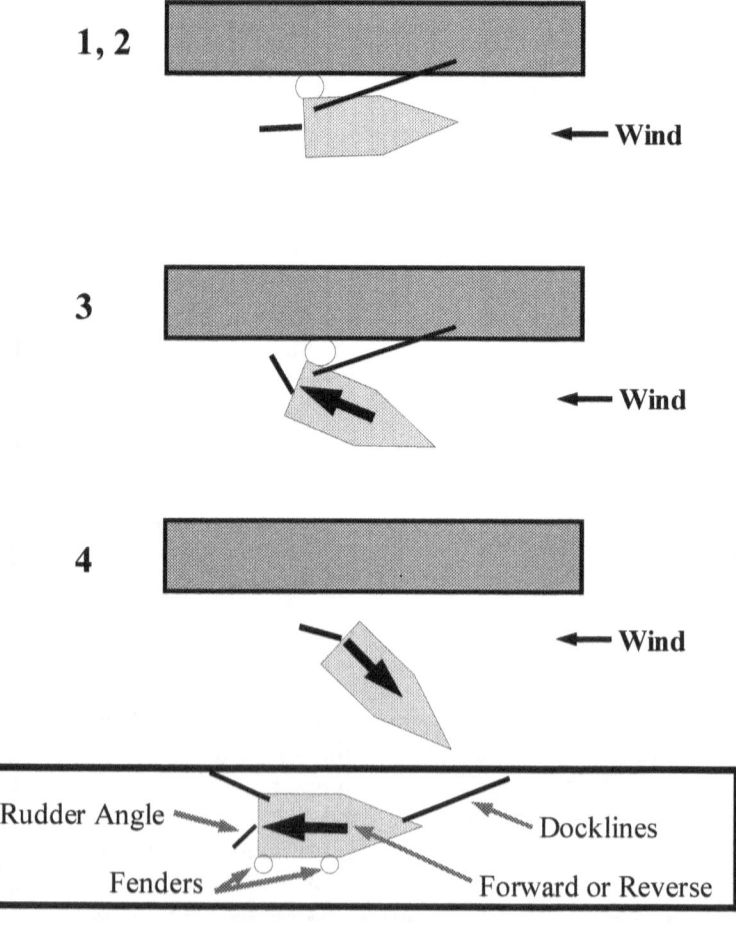

Approaching Dock From Leeward, or
Approaching Dock With Traffic:
1. Set out fenders on the docking side of the boat.
2. Slowly ease the vessel up to the dock in forward gear.
3. As the bow approaches the dock, have a crew member tie a bow spring line to the dock.
4. With rudder away from dock, move forward against the spring line. This will bring in the stern.
5. Tie off dock lines.

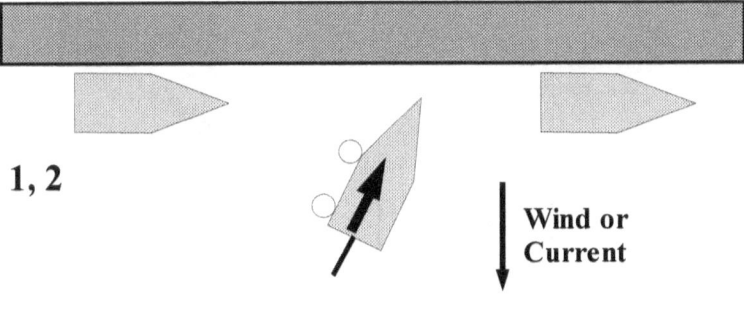

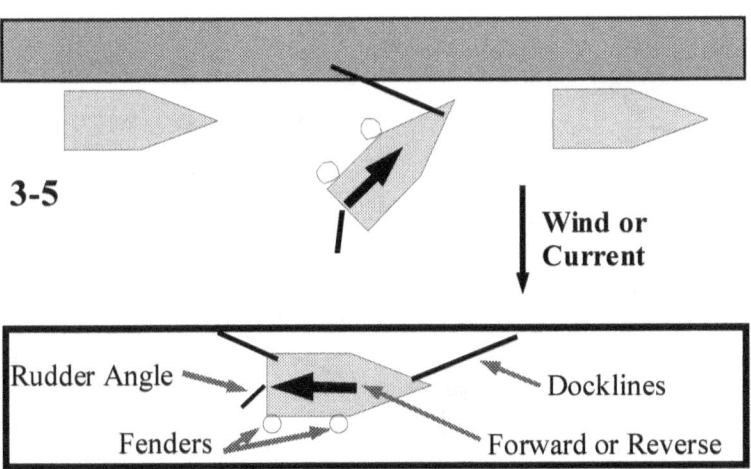

Approaching Dock By Backing, Limited Space:

1. Set out fenders on the docking side of the boat.
2. Slowly ease the vessel up to the end of dock in forward gear.
3. Reverse the engine and back up toward the side of the dock.
4. With rudder hard away from dock, engage forward gear. This will kick the stern toward the dock.
5. Repeat the reverse-then-forward process, until even with the dock. Tie off.

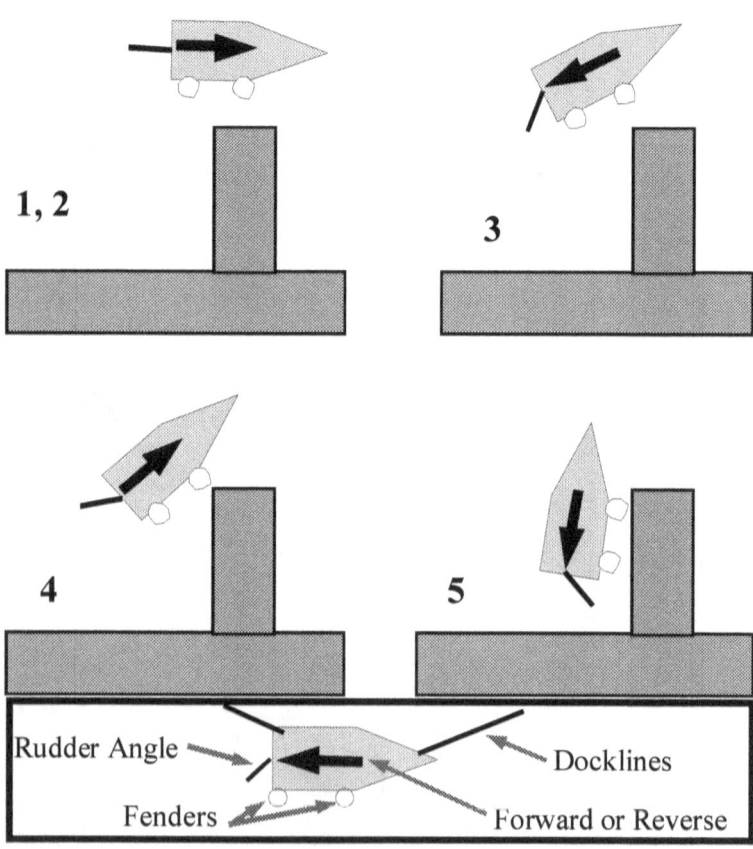

Leaving Dock Into Wind Or Current, Or Leaving A Crowded Dock:

1. Secure a forward quarter spring line to the dock.
2. Set out a fender near the cleat on the boat where the spring line is attached.
3. With the rudder turned into the dock, back against the spring line. The bow of the boat will swing out from the dock.
4. Release the dock line, and pull forward, away from the dock.

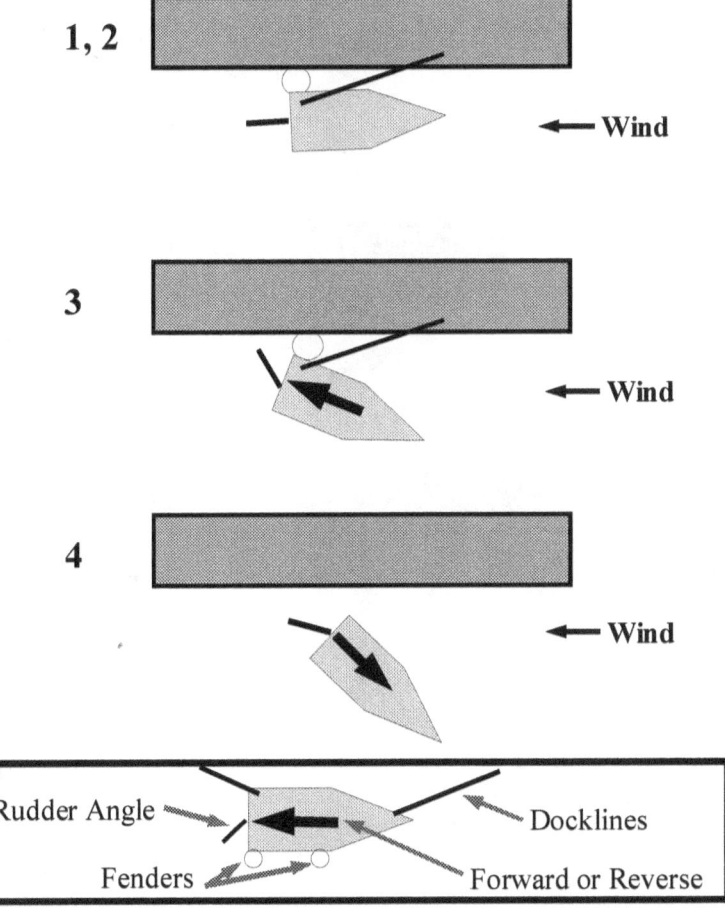

Leaving Dock With Wind Or Current Into Dock, Or With Wind Or Current From Astern:

1. Secure an after bow spring line to the dock.
2. Set out a fender near the cleat on the boat where the spring line is attached.
3. With the rudder turned into the dock, go forward against the spring line. The stern of the boat will swing out from the dock
4. Release the dock line, and back out, away from the dock.

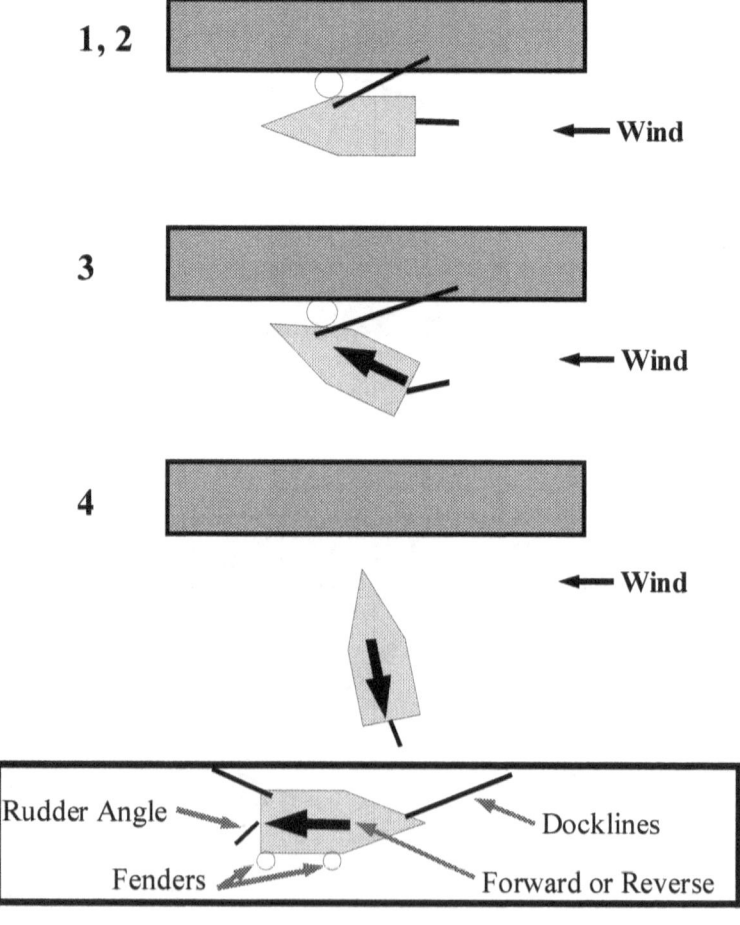

Backing Out Of A Slip:

1. Back out of the slip until the stern is just past the edge of the dock.
2. Secure a forward quarter spring line to the dock.
3. Set out a fender near the cleat on the boat where the spring line is attached.
4. With the rudder turned into the dock, back down against the spring line. The stern of the boat will pivot around the dock, allowing the bow to swing free of the slip.
5. Release the dock line. Pull forward, away from the slip.

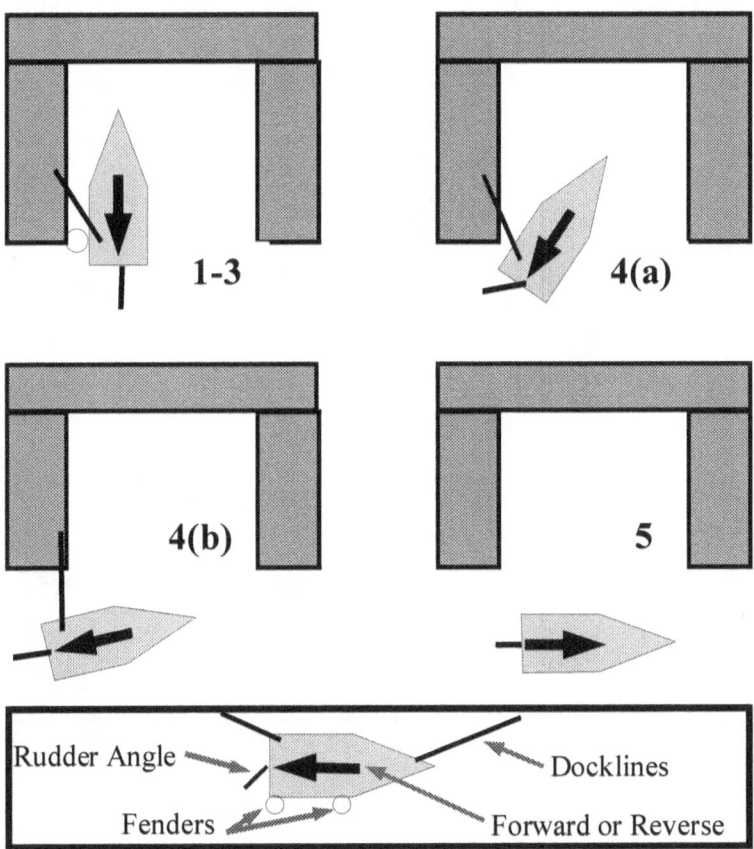

Tight-Radius Turning:

1. If turning to starboard, start at the left side of the channel. Leave enough room for the stern to swing out.
2. Initiate the turn in forward gear, with the rudder hard to starboard.
3. Engage reverse gear, keeping the rudder hard over to starboard. During backing, uneven blade pressure will move the stern to port.
4, 5. Alternate going ahead and backing as necessary to complete the turn.

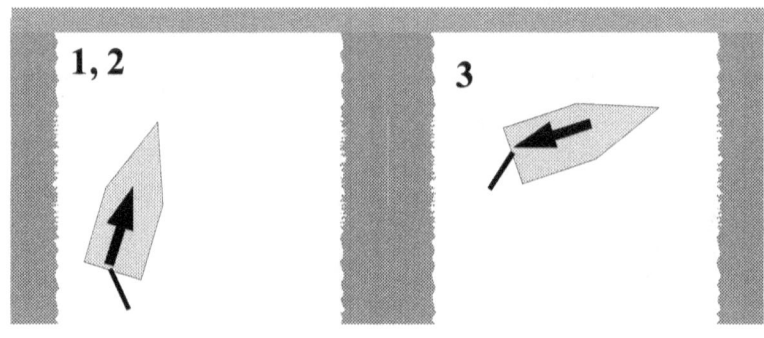

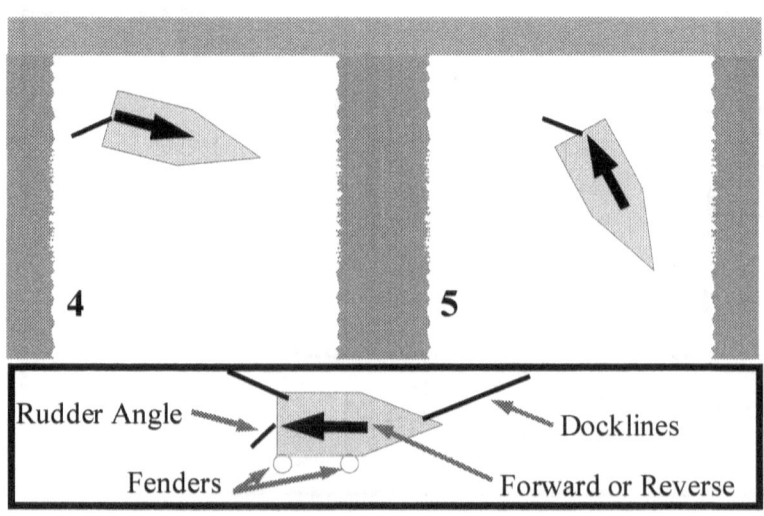

Turning On Pilings:

1. Loop a forward line around a piling or cleat, so that it may be retrieved.
2. Slowly, go ahead against the line. This will swing the boat around the piling.
3. When the boat is completely turned around, loop an aft line around another piling. Retrieve the first line.
4, Back down against the aft line, pivoting around the piling.
5. Continue backing against the line until the boat is in the desired position. Tie off the dock lines.

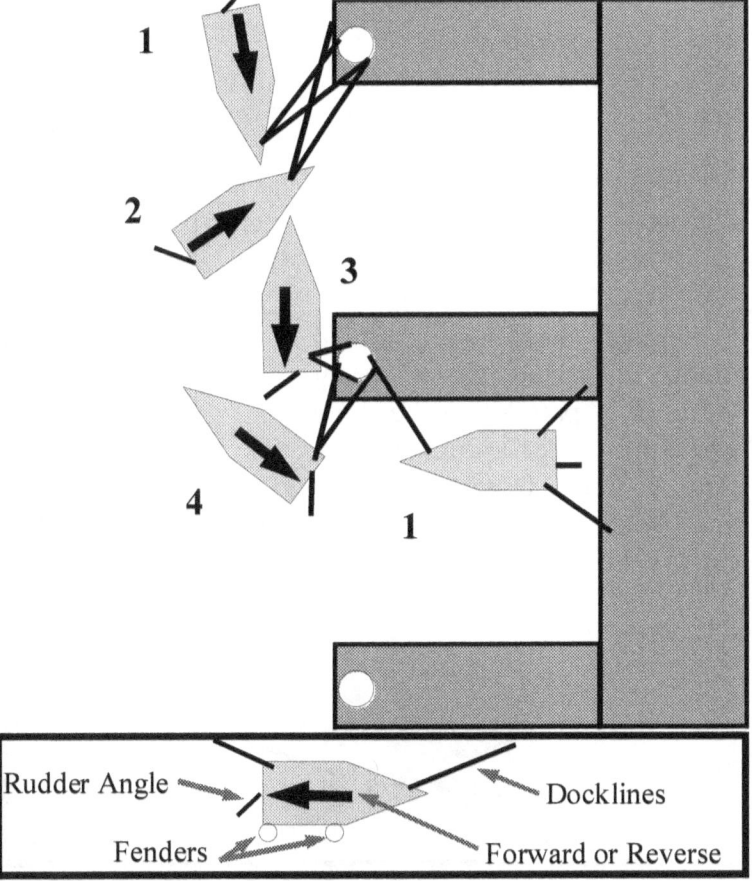

Using Spring Lines

Spring lines are very useful for maneuvering in tight areas and difficult docking situations. In each diagram below, #1 shows the initial vessel position and #2 shows the resulting position when a spring line is used.

1. Going ahead with straight rudder: this spring line will move the bow into the dock, and will swing the stern away from the dock. Use when backing out of a crowded dock, or to pivot into a berth.

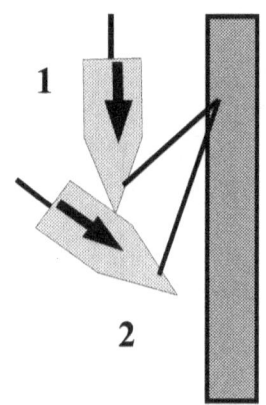

2. Going ahead with turned rudder: this spring line will bring the boat in parallel to the dock when the rudder is turned away from the dock. Use to pull into a dock when the wind or current blows off the dock.

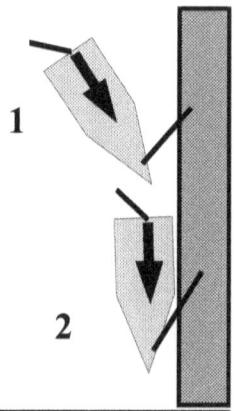

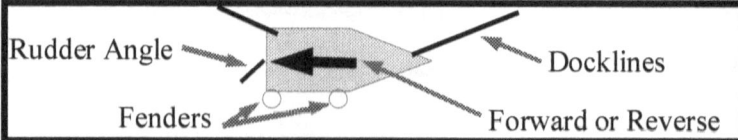

Using Spring Lines, continued

In each diagram below, #1 shows the initial vessel position, and #2 shows the result when a spring line is used.

3. Backing with straight rudder: this spring line will move the stern into the dock, and will swing the bow away from the dock. Use to pivot around a cleat or piling, when backing into a berth. This can also be used to leave a dock when the wind or current is pushing the boat into the dock.

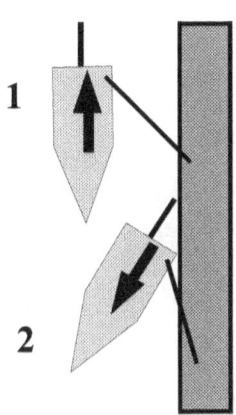

4. Backing with straight rudder: this spring line will bring the boat in parallel to the dock. Use to bring the boat closer to the dock, when wind or current pushes the boat away from the dock.

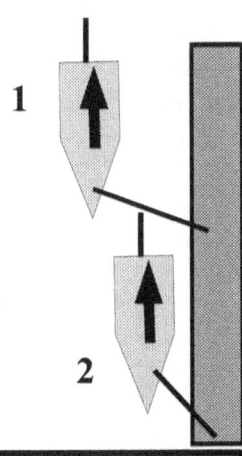

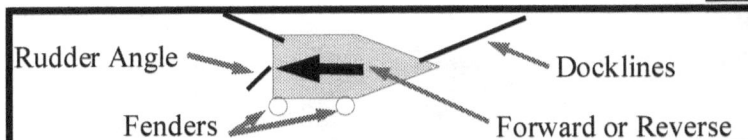

TWIN-SCREW VESSELS

A vessel equipped with two engines handles differently than a single-engine craft. Typically, the starboard propeller is right-handed and the port propeller is left-handed. Engines may be engaged independently of one another, allowing excellent maneuverability. At slow speeds, the two throttles can be used to maneuver the boat without turning the wheel.

Twin-Screw Basics
In each diagram below, #1 shows the initial vessel position and #2 shows the resulting position when the technique is applied. Each engine is depicted by an arrow.

1. Going forward with the port engine only. The boat turns to starboard much as a single-engine boat would. The stern swings to port as boat moves ahead. The boat will turn even if the rudder is straight.

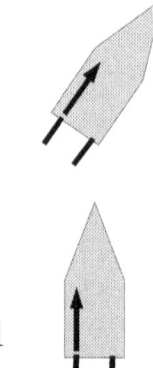

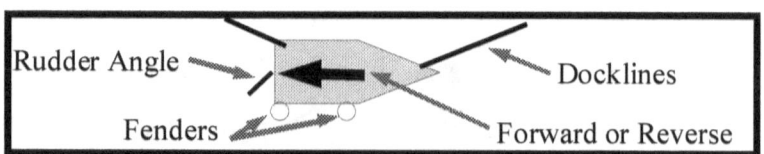

In each diagram below, #1 shows the initial vessel position and #2 shows the resulting position when the technique is applied. Each engine is depicted by an arrow.

2. Going forward with the starboard engine only. The boat turns to port much as a single-engine boat would. The stern swings to starboard as boat moves ahead. The boat will turn even if the rudder is straight.

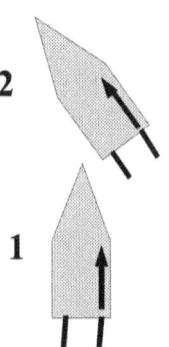

3. Backing with port propeller only. The stern moves to starboard as the boat moves back. The boat will turn even if the rudder is straight.

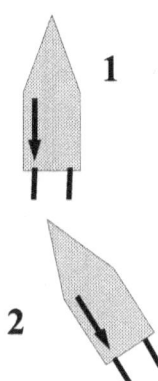

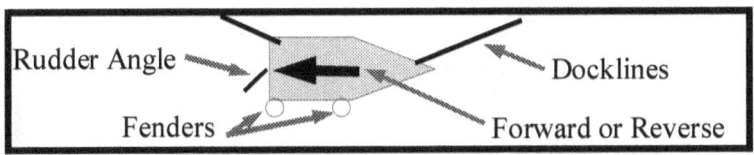

In each diagram below, #1 shows the initial vessel position and #2 shows the resulting position when the technique is applied. Each engine is depicted by an arrow.

4. Backing with starboard propeller only. The stern moves to port as the boat moves back. The boat will turn even if the rudder is straight.

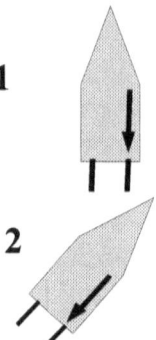

5. Forward with one engine while backing with the other engine. The great advantage of a twin-screw vessel is that it can turn in its own length.

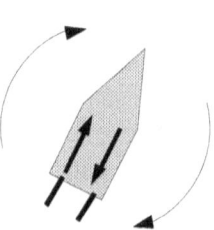

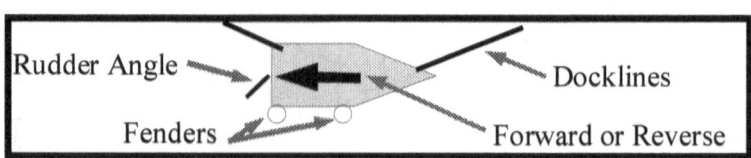

Twin-Screw Docking:
1. Set out fenders on the docking side of the boat.
2. Slowly ease the vessel up to the dock, with both engines ahead.
3. As the boat approaches the dock, put the dock-side engine in neutral, and the seaward engine in reverse. This will swing the stern parallel to the dock.
4. Tie off dock lines.

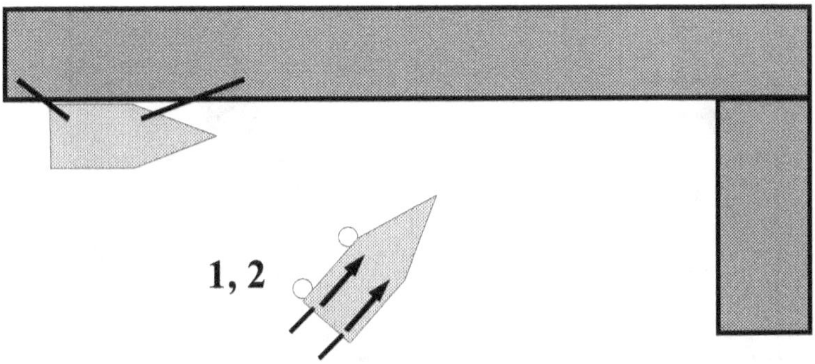

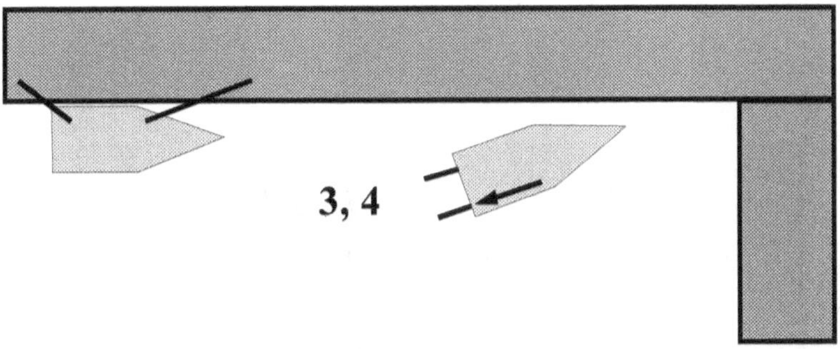

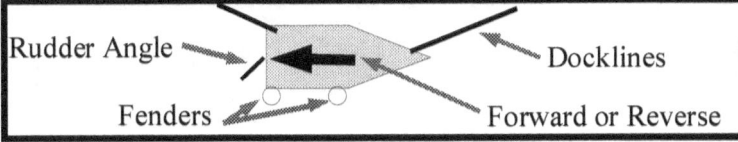

Twin-Screw, Backing Into A Slip:

1. Set out fenders on the docking side of the boat.
2. Pull forward to a position just past the slip.
3. With the dock-side engine ahead, put the outside (seaward) engine in reverse. This will rotate the vessel into position.
4. As the boat backs into the slip, pass a stern line to shore.
5. Put both engines in reverse to finish backing into the slip. Tie off dock lines.

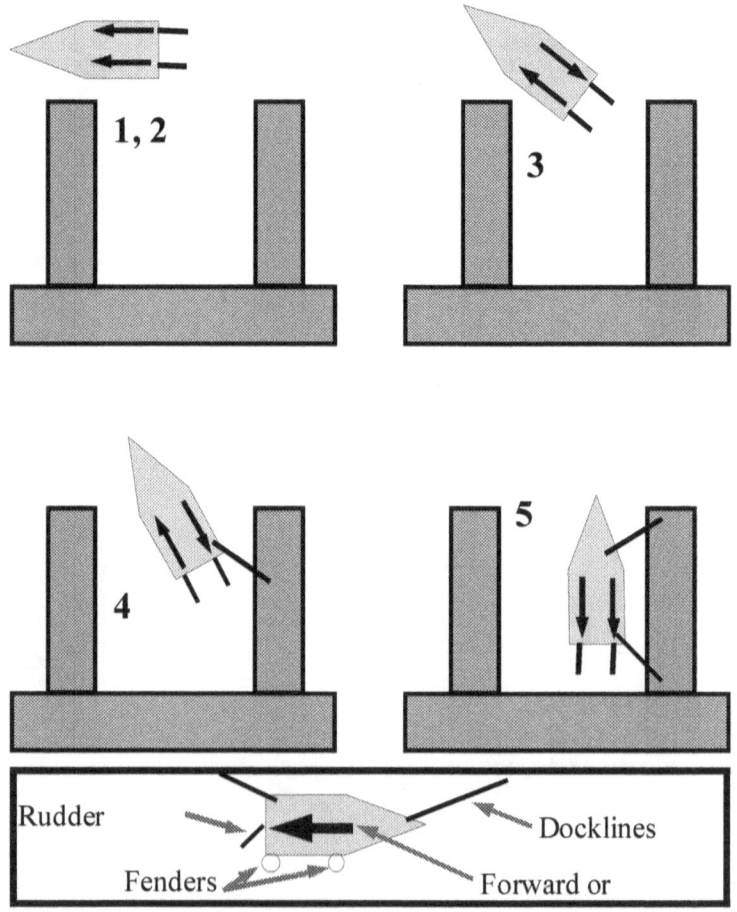

Twin-Screw, Leaving Dock With A Spring Line:

1. Secure an after bow spring line to the dock.
2. Set out a fender near the cleat on the boat where the spring line is attached.
3. With the outside (seaward) engine only, go forward against the spring line. Using just one propeller will assist in swinging out the stern. It is not necessary to turn the wheel.
4. Release the dock line, and back out, away from the dock.

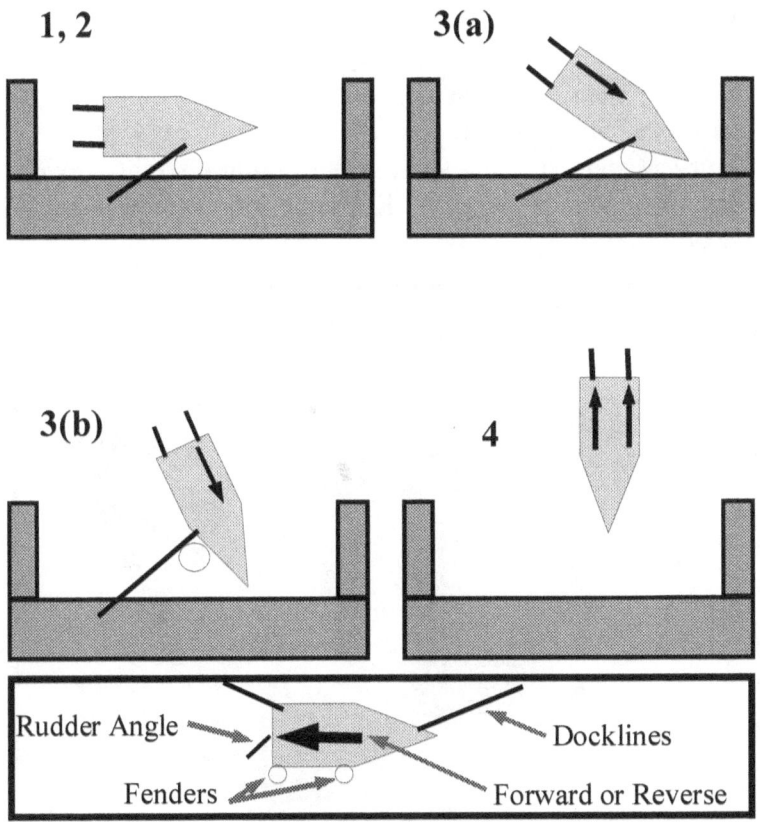

ROUGH SEAS

Boating in adverse weather or large waves demands **at least** the following precautions:
1. Confirm your position on a nautical chart.
2. Secure all hatches, windows, and loose gear.
3. Make ready all life preservers. Have everyone put them on if conditions worsens.
4. Keep the bilges dry. Pump them out as necessary.
5. Instruct the crew on safety procedures and radio use.
6. Head to sheltered water, if necessary.

The skipper is responsible for the safety of everyone on board.

Heading Into Large Waves
Large seas are best handled by heading directly into the waves. Quartering the waves (steering at a slight angle) may provide a better ride. Keep the boat below planing speed.

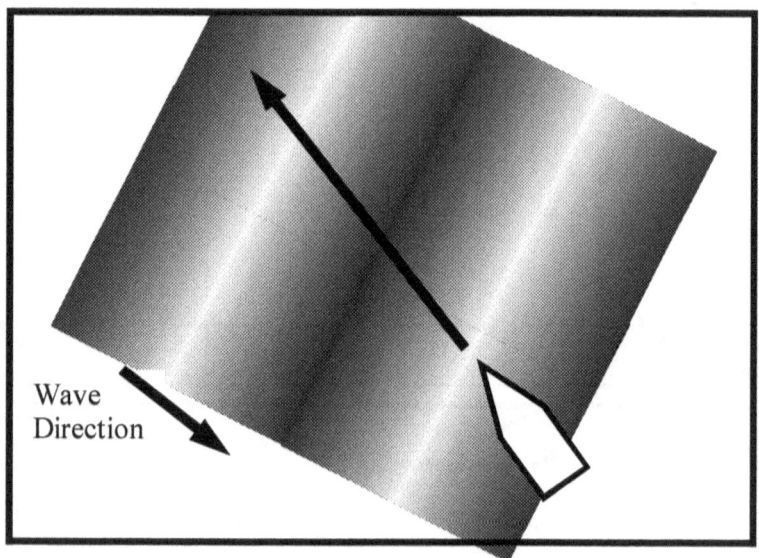

Running Parallel To Waves
Running parallel in steep seas can cause the vessel to capsize. The safest method to handle this situation is to tack back and forth toward your destination. Steer into the waves at an angle. After traveling some distance in that direction, turn and run with the waves at an angle. Make the turn as quickly as possible on the backside or trough of a wave. Continue zig-zagging in this fashion until the destination is reached. Keep the boat below planing speed.

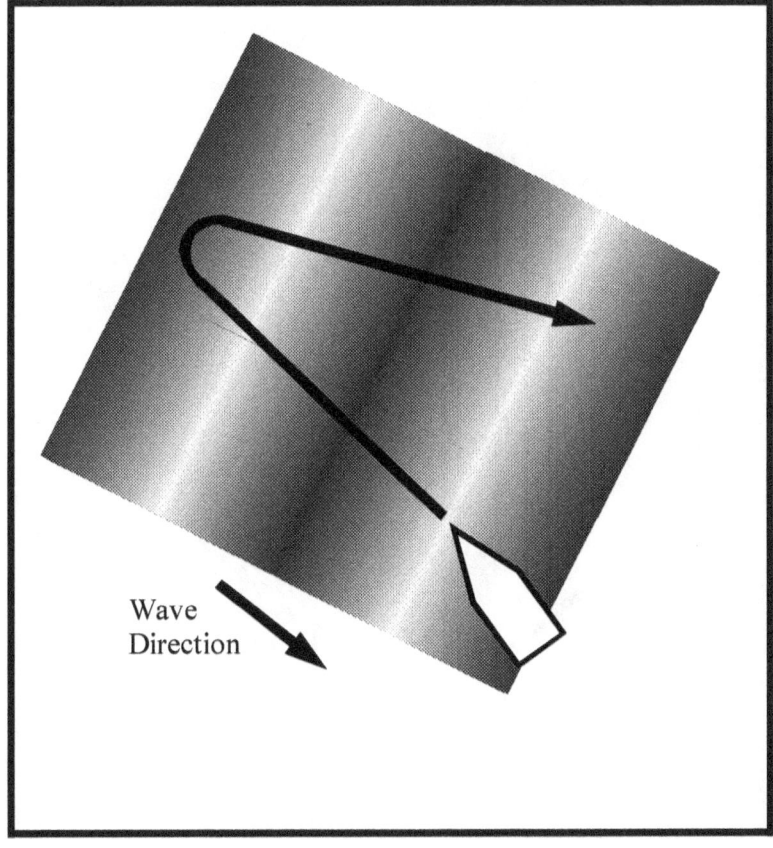

Running With The Waves

Running with the waves in steep seas can cause the vessel to pitchpole (be thrown end over end). The safest method to handle this situation is to stay on the backside of the wave that is in front of the vessel. Maintain enough speed to stay ahead of the crest that is behind the vessel. If the boat cannot keep up with the waves, quarter down the face of the wave as it passes under the vessel.

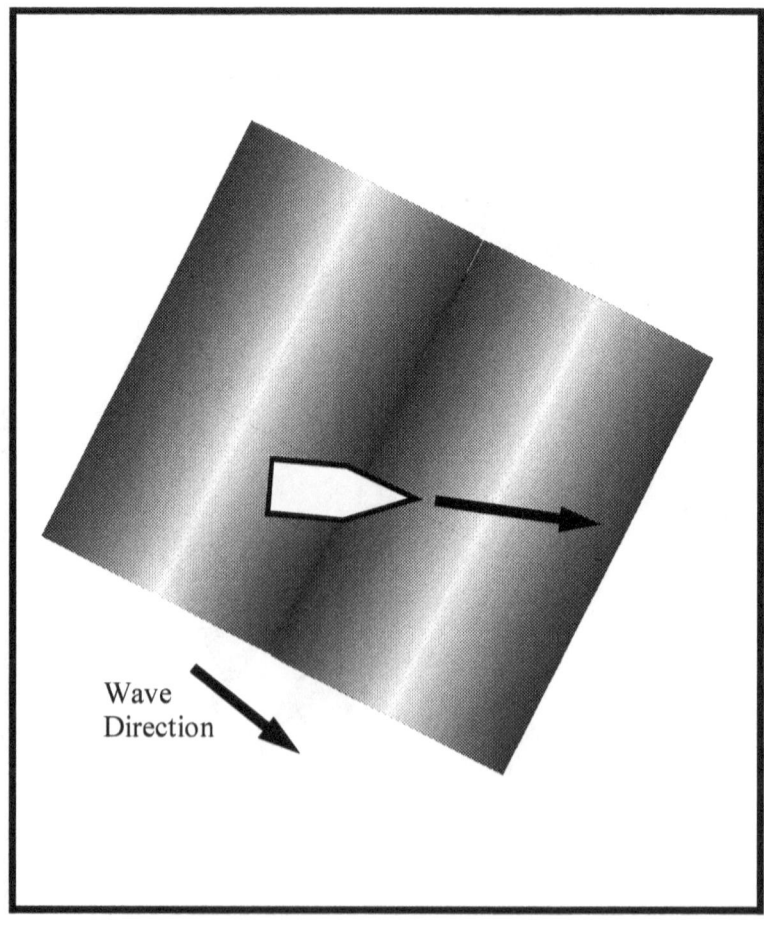

Turning Around

Turning around in large seas can be dangerous. It is important to not let the upcoming wave broadside the boat, so the turn should be made as quickly as possible. Execute the turn at the bottom of the trough, or on the backside of the wave ahead.

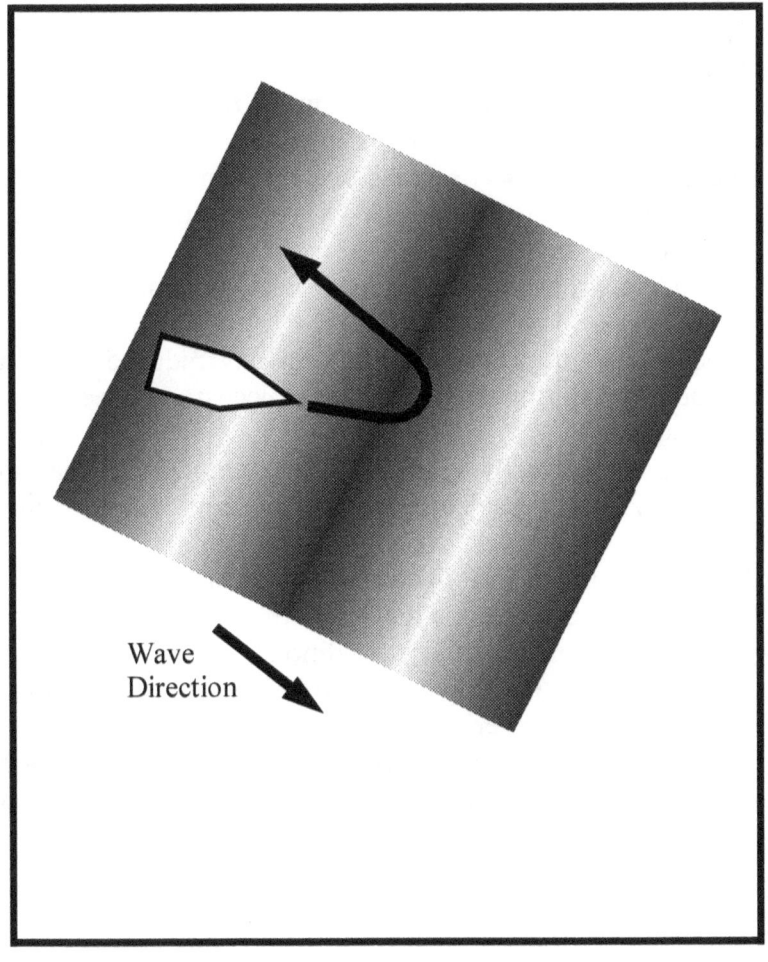

SPECIAL SITUATIONS

Running in Reduced Visibility:

1. These rules apply both night and day, whenever visibility is reduced. Reduced visibility could mean fog, snow, blowing dust, heavy rain, or low light conditions.
2. Reduce the speed appropriate for the conditions. A skipper must be able to avoid a collision.
3. Have a high-intensity spotlight available to illuminate buoys, docks, other vessels, and obstructions.
4. Post a lookout to look and listen. The lookout can be the skipper.
5. Navigation is more difficult during restricted visibility. The use of GPS or dead reckoning may become necessary. If available use the vessel's radar to help identify obstructions. Even if the radar is being used, a vessel must still have a posted lookout.
6. Sound appropriate fog signals (see section on sound signals).
7. Display the proper vessel lights in any reduced-visibility situation, even during daylight hours if necessary. (See section on light signals.)
8. In fog, periodically shut down the engines so that the skipper can hear fog signals from buoys, from shore, or from other vessels.
9. Hoist a passive radar reflector as high as possible.
10. If the skipper questions the safety of proceeding under the given weather and visibility conditions, consider anchoring until such conditions improve. The safety of the passengers and crew are the skipper's primary responsibility.
11. When laying over for better conditions, anchor in an area away from normal vessels traffic. Use the proper sound and light signals while anchored, if required.

Running an Inlet:

1. Entering an inlet from seaward can be extremely dangerous. It may be difficult to see large waves from seaward.

2. Wait near the entrance of the inlet before proceeding.

3. Study the wave sets. Typically the last wave of the set is the largest.

4. Prepare your boat as if for heavy weather. Close all hatches and windows, secure loose gear, and have everyone put on a personal flotation devise.

5. Wait until the wave set passes, and then follow the last wave in.

6. Try to stay on the backside of the last wave of the set.

7. Watch in front of and behind your boat, as you follow the wave in.

8. An ebb tide makes conditions worse. Consider waiting for a change in the tide. The best time is at the end of the flood tide.

9. It may be better to follow a local boat in, or even to call for a pilot.

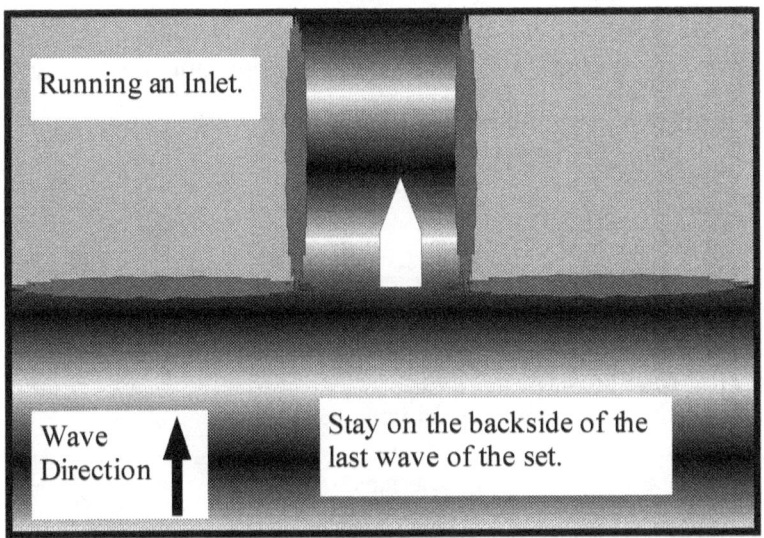

Water Skiing:
1. Always have an observer, always use a signal flag, and always have the skier wear a personal flotation device. State laws differ on the regulations and control of waterskiers and others in tow.
2. Competition ski lines start at 75' long, and are segmented to allow for shortening during competition.
3. Before getting started, agree on hand signals for "faster", "slower", "turn around" and "I am OK."
4. When starting from the water, have the skier sit up high facing the boat. Keep the knees bent, arms straight, and ski tips up. Remember to have the red signal flag up and visible.
5. Move the boat forward slowly, to take up all the slack in the tow line.
6. When the skier is ready, accelerate quickly and smoothly to the proper speed. The skier should stand up during acceleration. Lower the red signal flag when the skier is up.
7. The skier's weight should be centered over the skis, without leaning forward or back.
8. The proper towing speed depends on the ability of the skier, his weight, and whether he is using one ski or two.

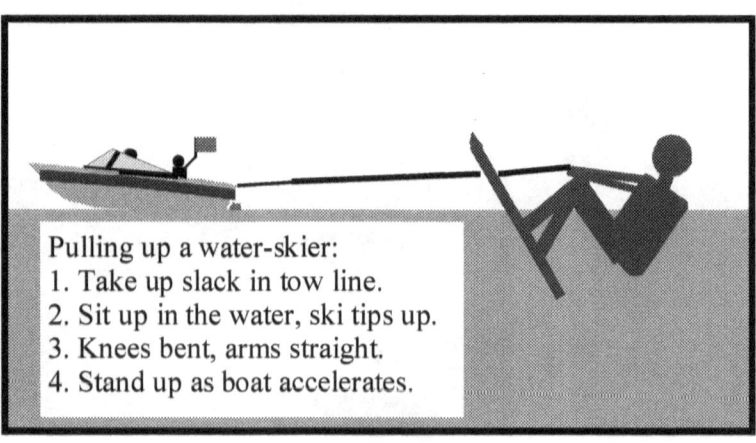

Pulling up a water-skier:
1. Take up slack in tow line.
2. Sit up in the water, ski tips up.
3. Knees bent, arms straight.
4. Stand up as boat accelerates.

9. Tow the skier on the smoothest water possible, away from other boats, jet skis, swimmers, obstructions, or floating debris.

10. Tow the skier in as straight a line as possible. Holding the boat steady in this manner allows the skier to make good slalom turns.

11. If the skier falls, turn the boat immediately, and raise the red signal flag. **The skier's safety is the skipper's responsibility.**

12. Always pick up the skier on the driver's side of the boat. This ensures that you can see the skier as you pull up alongside.

13. When returning the tow line to the skier, circle around the skier on the driver's side, and then straighten out. Be careful not to run over the tow line when circling.

14. When loading the skier back into the boat from the water, raise the red signal flag and turn off the engine. Take the tow line back aboard.

15. Stay out of 5 mph zones and no-wake coves. Many areas of lakes are off-limits to water-skiers.

16. Do not wave the red signal flag unless there is an emergency, and immediate assistance is required.

17. When not water-skiing, do not stir up otherwise calm water for nearby skiers. Hopefully, others will repay you with the same courtesy.

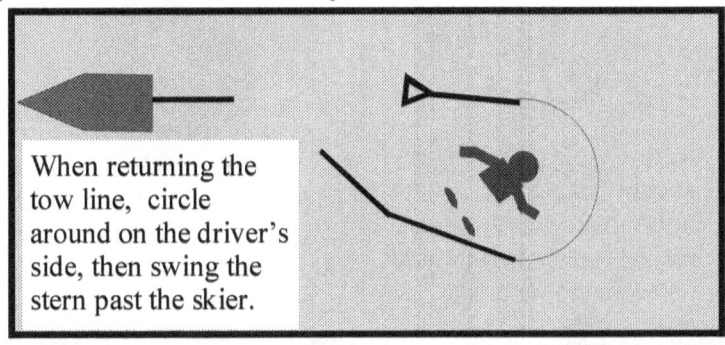

When returning the tow line, circle around on the driver's side, then swing the stern past the skier.

ANCHORING

Knowing how to use an anchor properly is a very useful skill for every skipper. Anchoring can be as simple as dropping a "lunch hook" over the side on a calm day, or as complicated as carefully placing two, three, or more anchors in a confined area during a blow.

Many different types of anchors are available. Each has its own application. Anchor selection should be based on the size (displacement) of the vessel, and its intended use.

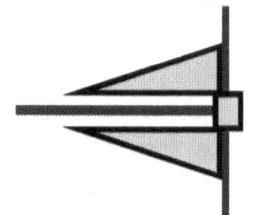 Fluke or Danforth Type. Light and strong. Made for soft bottoms, mud, and sand. Digs in to bottom. Not effective on rocks.	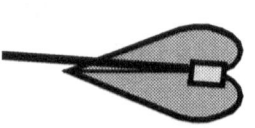 Plow Type. For grass, weeds, sand, and mud. Resists breaking out when direction changes. Will not foul anchor lines.
 Kedge Type. Heavy anchor used for hard bottoms, weeds, grass, and rocks. Not often used on recreational boats.	 Claw Type. The three-claw scoop is effective in mud, sand, and gravel. Sets quickly.

Ground Tackle

The sum of all the parts of an anchoring system is known as ground tackle. This includes the anchor, chain, line, and other fittings. A typical anchoring system is shown below.

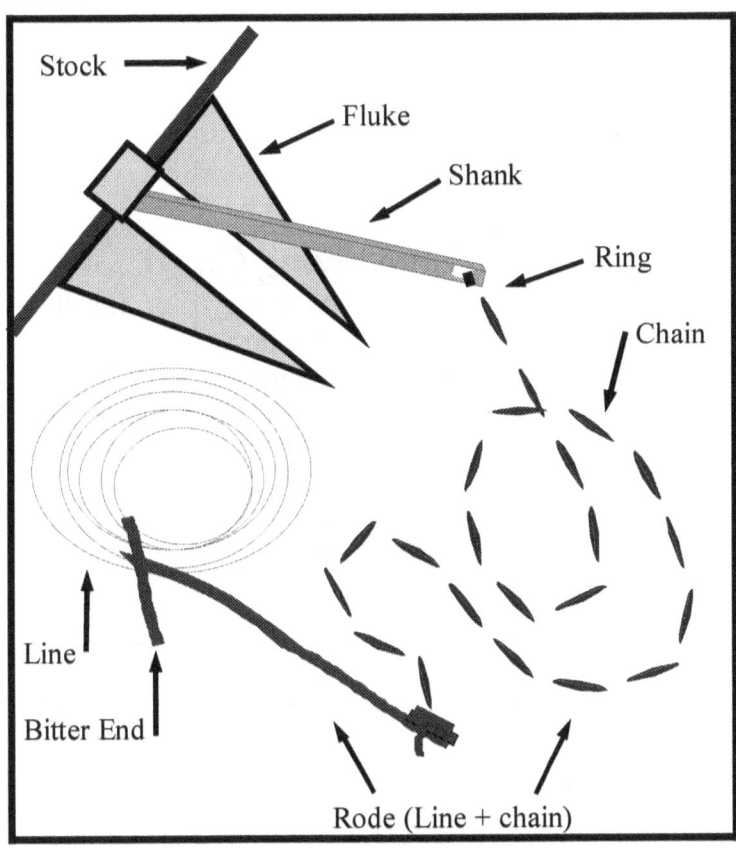

Anchor chain helps to set the anchor into the sea floor, and keeps the anchor from lifting out. The amount of chain between the anchor and line should weigh at least as much as the anchor, or it can be figured as half the boat length. The anchor line should be either three-strand or braided nylon, of a suitable diameter (see sizing chart).

Anchor Line Sizing Chart

Vessel Length (LOA)	Storm Anchor: Line Length/Size	Working Anchor: Line Length/Size	Lunch Hook: Line Length/Size
15'	125' 1/4"	100' 1/4"	80' 1/4"
20'	150' 3/8"	120' 1/4"	90' 1/4"
25'	200' 3/8"	150' 3/8"	100' 1/4"
30'	250' 7/16"	180' 3/8"	125' 1/4"
35'	300' 1/2"	200' 3/8"	150' 1/4"
40'	400' 5/8"	250' 7/16"	175' 3/8"
50'	500' 5/8"	300' 1/2"	200' 3/8"
60'	500' 3/4"	300' 1/2"	200' 3/8"

Anchoring With A Single Anchor:

1. Have ready a suitable anchor. Make sure an appropriate length of chain connects the anchor to the anchor line.
2. Approach the anchoring area traveling upwind or up-current.
3. Lower the anchor from a complete stop. Do not throw the anchor.
4. Reverse engine and back the vessel. Let out line until the proper scope (length of anchor line) has been let out.
5. Secure the anchor line to a cleat on the bow.
6. Back the vessel against the anchor line, setting the anchor into the bottom.
7. Make sure there is enough room for the boat to swing around with the wind, and not interfere with other boats, rocks, or other obstacles.
8. Do not overlap the swinging circles of other boats.
9. Note your exact position by lining up landmarks. This will allow you to tell if the anchor is dragging.
10. Display anchor ball, if necessary.

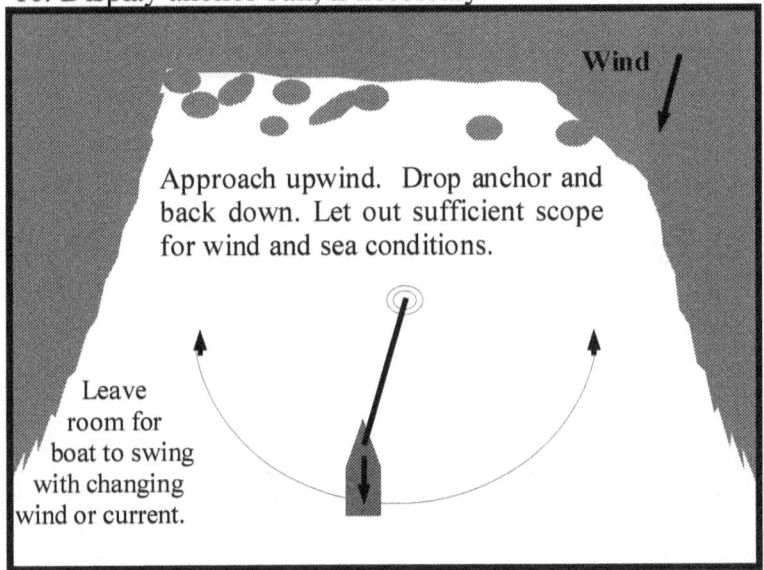

Weighing (Raising) Anchor:
1. Start up the engine before untying the anchor line from the cleat.
2. Under power, move up to a position directly over the anchor.
3. Lift up on the anchor line while the engine idles. If there is current or wind, use engine power to keep a position over the anchor.
4. If the anchor is stuck, fasten the anchor line to the bow cleat. Go ahead in the direction opposite to how the anchor was set. If that does not work, go ahead on a wide circle around the anchor, keeping enough strain on the anchor line to pull it free.
5. Secure all ground tackle before getting underway.

Lunch Hook
It is a good idea to have a smaller, lighter anchor available as your second or third anchor. A light anchor, often called a "lunch hook", will come in handy for short stays in calm weather. It can also be used together with a larger "working anchor" to secure a desired position.

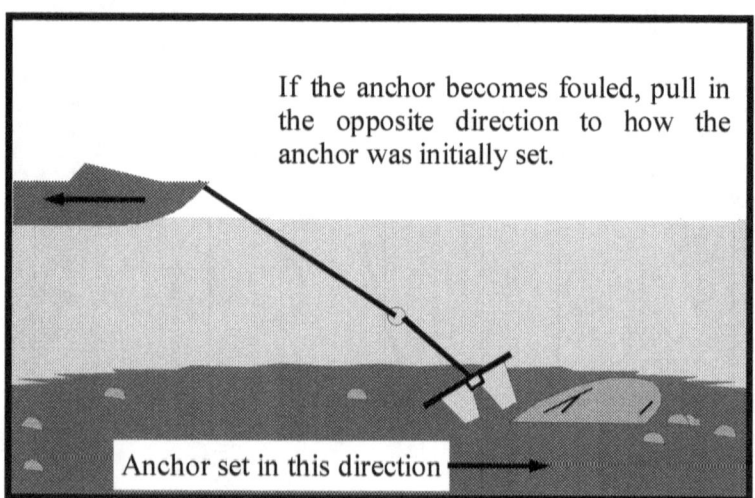

Using the Correct Scope
Scope is the length of anchor line, including chain, used in a given situation. It is often expressed as a ratio, where the length of anchor line is compared to the water depth. A longer scope provides greater holding power for the anchor. As the need for holding power increases, more anchor line can be let out. Also, to maintain proper scope in areas affected by tides, it may be necessary to let out more anchor line as water levels rise.

The chart below shows the scope used for varying anchoring conditions. Water depth is measured from the bow cleat of the vessel to the bottom of the water. A scope of 7:1 means that there should be seven feet of anchor line for every foot of water depth. If the water depth is 6 feet, there should be 42 feet of anchor line.

To keep track of anchor line length, mark the line in 10 foot increments with liquid plastic.

Recommended Scope	
Anchoring Conditions	Scope
Heavy Weather	10:1 to 15:1
Average Conditions	7:1 to 10:1
Calm Water	5:1 to 7:1
All Chain	3:1 to 5:1

Anchoring With Multiple Anchors

Having two or more anchors aboard will greatly increase the skipper's options. A desired anchoring spot may not offer enough room for the vessel to swing around. Differing conditions of weather, tides, and current may call for inventive anchoring strategies. As a minimum, a vessel should carry a strong "working" anchor and a smaller "lunch hook".

In the diagram below, a vessel is anchored in a narrow channel. A change in wind, tide or current could put the boat in an unfavorable position. In this case, set one anchor off the port bow and the other off the starboard bow. A third anchor could be set if necessary.

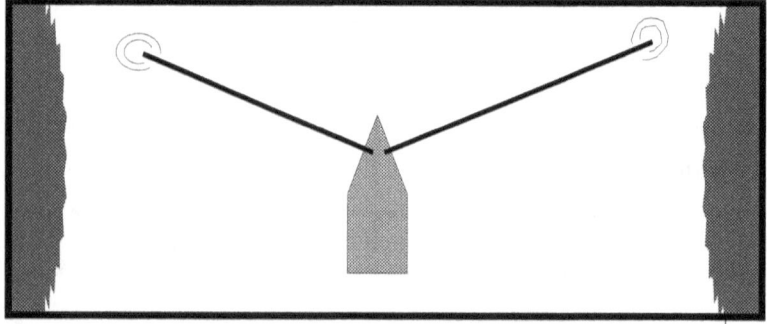

To set two anchors off the bow:
1. Bring the vessel up to the position that the first anchor is to be dropped. Send down the first anchor.
2. While paying out line from the first anchor, maneuver the boat to the position that the second anchor will be dropped. Lower the second anchor.
3. With the engine in reverse, back the vessel up to the desired spot, allowing for proper scope on both anchors.
4. Secure both anchor lines to bow cleats.
5. Visually line up (and take note of) several landmarks. They can be used to determine if the anchors are holding.

Anchoring by the stern and the bow can be useful when pulling up to shore. The object is to hold the vessel in a desired direction, far enough off the beach so that wind, waves and wakes do not cause the boat to hit bottom.

1. Set one anchor off shore, allowing for the proper scope. This can be either a bow or stern anchor.
2. While paying out line, maneuver the vessel close to the beach.
3. Send a crew member onto the beach with the second anchor. Set the anchor firmly in the sand.
4. Bring the boat back toward the offshore anchor, while paying out line from the beached anchor. This can be done under power for larger boats, or by hauling in the anchor line by hand on smaller boats.
5. When the boat is in the desired position, tie off both the bow and stern anchor lines.

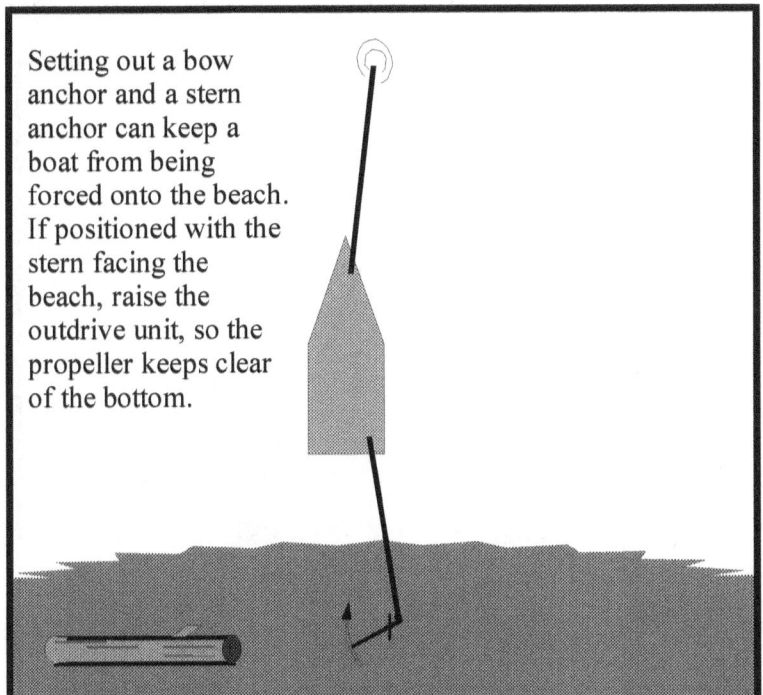

Setting out a bow anchor and a stern anchor can keep a boat from being forced onto the beach. If positioned with the stern facing the beach, raise the outdrive unit, so the propeller keeps clear of the bottom.

Vessels that are relatively small, or that have a shallow draft, may tend to yaw (tack back and forth) while at anchor. This behavior is more pronounced against a breeze or current, and it can be annoying. To prevent yawing at anchor, set out two anchors at an angle of about 45°. The procedure is the same as when setting two anchors off the bow:

1. Bring the vessel up to the position that the first anchor is to be dropped. Send down the first anchor.
2. While paying out line from the first anchor, maneuver the boat to the position that the second anchor will be dropped. Lower the second anchor.
3. With the engine in reverse, back the vessel up to the desired spot, allowing for proper scope on both anchors.
4. Secure both anchor lines to bow cleats.
5. Visually line up (and take note of) several landmarks. They can be used to determine if the anchors are holding.

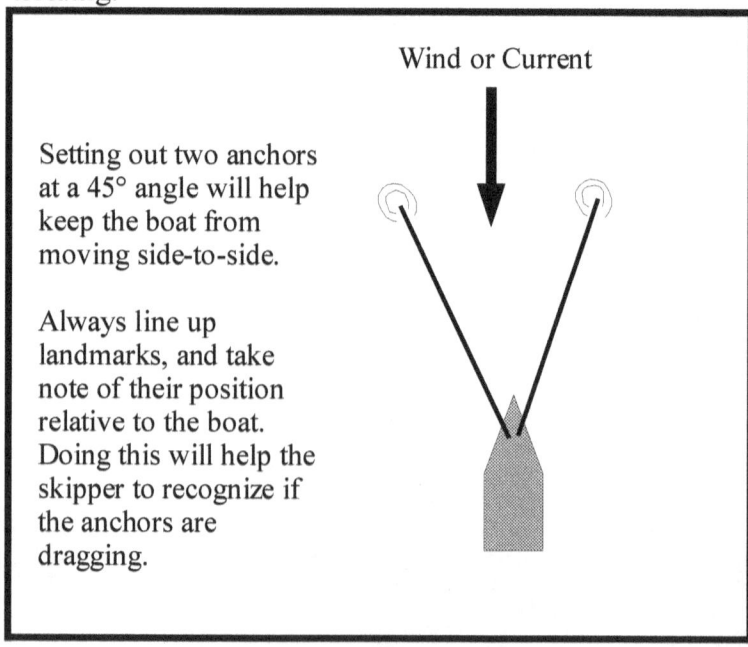

Setting out two anchors at a 45° angle will help keep the boat from moving side-to-side.

Always line up landmarks, and take note of their position relative to the boat. Doing this will help the skipper to recognize if the anchors are dragging.

BOAT LAUNCHING

Pre-Launch Check

A boating trip can easily be ruined by overlooking a few minor tasks. The items on the list that follow should be accomplished in the parking lot or the launch preparation area of the launch ramp. Finishing these tasks **before** backing the boat down the ramp will make launching easier and faster. It will identify the skipper as experienced and courteous.

1. Load all gear, food, clothes, and equipment aboard the boat.
2. Make sure the boat has gas. If not, bring enough money to buy gas while on the water.
3. Reconnect the battery cable, or set the battery selector switch to the starting cell.
4. Install and tighten the drain plug.
5. Raise the marine radio antenna, if lowered.
6. Disconnect and stow all stern trailer tie-down straps. **Do not disconnect the front trailer strap or safety chain at this time.**
7. Disconnect the trailer's taillight/electrical cable from the vehicle. This will prevent the trailer's bulbs from being damaged or shorting out when immersed in cold water.
8. Turn on the engine compartment blower to expel any fuel vapors. Always smell the engine compartment to insure it is free of fumes before starting the engine.
9. Make ready a bow line and a stern line. Assign a crew member the duty of holding the lines, if the boat is to be held at the dock.
10. Have passengers and crew stay near the boat. When a spot opens up on the launch ramp, everyone can be ready for launching.

Launching

Having finished all of the pre-launch procedures, the boat is now ready to launch. It is best not to be in a hurry. When it comes to launching, "smooth is fast".
1. Slowly back the boat down the ramp until the stern of the vessel is in the water. Keep the trailer strap firmly attached to the boat.
2. If the boat is to be backed off the trailer under power, the skipper should board the boat at this time. If the boat is to be "walked" off the trailer, have a crew member hold the bow and stern lines.
3. If the boat is to be backed off the trailer under power, lower the outdrive and start the engine(s).
4. Disconnect the front trailer strap and safety chain.
5. Slowly back the boat further into the water, until it floats free of the trailer.
6. If under power, the boat's engine can now be put in reverse, and backed out. Without power, the boat can be lead off the trailer with the bow and stern lines, and made fast to the floating dock.
7. Immediately after launching, drive the tow vehicle and trailer to a designated parking area. It may be advisable to lock the trailer to the hitch, to prevent trailer theft.
8. Some launching facilities use slings or cables, and have their own launching procedures. Local rules and customs should prevail at all launch facilities.

Inform a friend or relative if you are planning on staying out for an extended time, going offshore, or navigating to another location. Let them know where you are going, who is with you, and when you expect to return. A float plan can be filed with your marina, or given to some other responsible party. Carry a cell phone or marine radio. Let someone know if your plans change.

Skipper's Handbook – Robert Grossman

Trailering:
1. When trailering or storing your boat, it is best to have the battery disconnected and the drain plug removed.
2. Keep a safety chain connected from the trailer to the boat's bow eye-ring. The front trailer strap can break if it becomes worn or sun-damaged. It should be inspected regularly.
3. Secure the stern of the boat to the trailer with strong tie-down straps.
4. It is best to trailer a boat with all canvas tops stowed and secured. This includes the bimini top and mooring cover. Special boat covers are available that are designed to withstand the stress of towing.
5. Make sure the outdrive unit is fully raised, in its towing position.
6. Secure the outdrive unit with a strap or support designed for that purpose. This will alleviate some of the strain caused by bouncing during towing.
7. Keep a spare trailer tire mounted to the frame of the trailer. The spare tire will be useless without a tall jack and proper lug nut wrench. Wheel chocks are also useful.

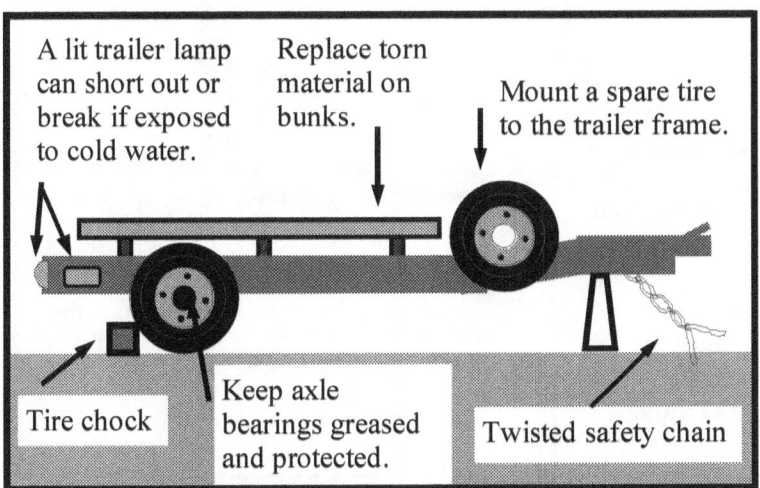

8. Before towing, check for proper tire pressure and check the axle hubs for proper lubrication (grease).
9. Insure proper, secure connection of the taillight/electrical cable.
10. Connect a safety chain from the trailer to the vehicle tow hitch. Local laws may require twisting the chain.
11. An improperly weighted trailer may fishtail. Weight distribution of a trailer is affected by how the boat sits on the trailer, whether the trailer is designed to carry that particular boat, the distribution of weight in the boat, and other factors.
12. Make wide turns. The trailer will cut corners.

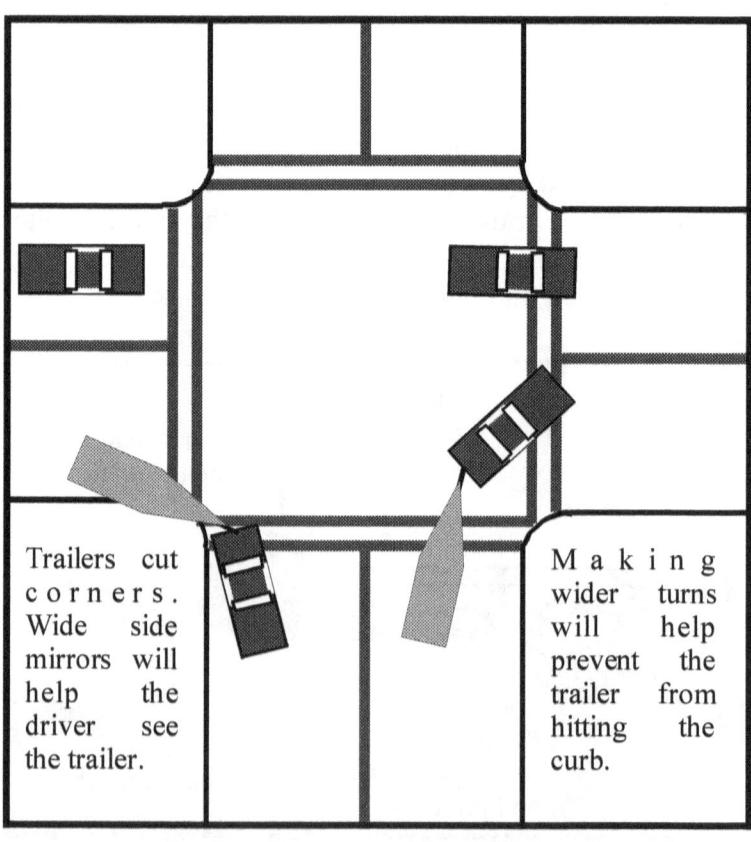

Trailers cut corners. Wide side mirrors will help the driver see the trailer.

Making wider turns will help prevent the trailer from hitting the curb.

13. Hard stops may cause the trailer to jackknife.

14. When backing, the rear of the trailer goes in the opposite direction than the rear of the vehicle. Turning the steering wheel to the right (clockwise) causes the trailer to move left. Turning the steering wheel to the left (counterclockwise) causes the trailer to move right.

15. When backing, overcorrecting turns are a major cause of problems. Small movements in the steering wheel are all that is usually needed.

16. Most vehicle manufacturers recommend towing without using the overdrive gear. Consult your vehicle owner's manual.

17. Specific towing regulations vary by state. Contact your local department of motor vehicles for more information.

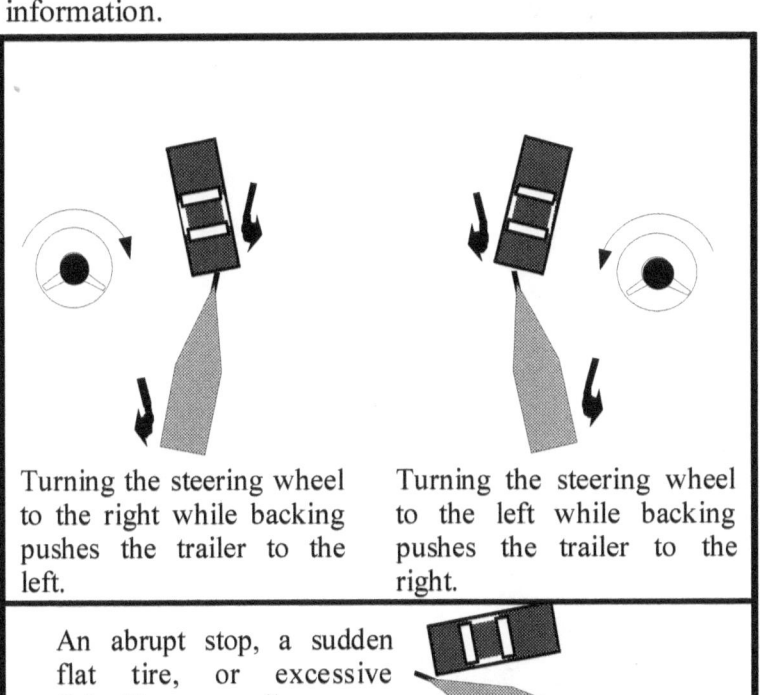

Turning the steering wheel to the right while backing pushes the trailer to the left.

Turning the steering wheel to the left while backing pushes the trailer to the right.

An abrupt stop, a sudden flat tire, or excessive fishtailing can all cause a trailer to jackknife.

Skipper's Handbook – Robert Grossman

SECTION 5
SEAMANSHIP

FIRE FIGHTING

Fires are classified as A (wood, paper, etc.), B (flammable liquids, gasoline), or C (electrical). Fire extinguishers on boats need to be Type B. Many commonly available fire extinguishers today will be effective on all three fire classifications.

Extinguishers can be dry chemical, carbon dioxide, Halon (vapor system), or foam. The dry chemical extinguisher is probably the most widely used because of its low cost and ease of use. A dry chemical extinguisher is pressurized. A pressure gauge on the unit will show if there is adequate pressure in the tank. Check the pressure regularly. If it is low, have the unit repressurized or have it replaced.

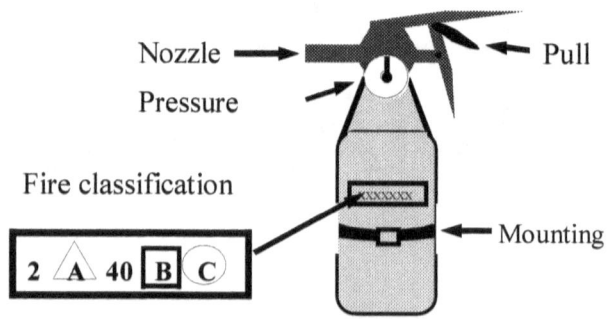

B-CLASS FIRE EXTINGUISHERS:				
Class:	Foam (gal.)	Dry CO_2 (lbs)	Chemical (lbs)	Halon (lbs)
B-I	1.25	4	2	2.5
B-II	2.5	15	10	10

Fighting Fires
Even a small fire aboard a boat should be considered an emergency. These actions should be taken immediately:
1. If the burning object is easily moved, throw it overboard.
2. If the burning area is below decks, close all hatches to limit oxygen availability.
3. If the fire is in the engine compartment, activate the fire extinguishing (Halon)system, if so equipped.
4. Grab a fire extinguisher. Pull the ring.
5. Aim the extinguisher toward the base of the flames. Squeeze the handgrips. A small fire extinguisher may discharge its contents in only 8 to 20 seconds.
6. Account for the crew and passengers.
7. If the vessel is damaged from the fire, or if the fire is not out, have everyone put on flotation devices.
8. If the fire is not out and the vessel is still under power, maneuver the boat so that the fire is downwind. This will help prevent the fire from spreading to the rest of the boat.
9. If the above actions have not put out the fire, and the vessel is in danger, get on the marine radio. Call "Mayday, Mayday, Mayday", and give your position.

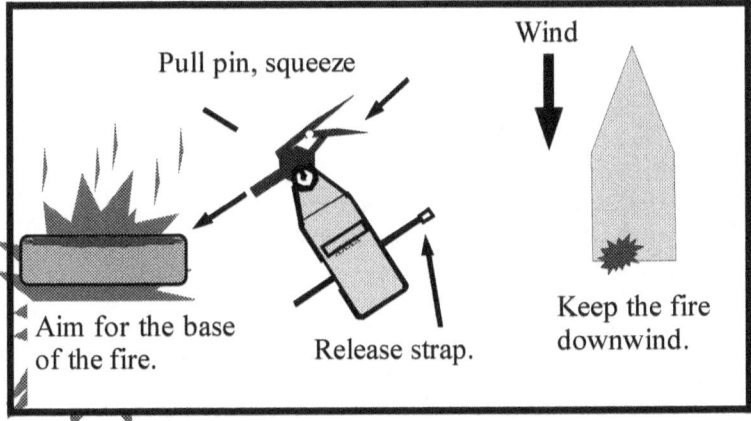

MARINE VHF RADIO CHANNELS
Portion of FCC Rules: 47 CFR 80.371 "c" and 80.373"f"

Type of Message	Appropriate Channel(s)
DISTRESS, SAFETY AND CALLING: To hail or get the attention of another vessel, and to use in emergencies.	16
INTERSHIP SAFETY: Use for ship-to-ship safety messages or for search and rescue messages. Also used by Coast Guard ships and aircraft.	6
COAST GUARD LIAISON: Use to talk to the Coast Guard (after first making contact on Channel 16).	22
NONCOMMERCIAL CHANNELS: For recreational boats. Messages must be about the needs of the vessel: fishing reports, rendezvous, scheduling repairs, docking and berthing information, etc.	$9^{(6)}$, $67^{(8)}$, 68, 69, 71, $72^{(8)}$, 78, $79^{(4)}$, 80^4

Footnotes
1. Not in Great Lakes, St. Lawrence, Puget Sound areas.
2. Only in Great Lakes, St. Lawrence, Puget Sound areas.
3. Only in New Orleans and Houston areas.
4. Only in Great Lakes.
5. Only in New Orleans area.
6. Only for intership, ship-ship, and ship-coast, noncommercial.
7. Only in Puget Sound and Strait of Juan de Fuca areas.
8. Ship-to-ship messages only.

Type of Message	Appropriate Channel(s)
COMMERCIAL WORKING CHANNELS: For working ships only. Must be about business or the needs of the ship.	$1^{(5)}$, 7, $8^{(8)}$, 9, 10, 11, 18, 19, $63^{(5)}$, $67^{(8)}$, $72^{(7,8)}$, 79, 80, $88^{(1,8)}$
PUBLIC TELEPHONE, MARINE OPERATOR: Use these channels to call a marine operator and make or receive telephone calls. There is usually a charge for this service (except for distress calls).	24, 25, 26, 27, 28, 84, 85, 86, 87, $88^{(2,8)}$
PORT OPERATIONS: Used in directing the movement of ships in or near ports, locks or waterways. Messages must be about the movement and safety of ships. Channels 11 and 12 may not be available for this use in some ports. Channel 20 is used only for ship-to-shore. Channel 77 is restricted to intership communication between pilots.	$1^{(5)}$, $5^{(3)}$, 12, 14, 20, $63^{(5)}$, 65, 66, 73, 74, $77^{(8)}$

1. Not in Great Lakes, St. Lawrence, Puget Sound areas.
2. Only in Great Lakes, St. Lawrence, Puget Sound areas.
3. Only in New Orleans and Houston areas.
4. Only in Great Lakes.
5. Only in New Orleans area.
6. Only for intership, ship-ship, and ship-coast, noncommercial.
7. Only in Puget Sound and Strait of Juan de Fuca areas.
8. Ship-to-ship messages only.

Type of Message	Appropriate Channel(s)
NAVIGATIONAL OR BRIDGE-TO-BRIDGE: Available to all vessels. Must be about navigation; passing or meeting other vessels. Messages must be short. Limited to 1-watt transmission. This is also the main working channel at most locks and drawbridges.	13, 67
MARITIME CONTROL: Used to talk to vessels and coast stations operated by state or local governments. Must pertain to regulations, controls, boating activities, or assistance to vessels.	17
DIGITAL SELECTIVE CALLING: For distress and safety calling, and for general-purpose calling, using digital selective calling techniques.	70
WEATHER: Receive weather broadcasts of NOAA. Receiving only.	WX-1, WX-2, WX-3

VHF Characteristics

The Very High Frequency (VHF) range of the radio spectrum goes from 30 to 300 MHz. Marine radios use only a small portion of the range, from 156 to 163 MHz. Signals on these frequencies are "line of sight", limited by the horizon or by mountains. The effective maximum transmission distance is about 20 miles, although it can be much further under certain atmospheric conditions. Distance is primarily a function of antenna height. Radio power will only slightly affect the transmission distance.

Emergency Radio Procedure

Use "Mayday" only if your vessel is in grave and imminent danger, and immediate assistance is required.
1. Call on channel 16: "Mayday, Mayday, Mayday."
2. Identify: "This is (vessel name)", repeat 3 times.
3. Location: give coordinates or bearings.
4. Problem: sinking, on fire, wounded personnel, etc.
5. Time: state how much time left until the boat sinks.
6. People: state how many people are aboard.
7. Description: vessel size, color, power or sail.
8. Monitor: stay on channel 16, unless told otherwise.

Non-emergencies

The signal "Pan-Pan", spoken three times, is used when assistance is needed, but not in a dire emergency. If the signal "Security" is heard, information will be broadcast involving vessel safety.

Personal and social conversations are not allowed on VHF marine radio frequencies. Messages should be kept short, and should only involve vessel safety, information, navigation, passing arrangements, docking, and other vessel-related activities.

Many radios allow selection to a lower power. The lowest power possible should be used on all transmissions, while still permitting clear reception. Use of obscene language is illegal, and violators can be taken to court. Radio traffic is often monitored.

A license is not required to operate a marine radio on recreational vessels, or on vessels with six or less paid passengers. Complete information and FCC forms can be accessed via the Internet by going to "fcc.gov."

Radio Calls
When calling someone on the marine radio:
1. Tune to the appropriate channel, and wait until the channel is not in use. Channel 16 can be used as a hailing frequency.
2. Broadcast the name of the vessel or party you are trying to reach, followed by "this is," followed by your vessel name. Example: "Coast Guard this is Papa's Pride."
3. The initial announcement can be made up to three times.
4. If the party responds on channel 16, agree to move to another channel to complete the communication.
5. Keep the conversation brief, and limit it to vessel-related activities. Personal and social conversations are not allowed on marine radio frequencies.
6. If the intended party did not respond to the hail, try again later. Do not "sign off" by announcing "negative contact."

Antenna Radiation Pattern
Radio antennas come in different lengths, typically 4', 8' and 16'. An 8' antenna is sufficient for most recreational boats. The antenna "gain," measured in decibels, determines the pattern of transmission. Higher gain antennas concentrate their energy in a flatter arc, increasing their range. If the gain is too high, the reception and transmission may fade in and out as the boat rocks on the waves. The coaxial cable should be kept short, to avoid excess power loss to and from the antenna.

WEATHER

Reading Weather Maps

Weather maps are available through many different sources, including the daily newspaper, and at dozens of locations on the Internet. Reading these maps is a valuable tool in deciding when and where to navigate.

Using a map of actual conditions and recent time, it is possible to forecast weather conditions for the following 6 to 12 hours. Weather maps are good for determining conditions over a wide area. Localized conditions can be very different than what is indicated on a map. Tune your marine radio to the WX stations for local conditions and weather advisories.

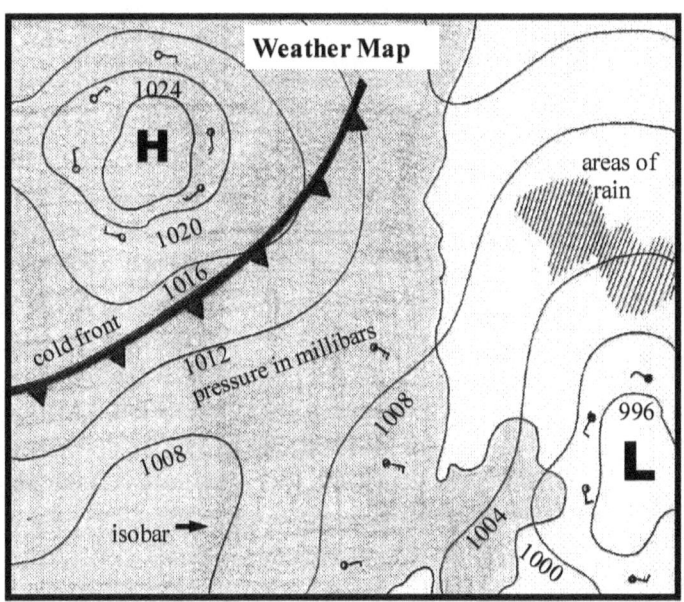

Weather Map Symbols

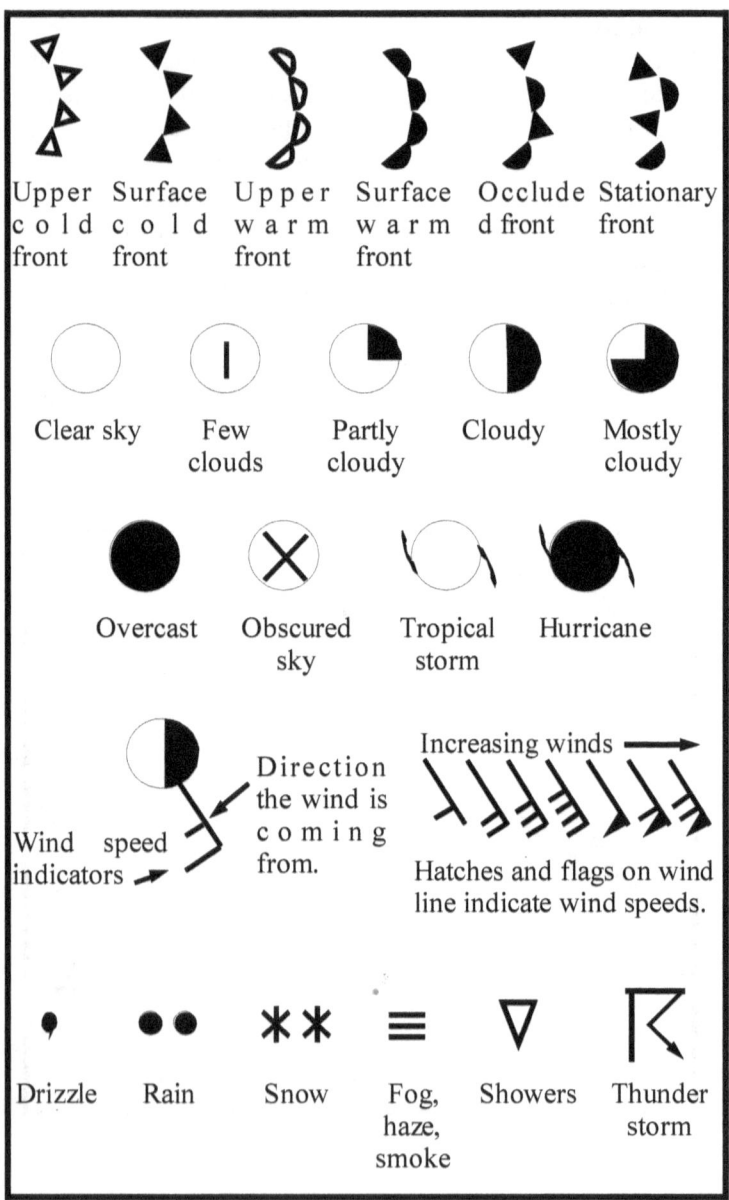

General Weather Information
- HIGH pressure area winds rotate clockwise.
- LOW pressure area winds rotate counter-clockwise.
- Winds move from HIGH pressure to LOW pressure.
- HIGH pressure generally brings fair weather.
- LOW pressure generally brings foul weather.
- In the Northern hemisphere, if you face the wind, the LOW pressure area will generally be behind you and toward the right.
- Wind direction is where the wind is coming from.
- Weather patterns in North America generally move from West to East.
- Winds will be stronger where isobar lines appear closer together on a weather map.
- Relative humidity is the percentage of moisture in the air compared to what the air can hold.
- Cold air holds less water than warm air.
- Expect higher winds underneath thunderheads.
- WX stations on your marine radio give 24 hour weather updates. Forecasts are provided for localized areas.

Protection From Lightning

During a lightning storm, passengers and crew should stay inside the cabin of the vessel. Stay out of the water. No one should contact items on the boat that connect to different parts of the grounding system.

The vessel itself should have all metal parts and electrical components protected from lightning by a grounding conductor. A metal VHS antenna can serve as a lightning rod. A lightning rod will protect a vessel underneath an imaginary 60° cone, the apex being at the top of the rod. A fiberglass antenna will not provide protection.

Weather Terms

Advection Fog - Caused by warm, moist air moving over a colder surface. This type of fog can form over the sea any time of the year.

Barometric Pressure - A measure of atmospheric pressure. The direction of the change in pressure, along with the rate of the change, are important indicators of changing weather.

Cold Front - Brings cooler air. May or may not cause precipitation. As a cold front approaches, wind will shift to the south, and the pressure will fall.

Isobars - Lines on a weather map that connect points of equal barometric pressure. Labeled in millibars or inches.

Occluded Front - Occurs when a cold front overtakes a warm front. Either the warm or cold front may rise. Look for winds moving counterclockwise.

Precipitation Fog - Occurs when warm rain falls through cold air at ground level.

Radiation Fog -   Occurs on calm, clear nights, when cool moist air at ground level loses temperature. The air is cooled below the dewpoint, forming ground fog.

Relative Humidity - The percentage of moisture in the air, as compared to the maximum amount of moisture that the air could hold at that temperature. Warmer air holds more moisture.

Stationary Front - When the movement of a weather front slows to a stop, it is called a stationary front. Expect weather similar to a warm front.

Steam Fog - Caused by cold air moving over much warmer water. It has the appearance of steaming water.

Warm Front - Brings warmer air. Weather changes not as extreme as a cold front. As a warm front approaches, pressure will drop, clouds will build, and rain may set in.

Cloud Chart

Warm air rises, as it is less dense than cold air. Warm air holds more moisture than cold air. As the warm air rises, it cools, causing the moisture to condense into clouds.

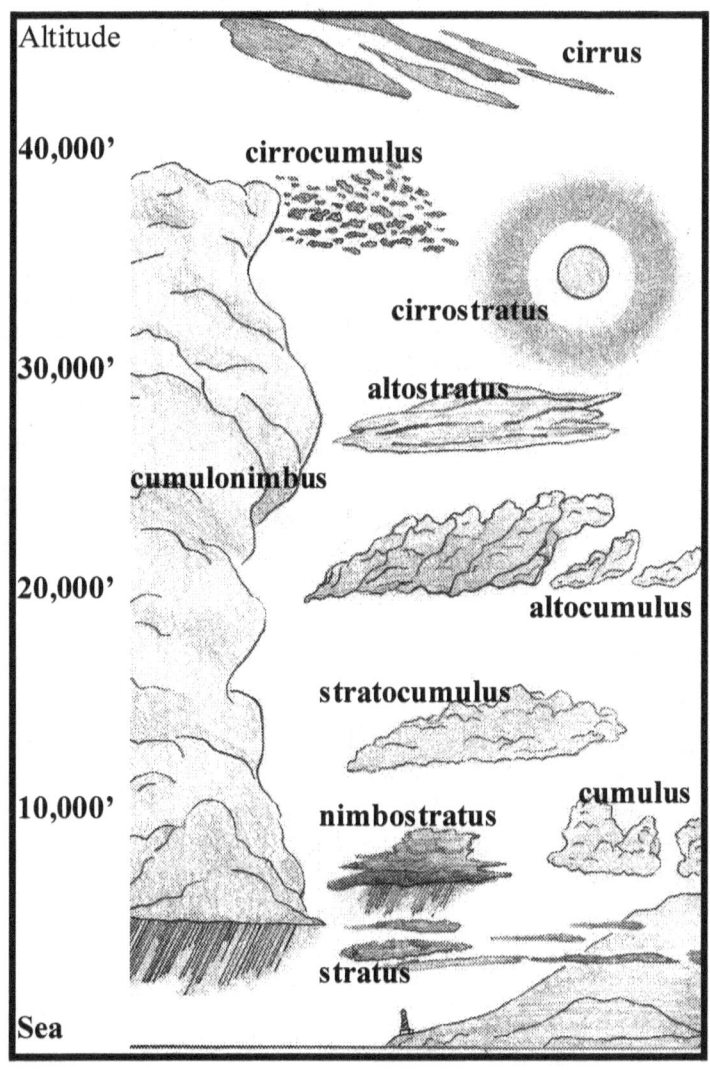

Beaufort Wind Scale			
Force	Wind Speed knots mph	WMO* Label	Effects at sea
0	Under 1	Calm	Like glass
1	1-3 1-3	Light Air	Ripples
2	4-6 4-7	Lt. Breeze	Wavelets
3	7-10 8-12	Gentle Brz	Large Wavelets
4	11-16 13-18	Mod. Brz	1'-4' waves, whitecaps
5	17-21 19-24	Fresh Brz	4'-8' waves, whitecaps
6	22-27 25-31	Strong Brz	8'-13' waves, whitecaps, spray
7	28-33 32-38	Near Gale	13'-20' waves, some foam
8	34-40 39-46	Gale	13'-20' waves, blowing foam
9	41-47 47-54	Strong Gale	20' waves, dense spray and foam
10	48-55 55-63	Storm	20'-30' waves, dense foam
11	56-63 64-72	Violent Storm	30'-46' waves, dense foam
12	64+ 73+	Hurricane	Waves over 46', driving foam, spray

* World Meteorological Organization

Knots for Boating and Fishing

Bowline - Use this knot to fix a line to an object or to form a loop at the end of a line. A bowline will not slip, jam, or come loose. It is easy to untie. It is probably the most important knot to the boater.

To tie:
1. Make a small loop near the end.
2. Pass the end through the small loop, forming a larger loop.
3. Pass the end behind the line and around to the front.
4. Pass the end back through the small loop.
5. Tighten the knot, leaving the larger loop.

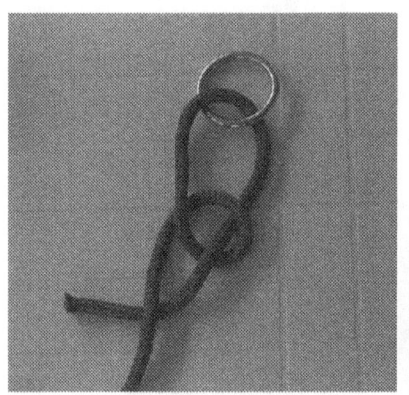

Starting a Bowline

Bowline
Finished Knot

Two Half Hitches - This is a quick and basic knot that is good for temporary use or to strengthen other knots.

To tie:
1. Loop the line around an object.
2. Pass the end behind the part of the loop that faces you. This is a "half hitch".
3. Once more, pass the end behind the part of the loop that faces you, but below the first half hitch.
4. Repeat as needed to add the number of half hitches desired.

Two Half Hitches
Tied Loose

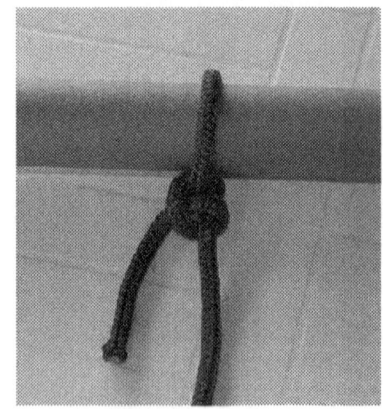

Two Half Hitches
Finished Knot

Anchor Hitch - This is a secure knot that is used to attach lines to another object. Use on an anchor or object on shore. Add an extra half hitch for insurance.

To Tie:
1. Loop the line line twice around object.
2. Pass the end behind both loops.
3. Make two or more Half-Hitches.

Starting an
Anchor Hitch

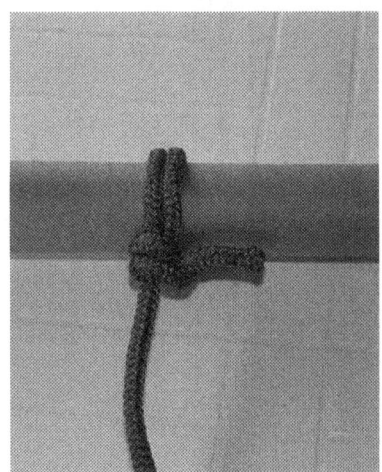

Anchor Hitch
Finished Knot

Rolling Hitch - This is a good knot for securing mooring lines to objects on shore, for attaching a smaller line to a larger one, and for general boating uses.

To tie:
1. Loop the line over the object.
2. Take two turns clockwise around the line, and tighten.
3. Bring the end below the first two loops and make a half hitch around the line.
4. Tighten the knot.

Starting a
Rolling Hitch

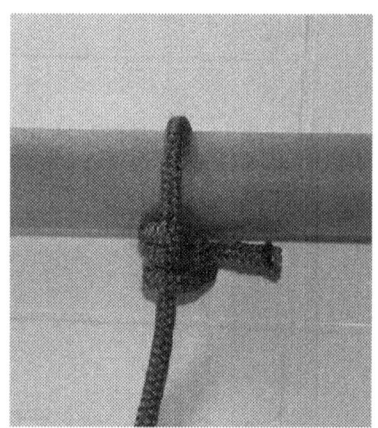

Rolling Hitch
Finished Knot

Clove Hitch - This knot works only for a line under strain, like mooring a boat against a current. It is simple and fast to tie, and can easily be untied when the strain is removed. Do not use this knot for long-term applications.

To tie:
1. Loop the line twice around a fixed object, such as a post, piling, or railing.
2. Form an "X" out of the two loops, with the "X" facing you.
3. Pass the end of the line up underneath the "X".

Starting a Clove Hitch

Clove Hitch Finished Knot

Belaying to a Cleat - This is the proper way to fix a mooring line to a cleat. The cleat can be on shore or on the vessel.

To tie:
1. Make a turn around the base of the cleat, starting with the end of the cleat that is farthest away from the boat.
2. Make several figure-8 turns around cleat.
3. Finish the knot with a half hitch.

Belaying to a cleat can also be done with all Half-Hitches. Twist each loop of the figure-8 before they are slipped over the ends of the cleat.

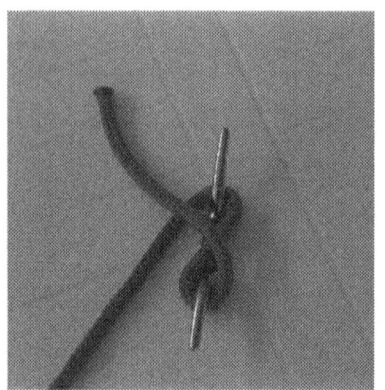

Starting a
Belay to a Cleat

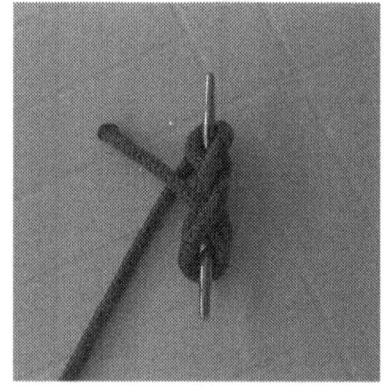

Belaying to a Cleat
Finished Knot

Sheet Bend - This knot is used for joining lines of different diameter and composition. The holding power of this knot increases with the strain, yet remains easy to untie. A sheet bend can be doubled or tripled (doubled in the photos below).

To tie:
1. Bend the end of the larger line back on itself.
2. Bring the lighter line through the loop formed in the heavier line.
3. Coil the lighter line around the doubled end of the heavier line one, two, or three times.
4. Pass the lighter line between the loop of the heavier line and the lighter line.
5. Tighten and apply strain.

Double Sheet Bend
Tied Loosely

Double Sheet Bend
Finished Knot

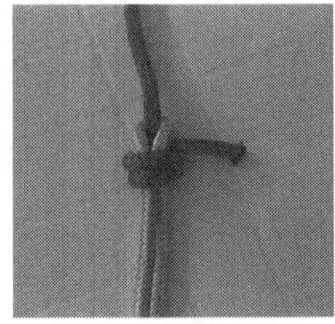

Square Knot - This is a good knot to know for temporarily joining lines of similar diameter. It should not be subjected to great strain. This knot is also called a Reef Knot.

To tie:
1. Make an overhand knot, by crossing one line around the other.
2. Bring the the ends of both lines around to face each other.
3. Make another overhand knot with the ends, so that the end of each line faces the direction it started from.
4. Tighten to finish.

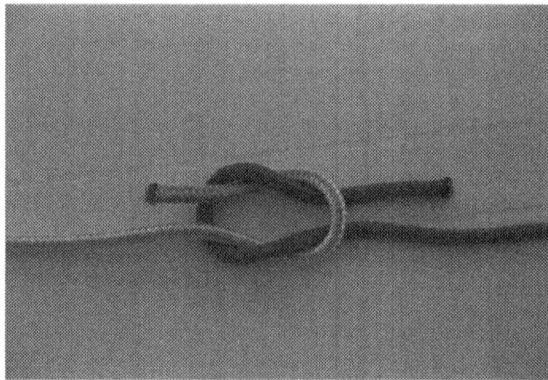

Square Knot Tied Loosely

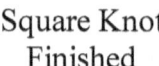

Square Knot Finished

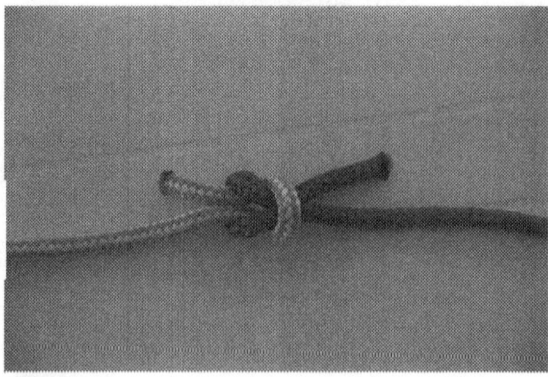

Carrick Bend - This knot is useful for joining together lines of roughly equal diameter. Although the knot will not slip, it may be difficult to untie.

To tie:
1. Form a loop with the first line.
2. With the second line, weave through the loop of the first line in an under-over pattern, as shown.
3. Pull both lines at the same time to tighten.

Starting a
Carrick Bend

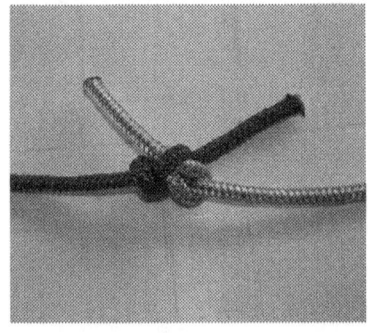

Carrick Bend
Finished Knot

Strait Bend - Use this knot to join together two different lines. This knot has good strength, and is easy to untie.

To tie:
1. Start with a clockwise loop in one line.
2. Pass the end of the other line through the loop.
3. Form a counterclockwise loop with the second line.
4. With the two loops held together, pass the ends of both lines through the loops. The line ends should point away from you.
5. Tighten the knot to finish.

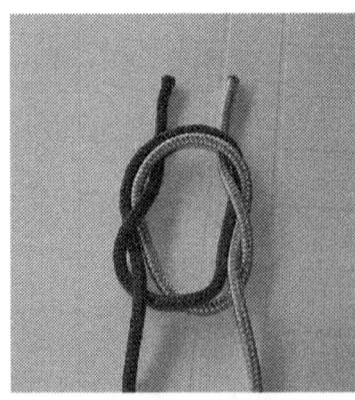

Starting a Strait Bend

Strait Bend Finished Knot

Water Knot - This is a good knot to use when joining together two thin-diameter lines, such as fishing line. It is not recommended for joining boating-diameter lines.

To tie:
1. Form a loose overhand knot with the first line, and pass the end of the second line through it.
2. Form a loose overhand knot with the second line, and pass the end of the first line through it.
3. Tighten both overhand knots, then pull the two lines together.

Starting a Water Knot

Water Knot
Finished Knot

Barrel Knot - This is a fishing knot, used for joining together fishing lines and other fine lines.

To tie:
1. Lay two lines together, with the ends overlapping in opposite directions.
2. Make several turns around the second line with the end of the first line.
3. Pass the end of the first line between the two lines, at the point where the two lines initially crossed.
4. Make several turns around the first line with the end of the second line.
5. Pass the end of the second line between the two lines, at the point where the two lines initially crossed. This is the same point that the end of the first line was passed in step 3. The end of the second line should be passed through this point in the direction opposite to the first line.
6. Pull the lines away from each other to tighten.
7. Trim any excess length from the ends.

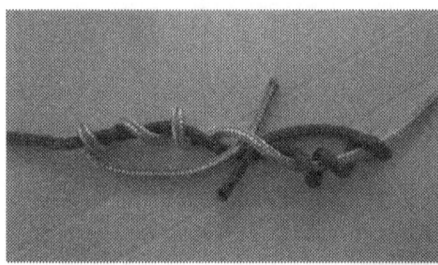

Starting a Barrel Knot

Barrel Knot Finished

Clinch Knot - Use this knot to join fishing line to hooks, flies, or swivels.

To tie:
1. Pass the end of the fishing line through the eye of the hook.
2. Wind the end back up around the line. Take six or seven turns.
3. Pass the end through the loop in the line formed just above the eye of the hook. This will form another, larger loop.
4. Pass the end back through the larger loop.
5. Tighten by pulling both ends of the line, and snugging the loops against the eye of the hook.

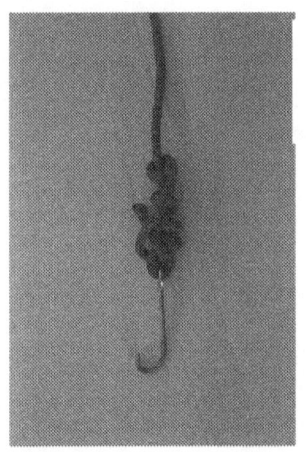

Clinch Knot
Tied Loosely

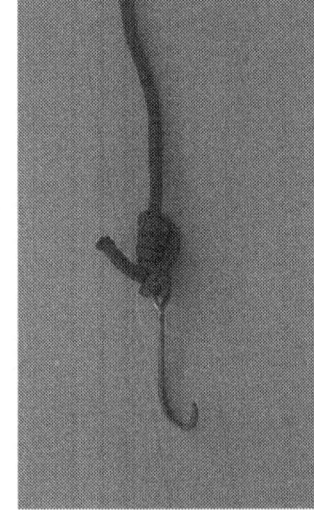

Clinch Knot
Finished

Skipper's Handbook – Robert Grossman

Figure Eight Knot - This knot can be used as a useful loop knot for tying a hook to a fishing line. It can also be used with larger diameter boating lines as a stopper or end-of-the-line knot, so that lines will not slip through your hands. This knot can jam.

To tie:
1. Bend the end of the line back on itself. If used to secure a fishing hook, pass the end of the line through the eye of the hook, before making the bend.
2. Give the loop one twist.
3. Pass the end through the loop.
4. Tighten to finish.
5. Trim the end of fishing line.

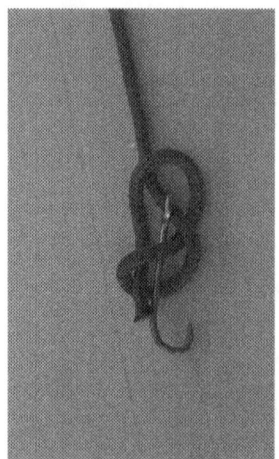

Figure Eight Knot
Tied Loosely

Figure Eight Knot
Finished

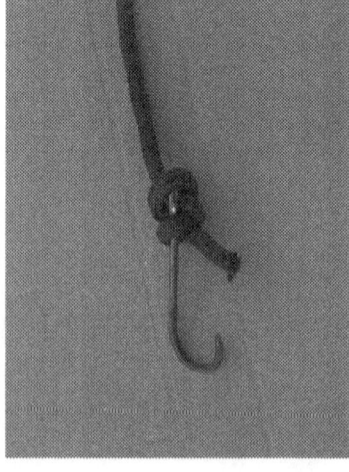

Palomar Knot - Use this knot to join fishing line to a hook. The knot is simple to tie, yet strong and elegant.

To tie:
1. Form a loop near the end of the fishing line.
2. Pass the loop through eye of the hook.
3. Form an overhand knot. Keep the hook in the loop of the overhand knot.
4. Pass the original loop up over the hook.
5. Tighten to finish.

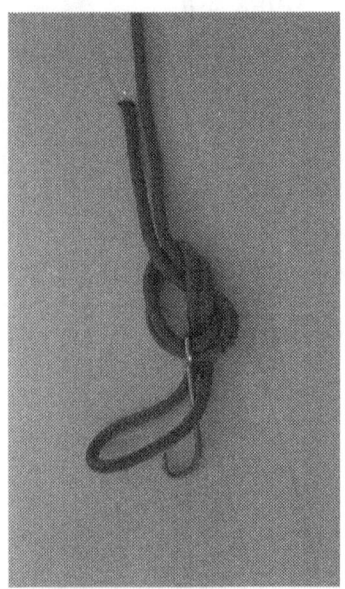

Starting a Palomar Knot

Palomar Knot Finished

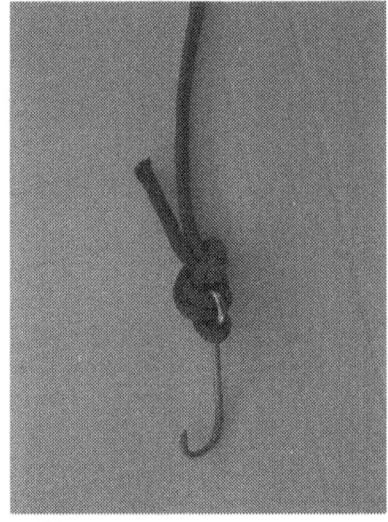

Quick Turn - Although this is not really a knot, it is a useful technique for the short-term stowage of often-used lines and extension cords. It will hold together well when hung up, and keeps lines stored neatly.

To tie:
1. Coil up the line.
2. Take the last 3-4 feet of the line and fold it back on itself, forming a "bight".
3. Pass the bight clockwise around the coil of line.
4. Pass the bight through the head of the coil.
5. Tighten and hang the coil of line by the bight, or stow the line laying flat.

Starting a Quick Turn

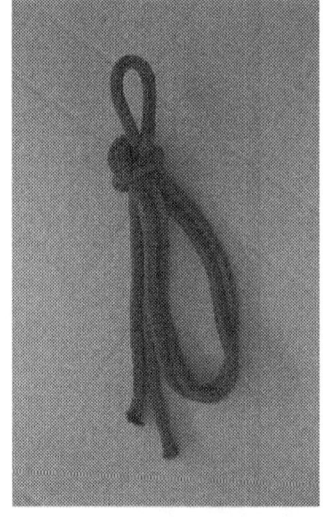

Quick Turn Finished Knot

USEFUL FORMULAS

Several formulas are important and useful to boaters. Five such formulas are described here.

Distance to Horizon: Use one of the following formulas to determine the distance to the horizon, given the height of the observer's eye above the water:

$$D = 1.17 \sqrt{h}$$

where D = distance in nautical miles, and h = height of observer in feet, or;

$$D = 1.145 \sqrt{h}$$

where D = distance in statute miles, and h = height of observer in feet, or;

$$D = 2.12 \sqrt{h}$$

where D = distance in nautical miles, and h = height of observer in meters.

Example: What is the distance (n mi) to the horizon if the observer's eyes are 10' above the water?

$$D = 1.17 \sqrt{10'} = 3.7 \text{ nautical miles}$$

In all formulas, the ** mark equals the square root of.

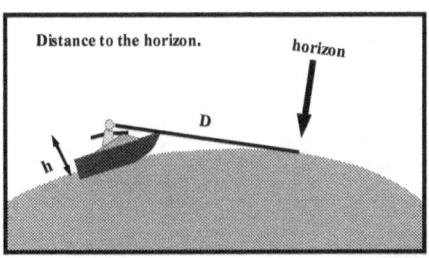
Distance to the horizon.

Distance to a Fixed Object of Known Height: The same formulas used to find the distance to the horizon can be used to determine the distance to a fixed object that lies beyond the horizon, when the height of the object is known. Heights of certain beacons, lighthouses, buoys, and other landmarks may be found in Coast Pilot, Light List, charts, and topo maps.

1) Find your distance to the horizon, using the one of the given formulas, to get D_1.
2) Find the distance from the object (lighthouse) to the horizon, using the same formula as in step 1. The height of this object will be known or given by a reference. This distance is D_2.
3) Add $D_1 + D_2$ to get the total distance to the object.

Example: What is the distance (n mi) to a 50' tall lighthouse, whose light can be seen on the horizon? Observer's height is 10'.
D_1 = 1.17 ** 10' = 3.7 n mi. D_2 = 1.17 ** 50' = 8.3 n mi. **Total Distance = 3.7 n mi + 8.3 n mi = 12 n mi.**

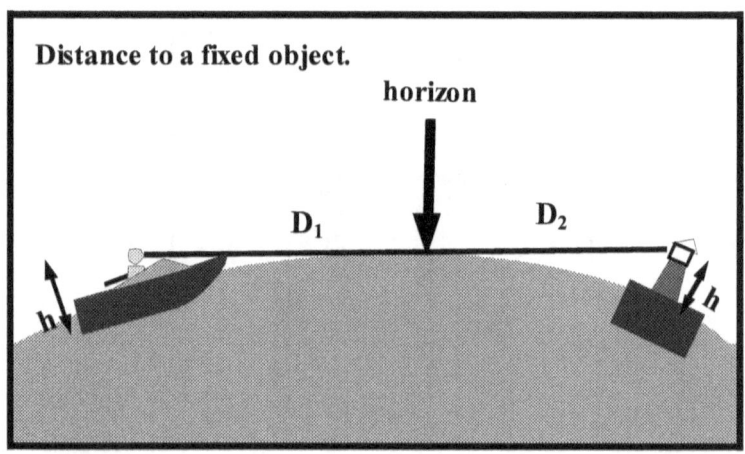

Distance to a fixed object.

Rule of 60: This formula is useful for quickly determining the number of degrees to change course, as necessary to avoid hitting an object. You must know the vessel's distance to the object, and choose how far off you wish to keep the object.

$$\alpha = (60/D) \cdot d$$

where: α = angle in degrees to change course
 D = distance in miles from you to the object
 d = distance in miles that you wish to keep away from the object

Example: A reef lies ahead 5 miles. You wish to keep it off your starboard bow by 1/2 mile. How many degrees to port should you steer?

$$\alpha = (60/5 \text{ mi}) \cdot 0.5 \text{ mi} = 6 \text{ degrees to port.}$$

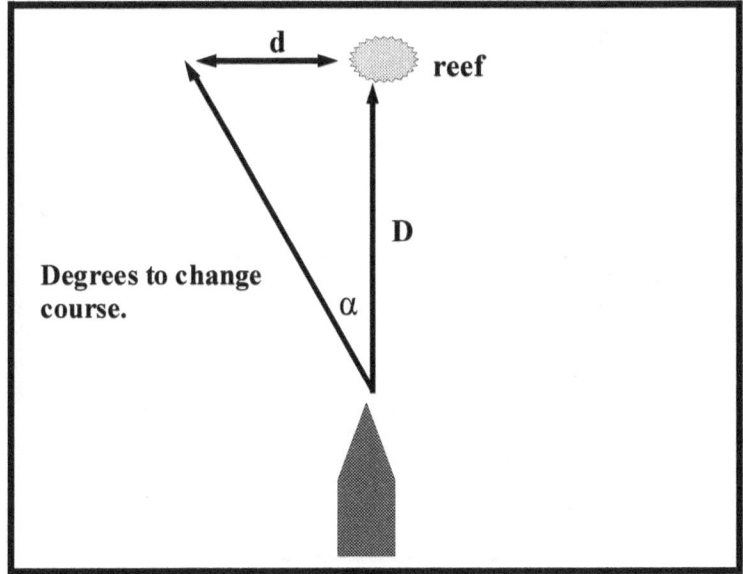

Electrical Power Calculations: Use these equations to determine your electrical requirements, power consumption, and to prevent overloading of fuses.

1) **watts = volts x amps**
2) **amps = watts divided by volts**
3) **volts = watts divided by amps**

Most boats operate on a 12 volt system. The amps or watts will be marked on each electrical appliance. Add the amps of each component that are connected to the same fuse to see if the fuse is overloaded. In the example below, a 12 amp fuse would be adequate for the listed appliances on the same circuit. A 5 or 10 amp fuse would not be adequate. To figure your battery requirements: take amps of an appliance and multiply by the hours it is used on an average day of boating, to give amp hours. Add up the total amp hours for all appliances normally used for one day. A deep-cycle battery (or bank of batteries) should offer 4 times the total amp hours.

Example: Draw a chart listing the appliances connected to one circuit. Add up the amps to find what size fuse to use in the circuit.

Appliance	Volts	Amps	Watts
Instruments	12	1.0	12
VHF Radio	12	6.0	72
Horn	12	3.5	42
Total	12	10.5	126

Mechanical Advantage - Lifting Force of Block and Tackle: Use this formula to determine how much force it will take to lift an object of a given weight off the deck. It can also be used to determine what kind of tackle to use.

$$F = \frac{(.05 \cdot W \cdot i) + W}{A_m}$$

where: F = force in lbs needed to lift an object
A_m = sum of all ascending and descending lines in the moving block
i = sum of openings in all blocks
W = weight of the object being lifted

Example: How many pounds are needed to lift a 400 lb object onto the deck of your boat, if there are 5 lines in the moving block and 4 total openings in both blocks?

$$F = \frac{(.05 \cdot 400 \text{ lb} \cdot 4) + 400}{5} = 96 \text{ pounds.}$$

Mechanical Advantage

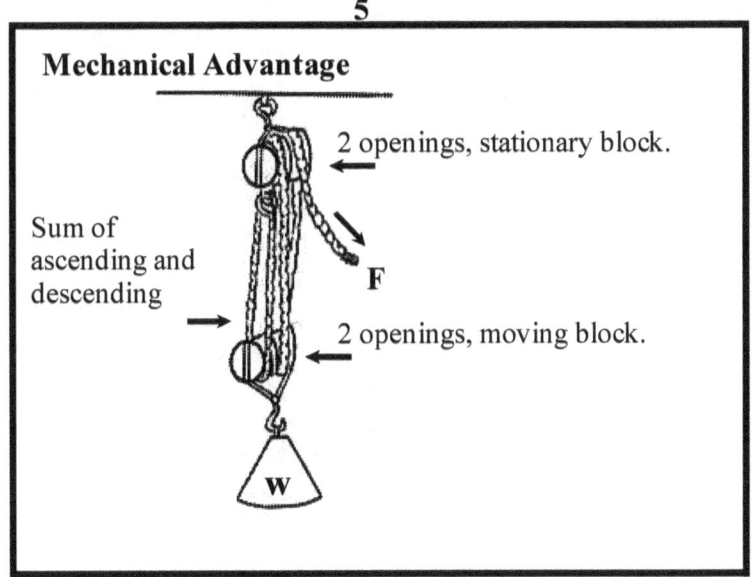

TYPES OF PERSONAL FLOTATION DEVICES

TYPE I Offshore
Buoyancy: 20 pounds or more. Designed to keep an unconscious person face up in the water. Good for open ocean use. Can be bulky and uncomfortable.

TYPE II Near-Shore
Buoyancy: 15.5 pounds or more. Designed to keep an unconscious person face up. More comfortable to wear than Type I. Best for use within sight of shore, and on inland

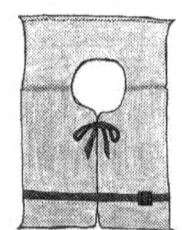

TYPE III Flotation Aid
Buoyancy: 15.5 pounds or more. Will not keep a person face up in the water. Designed for water-sports use, general boating wear, fishing, etc. Can be very comfortable. Do not use offshore, or in rough water.

TYPE IV Throwable Device
Buoyancy: 16.5 pounds or more. Designed to be thrown to a person in the water. It is advisable to tie a line from the device to the vessel.

U. S. Coast Guard Minimum Equipment Requirements

Equipment	Requirements for boats less than 16', canoes, and kayaks.
Personal Flotation Devices	One Type I, II, III, or IV for each person on board.
Fire Extinguishers	One Type B-I, except outboards.[1]
Visual Distress Signals	Only at night or with 6 or less paid passengers. Equipment same as larger boats.
Sound Signals	Boats up to 39.4 feet (12 m) must carry an efficient sound-producing device.
Ventilation – Boats built or decked over between 25 April 1940, and 1 August 1990	Two ventilator ducts, with cowls. Boats built after 31 July 1981 must have operable power blowers.[2]
Ventilation – Boats built after 1 August 1990	At least two ducts that must ventilate every closed compartment that contains a gas engine or gas tank.[3]
Backfire Flame Arrestor	A USCG approved back-fire control device installed on inboard engines.[4]

Equipment	Requirements for boats 16' to less than 26'.
Personal Flotation Devices	One Type I, II, or III for each person on board, + one Type IV available to be thrown.[5]
Fire Extinguishers	One Type B-I, except outboards.[1]
Visual Distress Signals	Three red flares, three orange smoke signals, or orange flag with black square and disk, + S-O-S light.[7]
Sound Signals	Boats up to 39.4 feet (12 m) must carry an efficient sound-producing device.
Ventilation – Boats built or decked over between 25 April 1940, and 1 August 1990	Two ventilator ducts, with cowls. Boats built after 31 July 1981 must have operable power blowers.[2]
Ventilation – Boats built after 1 August 1990	At least two ducts that must ventilate every closed compartment that contains a gas engine or gas tank.[3]
Backfire Flame Arrestor	A USCG approved backfire control device installed on inboard engines.[4]

Equipment	Requirements for boats 26' to less than 40'.
Personal Flotation Devices	One Type I, II, or III for each person on board, + one Type IV available to be thrown.[5]
Fire Extinguishers	Two Type B-I or one Type B-II.[6]
Visual Distress Signals	Three red flares, three orange smoke signals, or orange flag with black square and disk, + S-O-S light.[7]
Sound Signals	Boats up to 39.4 feet (12 m) must carry an efficient sound-producing device.
Ventilation – Boats built or decked over between 25 April 1940, and 1 August 1990	Two ventilator ducts, with cowls. Boats built after 31 July 1981 must have operable power blowers.[2]
Ventilation – Boats built after 1 August 1990	At least two ducts that must ventilate every closed compartment that contains a gas engine or gas tank.[3]
Backfire Flame Arrestor	A USCG approved backfire control device installed on inboard engines.[4]

Equipment	Requirements for boats 40' to not more than 65'.
Personal Flotation Devices	One Type I, II, or III for each person on board, + one Type IV available to be thrown.[5]
Fire Extinguishers	Three Type B-I, or One Type B-I + one Type B-II.[6]
Visual Distress Signals	Three red flares, three orange smoke signals, or orange flag with black square and disk, + S-O-S light.[7]
Sound Signals	Boats 39.4' to 65.7' must carry a bell, and either a power whistle (audible ½ naut. mile), or a power horn. Bell diameter at the mouth shall be at least 7.9".
Ventilation – Boats built or decked over between 25 April 1940, and 1 August 1990	Two ventilator ducts, with cowls. Boats built after 31 July 1981 must have operable power blowers.[2]
Ventilation – Boats built after 1 August 1990	At least two ducts that must ventilate every closed compartment that contains a gas engine or gas tank.[3]
Backfire Flame Arrestor	A USCG approved back-fire control device installed on inboard engines.[4]

Footnotes

1. Not required on outboard boats under 26', if not carrying passengers for hire, if boat has no permanently installed fuel tanks, and if boat is constructed so that flammable or explosive vapors cannot be entrapped. When a fixed fire extinguishing system is installed in machinery spaces, it will replace one B-I type portable extinguisher.
2. Must efficiently ventilate the bilges of all engine and fuel tank compartments of boat using gasoline or other fuel having a flashpoint lower than 110°.
3. Permanently installed gas tanks that vent outside the boat and that have no unprotected electrical devices are exempt. Engine compartments containing a gas engine with a remote-operated starter (cranking motor) must contain power-operated exhaust blowers, which can be controlled from the instrument panel.
4. Applies to all gas engines installed in a vessel after 25 April 1940.
5. A person "on board" includes anyone being towed behind the boat on water skis, inner tubes, wakeboards, or other towable equipment.
6. When a fixed fire extinguishing system is installed in machinery spaces, it will replace one B-I type portable extinguisher.
7. Flares can be handheld, meteor, or parachute type. Smoke signals can be hand held or floating.

RECOMMENDED EQUIPMENT LIST	
☐	Air Horn; handheld
☐	Anchor: foul weather, plus line
☐	Anchor: light duty, plus line
☐	Bailing Bucket
☐	Bilge Pump; electric
☐	Boathook
☐	CO Detector; for cabin
☐	Compass
☐	Depth Sounder or Fishfinder, electronic
☐	Dock Lines
☐	Drain Plug; spare
☐	Electrical Tape
☐	Emergency Blanket
☐	Fenders
☐	Fire Extinguisher(s); extra
☐	First Aid Kit; with CPR mask, gloves
☐	Flashlights; with spare batteries
☐	Fuses; spare
☐	GPS Unit

RECOMMENDED EQUIPMENT LIST
☐ Hour-Meter, for engine
☐ Knife; utility
☐ Lines; extra
☐ Offshore: Life raft, EPIRB, Type I PFDs
☐ Oars or Paddle
☐ Papers: logs, insurance, licenses, registration
☐ Parts: belts, hoses, spark plugs, oil, etc.
☐ Portable Head; plus toiletries, soap
☐ Propeller; spare, plus extra cotter pins
☐ Rags
☐ Spotlight
☐ Tool Kit, with WD-40
☐ Tow Line
☐ VHS Radio
☐ Visual Distress Signals; spare flares
☐ Water; emergency
☐ Other Items:

PERSONAL EQUIPMENT LIST	
☐	Boat keys
☐	Beach towels and beach chairs
☐	Car keys
☐	Clothes, extra
☐	Fishing gear, fishing license
☐	Food, snacks, drinks
☐	Food prep equipment, portable stove
☐	Gas for boat, spare gas can
☐	Hat, extra hats for passengers
☐	Ice, cooler
☐	Jackets, rain gear
☐	Overnight equipment
☐	Skis, wakeboard, towable toys, ski tow rope
☐	Sunglasses
☐	Sunscreen
☐	Towels
☐	Wallet, money
☐	Miscellaneous items
☐	Miscellaneous items

Skipper's Handbook – Robert Grossman

Alphanumeric Code Flags

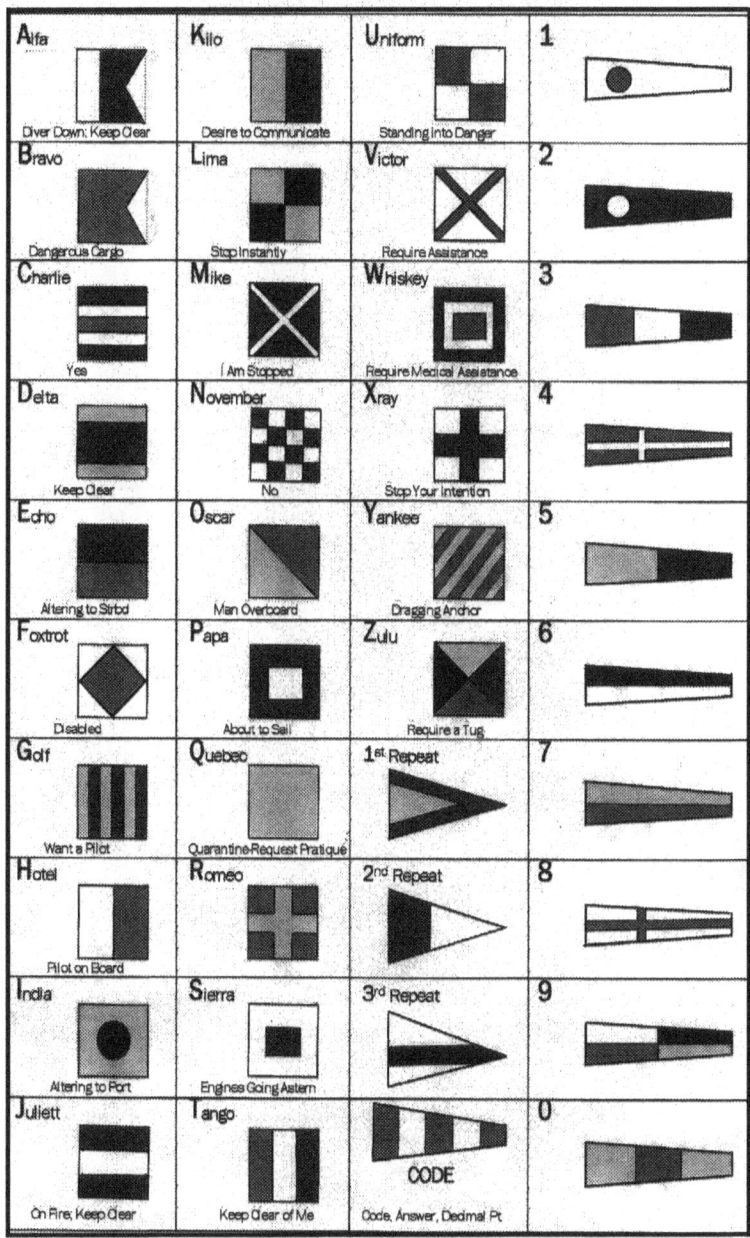

SYMBOLS, ABBREVIATIONS, & CONVERSION CHARTS

SYMBOLS AND ABBREVIATIONS	
atm = atmosphere	kg = kilogram
Btu = British thermal unit	km = kilometer
°C = degree Celsius	kW = kilowatt
cal = calorie	L = liter
cm = centimeter	lb = pound
°F = degree Fahrenheit	m = meter
ft = foot	MHz = megahertz
ft^2 = square feet	mi = mile
ft^3 = cubic feet	min = minute
g = gram	mm = millimeter
gal = gallon	n mi = nautical mile
h = hour	naut mi = nautical mile
hp = horsepower	oz = ounce
Hz = hertz	psi = lb/in^2
in = inch	qt = quart
in^2 = square inches	s or sec = second
in^3 = cubic inches	V = volt
J = joule	W = watt
	yd = yard

CONVERSION TABLES

AREA
1 in² = 6.452 cm²
1 ft² = 0.0929 m²
1 m² = 10.76 ft²

COMPASS
360° = 1 complete circle
1° (degree of arc) = 60' (minutes)
1' (minute of arc) = 60" (seconds)

ENERGY/POWER
1 hp = 550 ft·lb/s = 0.746 kW
1 W = 1 J/s = 0.746 kW
1 Btu/h = 0.293 W
1 J = 0.738 ft·lb
1 cal = 4.186 J

CONVERSION TABLES

LENGTH/DISTANCE
1 ft = 12 in
1 yd = 3 ft
1 mi = 1760 yd = 5280 ft
1 ft = 0.3048 m
1 yd = 0.9144 m
1 mi = 1.609 km
1 m = 3.281 ft
1 km = 0.621 mi
1 n mi = 1.15 mi = 6076.1 ft
1 mi = 0.869 n mi
1 n mi = 1.852 km

PRESSURE
1 atm = 760 mm Hg (mercury)
1 atm = 14.7 lb/in^2
1 bar = 14.5 lb/in^2
1 atm = 1.0133 bar
1 bar = 0.9869 atm = 750 mm Hg

CONVERSION TABLES

RADIO FREQUENCY
1 Hz = 1 cycle/s
1 kHz = 1,000 Hz
1 MHz = 1,000,000 Hz

SPEED
1 mi/h = 0.8695 knot
1 knot = 1.15 mi/h
1 mi/h = 1.61 km/h
1 knot = 1.852 km/h
1 km/h = 0.621 mi/h
1 km/h = 0.5405 knot

TEMPERATURE
32 °F = freezing point, water
212 °F = boiling point, water
0 °C = freezing point, water
100 °C = boiling point, water
°C = (°F - 32) x (5/9)
°F = (°C x 9/5) + 32

CONVERSION TABLES
TIME
1 min = 60 s
1 hr = 60 min
1 day = 24 hr
1 year = 365 days
VOLUME
1 qt = 32 oz
1 gal = 4 qt = 128 oz
1 gal = 231 in^3
1 ft^3 = 1728 in^3
1 ft^3 = 7.481 gal
1 qt = 0.9465 L
1 gal = 3.786 L
1 L = 1.0576 qt
1 L = 0.2642 gal

CONVERSION TABLES

WEIGHT/MASS

1 lb = 16 oz
1 ton = 2000 lb
1 long ton = 2240 lb
1 oz = 28.35 g
1 lb = 0.4536 kg
1 kg = 1000 g
1 g = 0.03527 oz
1 kg = 2.205 lb

WEIGHT OF FUEL

Fuel Type	Pounds Per Gallon
Diesel Fuel	7.1
Gasoline	6.0

WEIGHT OF WATER

Fresh:	1 cubic foot	62.39 lb
Fresh:	1 gallon	8.34 lb
Salt:	1 cubic foot	64.05 lb
Salt:	1 gallon	8.56 lb

VISIBILITY OF LIGHTS

Inland Waters Visibility given in statute miles			
Position Of Lights On Vessel	Boats Less Than 12 Meters	Boats 12 to Under 50 Meters	Boats 50 Meters And Over
Masthead	2	5*	6
Sidelights	1	2	3
Special Flashing	2	2	2
Vessels Being Towed	3	3	3
All Other Lights	2	2	3

* Masthead light on vessels 12 to under 20 meters is 3 miles

International Waters Visibility given in statute miles			
Position Of Lights On Vessel	Boats Less Than 12 Meters	Boats 12 to Under 50 Meters	Boats 50 Meters And Over
Masthead	2	5	6
Sidelights	1	2	3
Vessels Being Towed	3	3	3
All Other Lights	2	2	3

APPENDIX 1
STATE BOATING INFORMATION

Each state has its own set of rules and regulations that govern vessel traffic, water sports, fishing, and other boating related activities. In many states, boating regulations and services are handled by several different agencies. For example, the motor vehicle department may handle boat registration, the state police may oversee boating laws, and the department of natural resources may control boat access and fishing regulations.

The telephone numbers and web sites listed below provide a good starting point to obtain boating information. These numbers and web sites will not lead to every boating-related agency for each state. Be aware that telephone numbers and web site addresses frequently change.

Alabama - Dept. of Conservation and Natural Resources, 334 243-3673 or 334-242-3673, www.dcnr.state.al.us (go to Marine Police)

Alaska - Div. of Parks & Outdoor Recreation, Office of Boating Safety, 907 269-8705,
www.dnr.state.ak.us/parks/boating.

Arizona - Game & Fish Dept., 602 942-3000,
www.gf.state.az.us

Arkansas Game & Fish Commission, 501 223-6300,
www.agfc.state.ar.us/boating

California Dept. of Boating & Waterways, 916 263-4326, www.dbw.ca.gov

Colorado State Parks & Outdoor Recreation, 303 866-3437, www.dnr.state.co.us/parks/boating

Connecticut Dept. of Environmental Protection, Boating Division, 860 434-8638, http://dep.state.ct.us/

Delaware Div. of Fish & Wildlife, 302 739-3498, www.dnrec.state.de.us/fw/wildregs.htm

Florida Fish & Wildlife Conservation Commission, 850 488-1401, www.state.fl.us/fwc

Georgia Dept. of Natural Resources, 888 748-6887, www.dnr.state.ga.us/dnr/wild

Hawaii Div. of Boating & Ocean Recreation, 808 587-1966, www.hawaii.gov/dlnr/dbor/dbor.html

Idaho State Parks & Recreation, 208 334-4199, www.idahoparks.or/rec

Illinois Dept. of Natural Resources, 217 557-0180, http://dnr.state.il.us

Indiana Dept. of Natural Resources, 317 232-4020, www.state.in.us/dnr/lawenfor/boating

IowaDept. of Natural Resources, 515 281-9361, www.state.ia.us/government/dnr

Kansas Dept. of Wildlife & Parks, 785 296-2281, www.kdwp.state.ks.us

Kentucky Dept. of Fish & Wildlife Resources, 800 858-1549, www.kdfwr.state.ky.us

Louisiana Dept. of Wildlife & Fisheries, 225 765-2984, www.wlf.state.la.us

Maine Dept. of Inland Fisheries & Wildlife, 207 287-8000, http://janus.state.me.us/ifw/

Maryland Dept. of Natural Resources, 877 620-8367, www.dnr.state.md.us/boating

Massachusetts Dept. of Fisheries, Wildlife & Environmental Law Enforcement, 617 727-3905, www.magnet.state.ma.us/dfwele/dle

Michigan Dept. of Natural Resources, 517 373-1214,

www.dnr.state.mi.us
Minnesota Dept. of Natural Resources, 651 296-6157, www.dnr.state.mn.us
Mississippi Dept. of Wildlife, Fisheries & Parks, 601 362-9212, www.mdwfp.com
Missouri Dept. of Public Safety, State Water Patrol, 573 751-3333, www.dps.state.mo.us/dps/mswp/wp.htm
Montana Montana Fish Wildlife & Parks, 406 444-2950, http://fwp.state.mt.us
Nebraska Game & Parks Commission, 402 471-0641, http://ngp.ngpc.state.ne.us
Nevada Div. of Wildlife, 775 688-1500, www.state.nv.us/cnr/nvwildlife
New Hampshire Fish & Game Dept, .603 271-3211, www.wildlife.state.nh.us
New Jersey Div. of Fish, Game & Wildlife, 609 292-2965, www.state.nj.us/dep/fgw/lawhome.htm
New Mexico Motor Vehicle Div., 888 683-4636, www.state.nm.us/tax/mvd/mvd_home.htm
New York Div. of Fish, Wildlife & Marine Resources, 516 444-0430, www.dec.state.ny.us
North Carolina Wildlife Resources Commission, 919 733-3391, www.wildlifestate.nc.us
North Dakota Game & Fish Dept., 701 328-6300, www.state.nd.us/gnf
Ohio Dept. of Natural Resources, 614 265-6480, www.dnr.state.oh.us/odnr/watercraft
Oklahoma Dept. of Wildlife Conservation, Oklahoma Lake Patrol, 405 521-3851, http://title3.sde.state.ok.us/recreation/safety1.htm
Oregon State Marine Board, 503 378-8587, www.marinebd.osmb.state.or.us
Pennsylvania Fish & Boat Commission, 717 657-4515, www.fish.sate.pa.us
Rhode Island Dept. of Environmental Management, 401 222-6647, www.state.ri.us/dem

South Carolina Dept. of Natural Resources, 803 734-3888, http://water.dnr.state.sc.us

South Dakota Div. of Motor Vehicles, 800 829-9188, www.state.sd.us/revenue/motorvcl.htm

Tennessee Wildlife Resources Agency, 615 781-6682, www.state.tn.us/twra

Texas Texas Parks & Wildlife, 512 389-4828, www.tpwd.state.tx.us/boat/boat.htm

Utah Utah State Parks & Recreation, 801 538-7220, www.parks.state.ut.us/

Vermont State Police, Marine Div., 802 878-7111, www.boatsafe.com/vt

Virginia Dept. of Game & Inland Fisheries, 804 367-1000, www.dgif.state.va.us

Washington State Dept. of Licensing, 360 902-3600, www.wa.gov/dol/

West Virginia Div. of Natural Resources, Law Enforcement Section, 304 558-2784, www.boatsafe.com/West_Virginia

Wisconsin Dept. of Natural Resources, 608 266-2141, www.dnr.state.wi.us

Wyoming Wyoming Game & Fish, 303 777-4600. http://gf.state.wy.us/HTML/faq/faqboating.htm

APPENDIX 2
GLOSSARY OF BOATING TERMS

aft • Toward the rear of the vessel.
aids to navigation • Buoys and markers with charted positions, used to determine location and guide direction of travel.
ballast • Weight placed within the boat to improve stability.
barometer • Instrument used to measure atmospheric pressure.
beam • 1. The width of a vessel. 2. The direction to the side of a vessel.
bearing • The direction of an object from the observer.
Beaufort scale • A scale describing the force of winds.
belay • 1. To secure a line to a cleat. 2. An order to stop.
bend • A class of knots.
berth • A resting place for a vessel.
bight • 1. A loop made in a line. 2. Part of a knot.
bilge • The lowest interior part of a vessel's hull.
bitt • A strong post on the deck of a boat used to fasten towing, mooring, or anchor lines.
block-and-tackle • A system of pulleys and lines used to lift heavy objects.
bow • The front of a vessel.
bowline • A knot commonly used by boaters.
breast line • A dock line that controls lateral movement.
broach • A dangerous, unplanned movement of a boat that

throws the hull broadside to the waves.

bulkhead • A wall that creates an interior compartment in a boat.

burdened vessel • A vessel that must yield right of way to another vessel.

capsize • To roll a vessel over so the bottom side is up.

cavitation • Air bubbles that collapse on the blades of a spinning propeller, causing loss of efficiency and propeller damage.

chine • The corner or ridge where the bottom of a boat's hull meets the side of the hull or other lengthwise vertical surface.

cleat • An anvil-shaped piece of hardware to which lines are secured.

COLREGS • "International Regulations for Preventing Collisions at Sea", also known as "Rules of the Road".

come about • To change direction.

companionway • An entrance to the vessel's cabin.

compass card • A round card with markings in degrees, that pivots in a compass. One point of the card is attracted to magnetic north.

cuddy cabin • A small cabin under the forward deck.

daymark • A sign marking an obstruction or side the of a channel.

day shapes • An object hung from a boat to indicate its status.

dead reckoning • A technique used to approximate one's position, speed, or running time.

deviation • The number of degrees that a compass needle is deflected away from magnetic north, caused by metal or magnetized objects near the compass.

displacement • The weight of water that is displaced by a vessel.

displacement hull • A boat hull designed to plow through the water at cruising speeds.

documentation • The license or registration for a vessel.

draft • The maximum depth of the underwater portion of a boat's hull.

EPIRB • Emergency Position Indicating Radio Beacon, identifies the location of a vessel in trouble.

estimated position • A dead-reckoned position that takes into account current and wind.

fathom • A depth of six feet.

fender • A rubber cushion hung from the side of a boat to prevent damage.

fix • The position of a vessel, as obtained by reliable means such a GPS or bearings.

flame arrestor • A metal mesh fitted over the carburetor to prevent an explosion in the engine compartment.

fore • Forward, or the front part of a boat.

founder • To sink.

freeboard • The distance from the waterline to the top of the deck.

galley • The kitchen on a boat.

ground tackle • The entire anchoring apparatus.

gunwale • The upper portion of the side of the hull.

hard over • Turning the wheel or tiller all the way until it stops.

hatch • An opening in the deck, usually covered.

head • 1. The bow of a boat. 2. The bathroom on a boat.

heading • The direction that a boat is pointing.

head sea • Waves heading toward the bow of the boat.

heave to • Heading into the waves and slowing, to make minimum speed.

heel • Leaning of a boat to one side.

helm • The steering station on a vessel.

hitch • A type of knot that attaches a line to another object.

hull • The main structural body of a boat.

hydrofoil • 1. A wing-shaped devise added to the outdrive unit of a boat, that increases lift. 2. A type of vessel that rides on submerged "wings".

ICW • Intracoastal Waterways; protected waterways traversing the Atlantic and Gulf coasts.

Inland Rules • Rules of the Road that apply to waters not covered by the International Rules.

isobar • A line drawn on a weather map that connects areas of equal pressure.

isogonic line • A line drawn on a map or chart that connects areas of equal magnetic variation.

kedge • 1. A type of anchor. 2. Pulling on an anchor line to move a boat.

keel • The main structural member at the base of certain types of hulls. 2. The fore and aft centerline of a boat.

lee • The direction that the wind is blowing.

leeward • 1. Toward the lee side. 2. The direction away from the wind.

leeway • The sideways movement of a vessel caused by wind or current.

line • A rope used on a boat.

LOA • Length Over All, the total length of a vessel.

locker • A closet on a boat.

lubber's line • A line or mark on a compass that indicates the direction.

lunch hook • A small, convenient anchor used for short stops.

make fast • To secure or tie a line to an object.

mooring • The place where a boat is anchored, tied to a buoy, or secured to a pier.

nautical mile • A length of about 6,076 feet, or one minute of latitude.

nav lights • Lights used by a vessel to show position, direction of travel, and occupation.

neap tide • A tide of small rise and fall that occurs when the sun and moon are furthest from being lined up.

net tonnage • The carrying capacity of a vessel measured as the volume of the interior, less the volume of engines and equipment.

Notice to Mariners • Navigational safety updates available to boaters.

nun buoy • A cylindrical buoy with a tapered top, generally red with an even number.

outdrive • The exterior portion of the propulsion unit that is connected to an inboard engine. Also known as an I/O or sterndrive.

painter • A towline for a small boat or dinghy.

parallel rules • A device that is used on a nautical chart, that can "walk" a line from a compass rose to a vessel's position.

pennant • 1. A line that connects a boat to a mooring buoy. 2. A small flag.

PFD • Personal Flotation Device; a lifejacket.

pitch • 1. The angle of the blades on a propeller, which determine the theoretical distance the propeller will move in one revolution. 2. The rise and fall of the bow due to wave action.

pitchpole • A boat being thrown end over end by wave action.

planing hull • A boat hull designed to ride on top of the water at cruising speeds.

port • 1. The left side of a boat, or to the left. 2. An opening in the side of a boat for light and air. 3. A harbor.

privileged vessel • A vessel having the right of way.

pulpit • The railing and platform that projects forward of the bow of a boat.

radar • "Radio detecting and ranging," an instrument used to locate objects around a vessel.

rake • The fore and aft angle of a boat's bow or stern.

rhumb line • A straight course line on a chart that uses a "mercator projection". Suitable for short distances.

right-of-way • A vessel must yield to another vessel that has the right of way.

rode • The anchor line.

roll • The motion of a vessel where the sides move up and down with the waves.

rub rail • An impact-absorbing strip of material that runs around the hull of a boat.

rudder • A vertical fin at the stern, which steers a boat by deflecting water.

Rules of the Road • A system of regulations for collision avoidance, that boaters must follow.

running fix • A position on a chart obtained by using "lines of position" with a measured run.

running lights • Navigation lights used by a boat to indicate position, direction of travel, and occupation.

Samson post • A strong post on the deck of a boat used to fasten towing, mooring, or anchor lines.

scope • The length of the anchor line compared to the water depth, expressed as a ratio.

screw • The propeller.

scupper • A drain on deck that directs water overboard.

seacock • A one-way valve fitting in the hull of a boat.

sextant • A device used in navigation to measure the relative angle of stars or other fixed objects.

shear pin • A small metal pin that holds a propeller to its shaft, designed to break under stress. It helps protect the propeller from major damage caused by striking an underwater object.

sheave • The grooved wheel in a pulley, used with line to change the direction of force.

sheer • The fore and aft curvature of a vessel's deck.

side lights • The red port light and the green starboard light on a vessel.

slip • A berth between two floating piers.

sole • The floor of a boat's cabin or cockpit.

sounding • The depth of water as shown on a chart.

spar • A mast or boom used on a sailboat.

spring line • A dockline that controls for and aft movement.

squall • A strong, localized wind or rain storm at sea.

stanchion • A vertical metal post, affixed to the deck or gunwale, to which lifelines are secured.

standing part • The section of line that is not used in making a knot.

stand-on vessel • A vessel that has the right of way.

starboard • The right side of a boat, or to the right.
statute mile • A distance of 5,280 feet.
steerage way • Having enough speed relative to the water to be able to steer the boat.
stem • On wood-framed vessels, the forward most vertical structure of the hull, to which the keel and horizontal planks are attached.
stern • The rear of a vessel.
stern drive • A boat that has the engine inside the hull, and the propulsion unit outside the hull. The propulsion unit moves back and forth to steer the boat.
sternway • Moving in reverse through the water.
strake • A line formed by the planking on a boat's hull, running from the bow to the stern.
stuffing box • A fitting through which the drive shaft of an inboard engine passes to the exterior of a vessel.
swamp • To take on water over the side or transom of a vessel, but not to sink.
swell • A wave that does not crest.
tack • 1. A turn taken by a sailboat, putting the wind on the opposite side of the vessel. 2. A single segment of a zigzag path taken by a sailboat.
tender • A small dinghy attached to or towed by a pleasure boat. It is used to shuttle passengers, crew, and gear to and from the larger boat.
tiller • The handle on a rudder.
tonnage • A unit of measurement of the capacity or displacement of a vessel.
transom • The aft vertical wall of a boat's hull.
trim • The angle that a boat floats, relative to the water.
trough • The area between two adjacent waves.
true course • A vessel's direction, relative to the north pole. Corrections have been applied for variation and deviation.
underway • A vessel in motion.
variation • The angular difference between the direction of the north pole and magnetic north. It is measured in degrees

East or West.

veer • 1. To change direction. 2. A clockwise change in wind direction.

ventilation • The mixing of water and air or exhaust gasses at the propeller, causing engine over-revving.

VHF • Very High Frequency; the bandwidth between 156 and 163 MHz, on which marine radios operate.

V-hull • A hull design with the bottom shaped like a "V". Deeper "V"s offer a smoother ride on choppy water.

wake • 1. The waves caused by a vessel's movement through the water. 2. The path left in the water by a moving vessel.

way • The movement of a vessel.

weigh • To raise the anchor.

wharf • A pier or other structure at the shore, designed for vessels to dock alongside.

wheel • 1. The propeller. 2. The steering wheel.

whipping • Thin diameter line that is wound around the end of a larger diameter line to prevent fraying.

winch • A devise that pulls on a line, either by a rotating reel or a lever that provides mechanical advantage.

windlass • A winch mounted to a vessel's deck, used specifically for hauling in anchor line or chain.

windward • The direction from which the wind is coming; into the wind.

yaw • Rotational movement of a vessel on a horizontal plane, as caused by waves acting upon the surfaces of a vessel's hull.

APPENDIX 3
INDEX

24 Hour Clock	132, 133
Abbreviations	252
Adult CPR	15, 16
Alphanumeric Code Flags	251
Amputations	28
Anchor Line Chart	194
Anchoring	192-200
Antenna, Radio	214
Animal Bites	32
Asthma	43
Bearings	150-152
Blade Thrust	163
Block and Tackle	241
Brakes	165
Breathing, Rescue	14
Broken Bones	23
Buoys	65-73
Buoys, West Rivers	68, 69
Buoys, ICW	70-72
Buoys, Uniform State	73
Burns	22
Carbon Monoxide Poisoning	34
Cavitation	160
Charts	129
Child CPR	17
Childbirth	47-48

Cloud Chart	219
Compass Conversions	117, 124-128
Compass Degrees	117
Compass Deviation	119-123
Compass Points	117
Compass Rose	133
Compass Use	116-128
Compass Variation	118
Conversion Diagrams	124-128
Conversion Tables	131, 253-257
Area	253
Compass	253
Energy/Power	253
Length	254
Pressure	254
Radio Frequency	255
Speed	131, 255
Temperature	255
Time	256
Volume	256
Weight/Mass	257
Course Made Good	142-144
Course To Steer	147-148
CPR	14-18
Crossing	57
Cuts	26
Dayshapes	92-94
Dead Reckoning	130-131, 134-152
Deviation	119-123
Deviation Worksheets	122
Deviation Tables	119-123
Dislocations	24
Distance To Horizon	237
Distance T Object	238
Distress Signals	110-113
Diving Injuries	49-51
Dock Lines	166-167

Drowning	20
Electrical Power	240
Emergencies	154-157
Emergency Radio Use	213
Epileptic Seizure	44
Estimated Position	134-135, 145-146
Eviscerations	30
Eye Injuries	31
Find Position	134-135, 150-152
Find Distance	136-137
Find Speed	136-137
Find Time	138-139
Fire Fighting	208-209
Fishhook Removal	54
Fix With Bearings	150-152
Formulas	237-241
Glossary	265-272
Great Lakes	59
Gunshot Wounds	29
Heart Attack	21
Heat Stroke	40
Hierarchy	60-62
Hypothermia	42
ICW Bouyage	70-72
Illness, Sudden	35
Impaled Objects	27
Infant CPR	18
Insect Bites	38
Insulin Shock	45
Internal Injuries	36
Jellyfish Stings	39
Knots	131, 221-236, 255
Launching	201-202
Life Jackets	242-246
Marine Radio	210-214
Mechanical Advantage	241
Meeting	56

Motion Sickness	52
Multiple Anchors	198-200
Narrow Channels	61
Nautical Charts	129
Nav Lights Inland	74-82
Nav Lights International	83-91
Near Drowning	20
Open Wounds	26
Overtaking	58
Person Overboard	154
Personal Equipment	250
Personal Flotation Devices	242-246
Poisoning	33
Poisonous Plants	41
Propellers	158-160
Recommended Equipment	248-249
Reduced Visibility	103-109, 188
Required Equipment	243-247
Rescue Breathing	14
Responsibilities	63-64
Rest. Vis. Inland	103-106
Rest. Vis. International	103, 107-109
Restricted Visibility	103-109, 188
Rough Seas	184
Rule of 60	239
Running an Inlet	189
Sailing Vessels	62
Scope	197
Seasickness	52
Set and Drift	140-142, 145-146
Shock	19
Single-Screw Handling	168-177, 184-187
Snake Bites	37
Sound Signals Inland	95-98, 103-106
Sound Signals International	99-103, 107-109
Speed Made Good	142-144
Speed Made Good, Alt.	149

Sprains	25
Stab Wounds	29
State Boating Information	261-264
Steering	165
Stroke	46
Sudden Illness	35
Sunburn	53
Symbols	131, 252
Taking On Water	155
Towing	156
Trailering	203-205
Trim	161-162
Turning	164, 187
Twin-Screw Handling	178-187
Variation	118
Ventilation	160
Vessel Hierarchy	60-62
Vessel Aground	157
VHF Radio	210-214
Visibility of Lights	258-259
Water Skiing	190-191
Weather	215-220
Weather Map Symbols	215-216
Weight of Fuel	257
Weight of Water	257
Wind Scale	220

Books published by
Bristol Fashion Publications
Free catalog, phone 1-800-478-7147

Boat Repair Made Easy — Haul Out
Written By John P. Kaufman

Boat Repair Made Easy — Finishes
Written By John P. Kaufman

Boat Repair Made Easy — Systems
Written By John P. Kaufman

Boat Repair Made Easy — Engines
Written By John P. Kaufman

Standard Ship's Log
Designed By John P. Kaufman

Large Ship's Log
Designed By John P. Kaufman

Designing Power & Sail
Written By Arthur Edmunds

Building A Fiberglass Boat
Written By Arthur Edmunds

Buying A Great Boat
Written By Arthur Edmunds

Boater's Book of Nautical Terms
Written By David S. Yetman

Practical Seamanship
Written By David S. Yetman

Captain Jack's Basic Navigation
Written By Jack I. Davis

Creating Comfort Afloat
Written By Janet Groene

Living Aboard
Written By Janet Groene

Racing The Ice To Cape Horn
Written By Frank Guernsey & Cy Zoerner

Marine Weather Forecasting
Written By J. Frank Brumbaugh

Complete Guide To Gasoline Marine Engines
Written By John Fleming

Complete Guide To Outboard Engines
Written By John Fleming

Complete Guide To Diesel Marine Engines
Written By John Fleming

Trouble Shooting Gasoline Marine Engines
Written By John Fleming

Trailer Boats
Written By Alex Zidock

Skipper's Handbook
Written By Robert S. Grossman

White Squall - The Last Voyage Of Albatross
Written By Richard E. Langford

Skipper's Handbook – Robert Grossman

Cruising South
What to Expect Along The ICW
Written By Joan Healy

Electronics Aboard
Written By Stephen Fishman

Five Against The Sea
A True Story of Courage & Survival
Written By Ron Arias

Scuttlebutt
Seafarine History & Lore
Written By john Guest

Cruising The South Pacific
Written By Douglas Austin

VHF Marine Radio Handbook
Written By Mike Whitehead

Catch of The Day
How To Catch, Clean & Cook It
Written By Carla Johnson

About The Author

Robert Grossman has been an avid boater for nearly twenty years. Always interested in boating-oriented pastimes, he is also an active fisherman, scuba diver and water-skier. A graduate of Humboldt State University in Industrial Arts and Technology, he has since looked for ways to simplify and explain complex ideas. Understanding the profusion of rules and techniques of good seamanship presented a tempting challenge. Subsequent studies led him to earn his U.S. Coast Guard Masters' license, which he currently holds.

As an active Reserve Deputy Sheriff, Robert takes particular interest in boating safety and boating laws. He also serves as a board member of the Washoe County Reserve Deputy Association. Various memberships in boating, diving, and community organizations allow him to participate in charitable events, education, and public speaking.

Robert lives with his wife Julie, a teacher, avid boater and licensed Third Mate.

www.ingramcontent.com/pod-product-compliance
Lightning Source LLC
Chambersburg PA
CBHW032019230426
43671CB00005B/142